American Liberty & Justice

Gordon Morris Bakken
Series Editor

Editorial Board
Michal Belknap
Richard Griswold del Castillo
Rebecca Mead
Matthew Whitaker

Quite Contrary

Quite Contrary

The Litigious Life of Mary Bennett Love

David J. Langum, Sr.

Foreword by Gordon Morris Bakken

Texas Tech University Press

This book is typeset in Minion Pro. The paper used in this book meets the minimum requirements of ANSI/NISO Z39.48-1992 (R1997). ∞

Designed by Kasey McBeath
Cover photograph/illustration courtesy of the Conrado Family Archives.

Library of Congress Cataloging-in-Publication Data
Langum, David J., 1940- author.
    Quite contrary : the litigious life of Mary Bennett Love / David J. Langum, Sr. ; fore-word by Gordon Morris Bakken.
        pages cm — (American liberty and justice)
    Includes bibliographical references and index.
    ISBN 978-0-89672-874-5 (hardback) — ISBN 978-0-89672-875-2 (e-book) 1. Love, Mary Bennett, 1803-1868. 2. Women pioneers—California—Biography. 3. Pioneers—California—Biography. 4. Love, Mary Bennett, 1803-1868—Trials, litigation, etc. 5. Women farmers—California—History—19th century. 6. Squatters—California—Biography. 7. Land grants—California—History—19th century. 8. Public lands—California—History—19th century. 9. Santa Clara (Calif.)—Biography. 10. California—History—19th century—Biography. I. Title.
    F864.L89L36 2014
    979.4'04092—dc23   [B] 2014007755

14 15 16 17 18 19 20 21 22 / 9 8 7 6 5 4 3 2 1

Texas Tech University Press
Box 41037 | Lubbock, Texas 79409-1037 USA
800.832.4042 | ttup@ttu.edu | www.ttupress.org

I dedicate this book to two persons who have been of significant help to me: Grace Eskridge, *mi querida*, and a woman entirely unlike Mary Bennett Love, *and* William G. Ross, colleague, friend, and exemplary historian.

Contents

Illustrations

Acknowledgments

I have many persons to thank for various leads or material, and I have tried my best to remember them all and credit them in my citations. I apologize to anyone I have overlooked. However, I must especially thank Paul Conrado, a direct descendant of Mary Bennett Love, for the use of many Bennett family photographs and for furnishing a significant lead. Lorie García, Santa Clara's official historian, provided much insight into Mary Bennett Love's life in Santa Clara. William G. Ross, colleague and friend, read the entire manuscript and offered several suggestions. Formerly a newspaper editor, he insists that he enjoys close editing, and I am very grateful that he shared with me his suggestions in that regard.

Erin N. Boggan, my secretary, has been helpful in many ways, and Jeffrey M. Whitcomb, the computer expert at Cumberland School of Law, has helped me through several crises with a technology I am sure I will never really understand.

I would also like to thank Bernadette, my first wife. She had a great interest in Mary Bennett Love and enthusiastically accompanied me on my initial research forays in the 1970s.

David J. Langum, Sr.
Birmingham, Alabama

Foreword

Mary Bennett Love's California experience demonstrates the law-mindedness of nineteenth-century emigrants. Love, like so many other emigrants, had extensive knowledge of law. John Phillip Reid suggested, "If we find they acted on this knowledge to guide their conduct not only toward property but in dealing with fellow emigrants, then we may draw conclusions more far reaching." In Love and other emigrants, their "habits, actions, and values . . . were formed by a behaviorism based on law."[1] David Langum's book makes clear that Love's actions were part of this nineteenth-century culture. More importantly, Love knew law without the benefit of literacy. It was part of her experience, and she applied it well in dealings in business in California.

Further, Langum's book paints the amazing portrait of a female entrepreneur who paid attention to business although she was a lower-class emigrant to California. This is a substantial contribution to women's history, particularly female entrepreneurs. To give greater voice to women and to put their voices in an accessible form, Brenda Farrington and I edited *Encyclopedia of Women in the American West* (Thousand Oaks, CA: Sage Reference, 2003), which included a selection of female entrepreneurs. We included chapters on cowgirls, homesteaders, vintibusiness, and entrepreneurs.

Some of the biographical chapters resonate powerfully with Mary Bennett Love. Rhoda May Knight Rindge moved to California from Michigan with her husband and ranched near Malibu. After her husband died, she had to found a business, Malibu Potteries. Her handiwork was profitable, and she converted her profits into Rindge Castle at Laudamus Hill in Malibu, housing all three of her children's families. The Great Depression ruined her financially, and she died in poverty in 1941.[2] Love too went into business to save her family financially.

Another entrepreneur by necessity was Freda Ehmann, who immigrated from Germany. At age fifty-six she had just buried her husband and daughter near Oroville, California, and was impoverished. She had twenty acres of olives and turned to science to market her product. With the help of Professor Eugene

Hilgard at the University of California, Berkeley, she developed the process for curing ripe olives. In 1898 she founded the Ehmann Olive Company, with her son working in marketing and her son-in-law helping her with production. She hired Asian and female workers. She was generous to her employees and gained their loyalty. Ehmann personally marketed her product in Canada and throughout the United States. In 1911 she built a home known as the House the Olives Built that is today maintained by the Butte County Historical Society.[3] Like Ehmann, Love took personal responsibility for her products.

Marie Callender started baking pies in a southern California delicatessen and moved her expertise to the home, selling pies to the delicatessen owner. In 1948 with capital from the sale of the family car, she opened for business in Long Beach. The family baked the pies and sold them to local restaurants. In 1962 she opened a Marie Callender's restaurant in Orange County and put a working pie oven in the front window of the shop. The pie shop matured into a full-menu restaurant, and by the end of the decade, Marie Callender had over one hundred shops. She guarded her recipes, and loyal customers returned regularly once they tasted the products. Her husband's death in 1984 precipitated the sale of the business.[4]

Mary Ellen Pleasant was a San Francisco Bay area entrepreneur born into slavery in Georgia. Pleasant aggressively sought education, the liberation of her race, and equal rights. She arrived in gold-rush San Francisco and used her knowledge and money to desegregate public transportation. She could have been the richest woman in California but for her philanthropy.[5]

Love's financial fortunes were weak because of her first husband's lack of savvy—very much like Evelyn Cameron's husband's failure to take care of business while studying birds.[6] Love would shed her first husband because he lacked "sufficient ambition." Mary Bennett Love wanted better and obtained land.

Jeannette M. Oppedisano's *Historical Encyclopedia of American Women Entrepreneurs, 1776 to the Present* explored the lives of several women in the food business. Helene, Hannah, Elizabeth, and Monique An established the "Secret Kitchen" restaurants in California, creating special Vietnamese dishes.[7] Hattie Mosely Austin (1900–1998) founded Hattie's Chicken Shack in Saratoga Springs, New York, and for sixty years served ribs, cobbler, collards, corn bread, and chicken to loyal customers.[8] Anne Beiler, after almost nineteen years of marriage, found her husband in trouble in his auto-repair business. She took up part-time work in a local farmer's market and entertained customers by hand rolling pretzels. In 1988 she set up shop in Downingtown, Pennsylvania, with borrowed money, selling pretzels under the name Auntie Ann's. The pretzels sold; by 1989 she had seven stores, and within eleven years she had a franchise business with about 600 stores selling her pretzels.[9]

Rita D'Angelo and Marisa Iocco took their love of cooking into Boston's combat zone and opened a breakfast and lunch place in 1990. Three years later they were served dinner in Galleria Italiana, their award winning restaurant.[10] Susan Feniger and Mary Sue Milliken opened the City Café in Los Angeles in 1981 and a larger restaurant in 1985. That year they christened their first place Border Grill and opened another by that name in Santa Monica in 1990. A guest spot on *The Food Network* made them nationally famous as the "Too Hot Tamales." Soon they had four cookbooks, a weekly radio show, more Border Grill locations, a dishware and peppermill line, and further public acclaim in the food business.[11] Cathy Hamilton and her sister Gloria Griskowitz opened the Putnam Street Market in Saratoga, New York, in 1995, where they offered domestic and imported products, deli sandwiches, soups, baked goods, and wine. Three years later they were grossing a million dollars, and after just four years they branched out into catering. The sisters made it a priority to be on the floor of the market with their children as part of the fun experience of serving customers.[12] Judy Wicks was a single parent working in a Philadelphia restaurant, La Terrasse, for thirteen years when she was terminated for expressing her values regarding the business. She started selling muffins and coffee from her house in 1983, expanded to cooking in the backyard on the barbecue, and branched out to a row house facility with a bank loan. The business became the White Dog Café, one of Philadelphia's most famous restaurants. Wicks coupled business with community action, feeding the needy and providing spiritual uplift. She believed fully in serving customers, one another, community, and nature.[13]

Many of the attributes of these entrepreneurs resonate with Mary Bennett Love's story. When she shed her first husband, she was a single parent looking for a business opportunity. She found it in a land grant and started acquiring more land. Her crops, vegetables, and grapes were the main food of gold-rush California.

The most sophisticated work on women in business in California is Edith Sparks's *Capital Intentions: Female Proprietors in San Francisco, 1850–1920.* Many of her findings resonate powerfully with Love's experience. To be successful women had to be "financially and legally savvy enough to know how to maneuver" in their environment.[14] Sparks found that competition "required female proprietors to invest not just in lavish interiors but also in window displays.

For it was through these, after all, that customers' first impression of a business would be formed."[15] From a window display, common in department stores, entrepreneurs invested in advertising. Sparks noted, "By the early twentieth century, some female proprietors turned the job of advertising over to professionals, a decision that of course involved more money but which they no doubt expected to yield them more satisfying results." Further, "with the professionalization of advertising came added attention to elements of design, copy, and cost, all part of the shift" to influencing buyers to buy the product.[16] Sparks opined, "Women's contributions to their families' businesses included everything from tending to customers to minding the books. Such tasks may have been informally assigned instead of formally designated, but they exposed women to a wide variety of management skills."[17] Mary Bennett Love learned the financial trap of mismanagement from her first husband. She learned the mechanics of finance and the virtue of producing quality products. She personally cleaned the wheat after threshing.

Sparks concluded, "Scholarly literature confirms, in fact, that the story of women's small-business ownership in San Francisco during the late nineteenth and early twentieth centuries is not a story of western exceptionalism but one of female determination and innovation more generally."[18] Mary Bennett Love's story adds to this conclusion for the nineteenth century. She was tenacious in business and in her use of the law.

Gordon Morris Bakken
California State University, Fullerton

Quite Contrary

Chapter 1

Introduction

This is an account of a rambunctious woman—with a long glance at her equally unruly daughter—who traveled the plains by covered wagon to Oregon, then to California, where they led unusually independent lives for women of the mid-nineteenth century. Mary Bennett, later Mary Bennett Love, and her daughter Catherine Bennett left behind no record of remarkable behavior in the Southeast, from which they hailed. Yet probably this was only because local scribes lacked the initiative to describe them. In 1842, when Mary moved from Arkansas to Oregon, her fellow travelers on the Oregon Trail were very interested in noting her behavior in their diaries and reminiscences. The following year the family moved on to California, still a Mexican territory. Although Catherine's full name was Tillatha Catherine Bennett, she went by Catherine alone. They came as a large family, Mary with her husband Vardamon, accompanied by their eight children, Winston (twenty years old), Catherine (eighteen), Dennis (seventeen), Jack (fifteen), Mary Ann (eleven), Mansel (six), Julia Ann (four), and Samantha (two). They left behind in Arkansas twins who had just died.

Partly by her voice, also by her dress, but primarily by her actions, Mary Bennett captured the attention of many of her contemporaries, on the overland trail and then in the localities where she lived in California. Many observers recorded their impressions, leaving us vivid descriptions. We can still hear her loud, profane speech. We can still see Mary, gargantuan in size, about six feet tall and more than 300 pounds, as she stands in a gunfight with Indians or provokes a water fight with her San Francisco neighbors. Observations of her dress are less vivid, and in the only extant photograph she is dressed conventionally. However, the women who met Mary often described her attire as amusing or humorous. To balance this, her contemporaries also recorded many acts of her kindness and generosity.

Catherine Bennett did not attract recorded observations as readily as did her mother. However, there is no doubt that she was equally daring in her deeds. When she found a colorful male adventurer who appealed to her, Catherine defied social convention, government orders, and her formidable mother by simply moving in with him. She then declared before his friends and one of her brothers that she and her paramour, Isaac Graham, were married. Very few women had the nerve to do this in 1845. A few years later things were not working out well between them. Then she suddenly learned the shocking news that Isaac's first wife, whom he had abandoned in the East many years earlier, was still alive. She waited until Isaac was on a trip, then gathered up their children and several thousands of dollars of his gold, and set off for Hawaii. A feud developed between Isaac Graham's family and Mary Bennett's, during which Isaac's son Jesse shot and wounded Mary and then killed her son Dennis.

Mary demonstrated her audacity in many ways. Dissatisfied with her marriage, in 1845 she took her six children who remained minors and moved to another town, found a place to live, and by hard work supported herself and her children. Again, few women, if any others, acted so independently at this time, especially in the Roman Catholic culture of Mexican California. She did this without knowledge of Spanish and while illiterate in English. Yet she thrived and even obtained a small Mexican land grant. Later, Mary Bennett began to operate sawmills in the Santa Cruz Mountains and engaged in much litigation. In 1854 she married Harry Love, prominent for killing a local bandit, and as rough cut as herself. After a turbulent marriage they separated. Amid violence and Harry's accusation of her infidelity, the gunman Mary had hired for protection killed her husband in a shoot-out.

What was the central character of Mary Bennett? Was this woman a loudmouthed redneck or hell-raising hillbilly, to use more modern terms, or was she a shrewd, self-governed, independent woman? In truth she was both. Her neighbors saw her as a colorful "cracker," more or less today's hillbilly. Yet she was also an independent, gutsy woman, as was her daughter Catherine, more so than usual for their day. Those considerations alone make them interesting enough to look at more closely. Still other reasons compel our attention.

Mary's life provides an excellent and almost unique view of the American working class of pre-gold-rush California. American merchants in California during the 1830s and 1840s have many biographers, including myself.[1] Similarly, Americans who ranched on large estates have received attention. In contrast, almost nothing has been written about the poorer Americans who engaged in marginal business activities in the small towns or planted garden farms on small plots. Isaac Graham, Catherine Bennett's common-law husband, is an exception to this generality. Because of his notoriety, he attracted attention and has garnered journal articles and even a book.[2] In general, observers paid little attention to members of the poorer class of immigrant, and because of the absence of primary sources, most have disappeared as individuals from historical notice.

However, because of her personality and outlandish ways, people did notice Mary Bennett, and they recorded what they saw. In addition, because she had a Mexican land grant, the confirmation proceedings produced dozens of statements and depositions concerning her activities. These observers often expanded their remarks to include material about her family, what they were doing, how they made their living. So, for example, we have considerable detail about a horse-rental business that Vardamon Bennett operated in 1844 San Francisco for the patronage of foreign sailors, especially Americans, who were visiting that port. When Mary Bennett operated a small truck farm in the shadow of the old Santa Clara Mission, we have precise information about her crops. We simply do not have that detail about many working-class activities, and the richness of material on the Bennett family provides valuable insight.

The Bennett women can inform our more general understanding of gender relations in the far west of the nineteenth century. The most provocative analytical tool for understanding nineteenth-century women is the concept of the "Cult of True Womanhood," the title of a leading article by historian Barbara Welter.[3] This notion held that a "true" woman embodied four primary virtues of piety, purity, domesticity, and submissiveness. A necessary corollary of this thesis is that men and women occupied separate spheres of influence, men in the public arena and women in the private world. Perhaps this differentiation of spheres was the result of the industrial revolution, when men no longer worked in their homes as independent artisans alongside their wives but instead went off to factories, offices, and shops. However, this has been questioned and is not agreed upon.[4]

The relative unsettledness of the American West challenged the image of women as devoted to domesticity and operating in a separate sphere. In many settings all family members needed to work to provide a subsistence, and the lines between home and work once again became blurry. Pioneer women regained the economic importance they once held, and this model of appropriate behavior for "true" women had to be set aside.[5] Not only were women players within the traditional female occupations of schoolteacher and nurse but in more typically masculine activities. Women even became homesteaders, not just as the wives of entrants but as the actual entrants and occupiers.[6]

Perhaps some western women retained a belief in domesticity and the cult of true womanhood, even as they cooked with buffalo chips on the trail and hoed their gardens when once in the West. However this duality of moral precepts and actual behavior is a difficult conceptual tool, and some historians employ class as an analytical tool to interpret women's history in the American West. For example, Elizabeth Jameson suggests, "we need to stop assuming that all westerners believed in the Cult of True Womanhood. Instead, we need to define the beliefs about sex roles that westerners of different classes, races, and ethnic backgrounds expressed."[7]

Mary and Catherine Bennett would scoff at notions of "true womanhood." Nor did they act in accordance with ideals of piety, purity, domesticity, or submissiveness to husbands or anyone else for that matter. It is likely that social class, a factor suggested by Professor Jameson, may have played a role in their behavior. The Bennett women came out of the working class of the American South, as a group accustomed to physical work and therefore less concerned with ideals of domesticity and submissiveness.

What is striking is that *males* in mid-nineteenth century California judged Mary Bennett on these standards of "true womanhood," even while she made no pretense to honor them herself. In other words, the men thought that women *ought* to act in conformity with the principles of piety, purity, domesticity, and submissiveness and that there was something off with them if they did not. Mary Bennett, of the two women especially, was a hell-raiser and did cause disturbances. However, she was not riotous, nor was actual violence involved. Indeed, her oldest son, Winston Bennett, recalled that "my mother never carried a pistol. She was always afraid of firearms."[8] Her identical actions, if perpetrated by a male, would probably brand such a man as a "character," and little more.

In an 1888 trial Mary's reputation became relevant, even though she was long dead. Five men who had been residents of Santa Cruz County since 1847 and 1850, and who had known Mary in either Santa Cruz and Santa Clara Counties or both during the years 1847–1850, testified that her reputation for peace and quietness was "poor" or "bad." A sixth male witness, John Daubenbiss, who had crossed the plains in the same wagon train with Mary in 1842, testified that Mary Bennett Love's "reputation for peace and quietness was not very good."[9] These men expected more domesticity and submissiveness from women than Mary Bennett Love was prepared to offer.

Of course, the absolute zaniness of this woman provokes interest. Just how did she pull off her many shenanigans?

I cannot claim Mary Bennett Love as a fresh discovery; many other writers have written about her—and almost always very inaccurately. Moreover, almost all the other studies have viewed her in connection with somebody or something else. Both Joan B. Barriga (in 1990) and William B. Secrest (in 2005) wrote about Mary Bennett Love, but it was in connection with her second husband, Harry Love.[10] A 2002 study of the City of Santa Clara devoted an entire chapter to Mary Bennett, but unsurprisingly, it was largely about her in connection with the City of Santa Clara.[11] Doyce B. Nunis, Jr., in 1967 wrote extensively and accurately about Catherine Bennett, but again it was in connection with someone else, in her case Isaac Graham.[12] There is only one extensive study focused on Mary Bennett Love, and that was published by Catherine's granddaughter and Mary's great-granddaughter, Mabel Dorn Early, in 1950.[13] That study was undocumented and based primarily on family lore. It is best viewed as a primary source on the Bennett family's tradition, and where I refer to family lore or family tradition, it is to Ms. Early's writing.

Mary Bennett Love deserves better. She is an interesting person and deserves a book where her viewpoints and her activities are primary. She also deserves a sharper historical focus. Most of the existing literature on Mary has been written by amateur historians who relied on secondary sources written by other amateur historians. Inevitably that has introduced substantial errors into the stories.

Then too various traditions have arisen among her descendants or admirers that have acquired lives of their own. For example, there is a solid tradition that Mary received her Mexican land grant out of gratitude that she had provided midwifery and nursing services to poor Californio women. That is a nice thought, but there is no evidence for it whatsoever, either as to motive or that she provided those services. Indeed, there is every reason to believe that the grant was made for the very purposes specified in its documentation: to provide support for Mary Bennett's family.

I have ignored these traditions and secondary sources and have attempted to rc-create Mary Bennett Love's life by relying, to the greatest extent possible, on primary documents. I cite nineteenth-century observers or documentation for almost every statement made about Mary or her family except in a few cases, mostly concerning family background, where reliance must be made on family tradition.

I have been interested in Mary for a long time. In fact, I did some of the basic research for her biography in the mid-1970s while I was still practicing law. When I became a full-time law professor in 1978 I set aside the project as insufficiently scholarly in nature for an aspiring legal historian. Now, with six published books and dozens of articles to my credit, I have no insecurities about being sufficiently scholarly. I can return to the joy of telling the fascinating story of Mary Bennett Love. However, I was wrong about the study's lacking scholarly interest.

It became apparent while writing this biography that Mary Bennett Love was quite aware of law and legal concepts. She engaged in considerable litigation. This is important information for our understanding of nineteenth-century legal culture. John Phillip Reid, a noted historian of American law, is fond of saying that every chapter of history ought to have a page of law. By that he means that law can become a behavioral part of a national culture, and therefore people's actions and the historical explanations for them should be based, in part, on their understandings of law.

Reid is of the view that mid-nineteenth-century Americans were very law-conscious and that law had become a part of American culture. He described how the immigrants on the overland trail took actions dealing with their personal property in accordance with a reasonable familiarity with common-law legal principles, even though they were hundreds, sometimes thousands, of miles from a court or a lawyer.[14] In a similar vein I showed—or at least I think I did—that the American and British expatriates living in Mexican California in the 1830s and 1840s had a serviceable understanding of the common law, sufficient to enable them to govern their affairs without recourse to the Mexican courts that they did not trust or esteem.[15] A recent study of the jury in antebellum Illinois noted that "antebellum Americans were preoccupied with the law, understood its importance, and were engaged in a constant dialogue about it; the law mattered to them."[16]

The study of Mary Bennett Love's awareness and conscious thought about law advances these previous studies. The American and British expatriates were largely merchants or ranchers. The costs of outfitting a wagon, animals, and supplies for the trail meant that most overland trekkers were middle class, although in fact a few wealthy and poor persons somehow joined wagon parties. Mary Bennett Love was distinctly working class, and a study of her awareness and use of law advances the understanding of American nineteenth-century legal consciousness by extending it to a social class not clearly included in earlier studies.

I intend this biography to be of interest to and accessible by the general reader as well as those interested specifically in legal history. However, because of the nature of what I learned of Mary Bennett Love's use of law, I necessarily had to include much more discussion of law than might be expected in a biography of nonlegal figures. I have tried to keep such "law talk" to a nontechnical level, bearing in mind the intended audience.

Chapter Two
Bennett Family Background

Bennett family lore maintains[1] that Mary Bennett was born, in 1803, into the McSwain family, an Irish working-class family whose American ancestors reached into the colonial period. Apparently, Mary's grandfather fought for independence in the American Revolution. Her father had died prematurely, leaving a widow and thirteen children. They lived in Virginia, and Mary worked as a maid to help her mother support the large family that was near destitution. At some point her mother sent Mary to Georgia to work for the wealthy Bennett family. Vardamon Bennett, one of the family's sons, fell in love with Mary. They married, over the extreme objections of his parents, who after the marriage had nothing to do with either Mary or their son. Such is the family account.

There are kernels of truth in this family history, but it is difficult to sort them out precisely. We know that Mary McSwain was born in 1803. The United States census of 1850 indicates that she was then forty-seven, suggesting a birth date of 1803, and that she was born in North Carolina.[2] When she sought the aid of the American consul after her separation from Vardamon, she stated in her petition that she was a native of the state of Georgia.[3] However, in the special California census of 1852, she declared that she was born in North Carolina.[4] North Carolina is probably correct. Perhaps she was asked an ambiguous question for the Larkin petition, interpreted it as "where were you married," and because she was illiterate, did not spot the error in the final written petition.

In any event, it is true that Mary and Vardamon were married and lived in Georgia. Their first child, Winston, was born in 1822, when the family was living on a farm in Walton County, Georgia.[5] The second, Tillatha Catherine, known commonly as Catherine, arrived about 1824. Although this birth date is based only on the Bennett family lore, the year fits. The family's third and forth children, Dennis and David Jackson, sometimes Jack or just Jackson, were also Georgia natives of 1825 and 1828, respectively.[6]

Family lore has it that Mary was quite unhappy in Georgia because of the treatment by her husband's parents and their family. She eventually persuaded him to move to Tennessee. They found poor fortune in Tennessee and after only a year or so moved to Arkansas, where they had much better luck. They acquired a large farm approximately twenty miles from Little Rock, Arkansas, and improved it with pastures and an orchard.

Their fifth child, Mary Ann, sometimes called Amanda, was definitely born in Tennessee in 1831.[7] Winston Bennett, the eldest son, published memoirs that confirm that the family moved to Conway, Arkansas, in 1830 and engaged in farming until they left for the Pacific coast in 1842.[8] Conway is located twenty-five miles north of Little Rock. Here Mansel, Julia Ann, and Samantha, the last three of the family's eight surviving children, were born in 1836, 1838, and 1840 respectively.[9]

Before the Bennetts even considered moving across the continent to Oregon and then to California they had already traveled quite a bit. Mary had perhaps moved from North Carolina to Virginia, but she certainly had removed to Georgia. As a couple the Bennetts had already gone from Georgia to Tennessee, thence to Arkansas, and in 1842 stood on the brink of their longest move, to Oregon and then to California. Many Americans in the antebellum years shared this restless movement, and especially its westward tilt. Two emblematic Americans of the period demonstrate this. Abraham Lincoln and Jefferson Davis, respective presidents of their opposing nations in the War for Southern Independence, were both born in Kentucky locales of reasonable proximity. Lincoln's family took young Abraham north to Indiana, from whence he moved west as a young man to Illinois. In contrast, Davis's family took young Jefferson west but also south to Mississippi.

In the early nineteenth century, Americans were westward-moving people. With considerable individual variation, as a general pattern New Englanders and New Yorkers went to the Midwest, the mid-Atlantic state residents to Tennessee and Kentucky, and those in the lower south to Alabama, Mississippi, and Arkansas. Then in the 1840s and 1850s many moved even further west, across the continent to Oregon and California. The Bennetts were in the mainstream of the general westward movement and actual pioneers in the extended overland movement. It was a time of restless energy in America, and this westward travel was a part of the general romantic impulse to explore new worlds. As we shall see, Mary carried that restlessness with her to California and continued its practice.

The family traditions cover several other matters in connection with the Bennetts' Arkansas stay and the circumstances of their leaving. One tradition is that Mary became an accomplished midwife in Arkansas, carried that practice into California, and extended it into general nursing for immigrants arriving in California.[10] No written evidence exists for this claim. Another tradition is that Mary and Vardamon had suffered the loss of infant twins just prior to their move. No other evidence exists for this claim either, but if true that type of loss might be itself some motivation for departure. The family lore as to their immediate motivation for leaving points to the violent activities of a vigilante gang known, because of their disguise, as the "White Caps." They went around issuing warnings and punishments for what they regarded as offenses against the community, and Vardamon became anxious about his family's safety. However, the only historical records in Arkansas dealing with the White Caps dates them from the 1890s, too late to provide motivation in 1842.

When Captain Lansford W. Hastings's party came along with 150 people bound for the west coast, family tradition says that the Bennetts joined with them, making their preparations in only one day. There is evidence, however, that strongly suggests a contradictory account of their departure. In any event, when they did leave, they took with them horses, oxen, cattle, and wagons loaded with necessities for their trip. According to family lore they left behind everything else, including a cherry orchard in full bloom, departing their Conway, Arkansas, farm on April 1, 1842. The dogwoods were in flower, the countryside beautiful. Catherine, then seventeen or eighteen, cried for days, and to the end of her life maintained, again according to family tradition, that Arkansas was more beautiful than California.

Some of that can be verified. They had wagons, because we know of the sale of one and the abandonment of another along the trail, and horses too, for riding and packing supplies. They were in fact members of the wagon train captained by Lansford W. Hastings, who was taking the trip in order to write a book, which became hugely popular: *The Emigrants' Guide to Oregon and California* (1845). However, Hastings lived in Mount Vernon, Ohio, and joined with Dr. Elijah White and a small group of immigrants who passed through Ohio on their way to Independence, Missouri, the kickoff point for most wagon trains.[11] Arkansas is not on the route from Ohio to Independence, Missouri. Hastings did not himself expect a large group of immigrants but hoped only to hire trappers to guide them. He expressed surprise that

> having arrived at Independence, he was so fortunate as to find, not only the Santa Fe traders, and the Rocky mountain trappers, but also a number of emigrants, consisting of families and young men, who had convened there with the view of crossing the Rocky mountains, and were waiting very patiently until their number should be so increased as to afford protection and insure the safety of all.[12]

Winston Bennett's memoirs state that they started out on April 20, 1842, reached Independence on May 1, "halted and made up a train," and bought supplies before their final push off on May 16, 1842.[13] Taken together, all of this makes it clear that no one, or no group, came through Arkansas, that the Bennetts merely joined. Instead, they made a conscious decision on their own to go across the plains and then traveled as a family to the place where they could meet like-minded folks. Then they set off as a group. This makes the Bennetts' decision to travel to the West all the more special, since it was made by them independently of any external persuasion.

We must not minimize the courage and spunk of this decision. In traveling across the plains, they were not, either literally or figuratively, following a well-worn trail. Prior to 1840 only a few exploring parties, missionaries and their wives, and other adventurers had crossed the plains, usually guided by mountain men or trappers. When Joel Walker took his family to Oregon in 1840, accompanied by missionaries and the usual complement of trappers, he really became the first of a kind, an ordinary immigrant seeking a new life for himself and his family. Historians generally consider this the first of the overland emigrations. From that 1840 trip until Abraham Lincoln was elected president in 1860, approximately 250,000 overlanders had crossed the plains. Such emigration started out very slowly. The year 1840 saw thirteen emigrants to Oregon; 1841 witnessed twenty-four emigrants to

Oregon and thirty-four going directly to California. The year 1842 had 125 for Oregon, of which the Hastings party, which included the Bennett family, constituted slightly less than half. Up through 1848 the traffic increased steadily, and then in 1849, after the discovery of gold in California became known in the East, it exploded.[14] The Bennetts were not the very first in this quintessentially American adventure of overland travel, but they are right up there. It made their decision to go courageous, their adventure significant.

Chapter 3

Overland to Oregon in 1842

Independence, Missouri, to Fort Laramie, Wyoming

The 1842 emigrants tarried in Independence, allowing time to obtain last minute supplies, to adopt a code of regulations governing the wagon train, and to allow time for latecomers to arrive. The six diaries or recollections[1] prepared by participants that describe this wagon train generally agree that they pushed off on May 16, 1842, but they are in greater disagreement as to the size of their party, with participation ranging from 100 persons to 160. There were several families, and the Bennetts were not alone.

The diaries and reminiscences of this trip, of course, did not mention Mary or her family on a daily basis. However, as they discuss the hazards and excitements along their route, we must remember that Mary was present and participating in each one of them.

The path that the party took became a standard route. They struck out west across the plains (in present-day Kansas), forded the Kaw River (sometimes rendered Caw, today the Kansas River), then bore in a northwest direction along a small stream called, appropriately, the Little River, until it connected with the Platte River. The wagon train followed the south bank of the Platte until the Platte River forked. At that point they forded the Platte, always a difficult crossing, and followed the North Platte, continuing in a northwest direction, until they reached Fort Laramie at the confluence of the Laramie and North Platte Rivers in southeast Wyoming.

On May 21, only five days into the journey, a young couple's only child, a sixteen-month-old girl, died from illness. Her mother then became very ill herself. After a delay of a day or so, some men on fast horses escorted the couple back to civilization. Rain was heavy in late May and early June, and mosquitoes were plentiful. A huge controversy erupted over the numerous domestic dogs accompanying the party. Some thought that the dogs would give them away to Indians, others thought that the dogs might become rabid and attack their cattle or perhaps even themselves, while a third group thought the dogs might drive the cattle off. At a called meeting, the majority voted to execute all dogs. As the executions progressed, the emigrants' distress and angst became so great that at some point short of totality the killing was called off. Nevertheless, dissatisfactions, largely triggered by the dog controversy, led to a separation in the company. Until Fort Laramie, where they reconciled, two separate groups traveled and camped with a mile or two distance between them. No record reveals where the Bennett family stood on the dog controversy. Winston Bennett briefly mentions the incident and states that it was controversial, but he gives no opinion other than that the executions were pursuant to the will of the majority.

The diarists recorded positive experiences alongside reports of poor weather, mosquitoes, dogs, and a death. So far, food was bountiful. Before they reached the Platte River in early June, there was a multitude of deer, elk, hare, and wild fowl, all feeding on abundant prairie grass. After the Platte they saw buffalo by the thousands. Several diarists were taken with the scenery, especially the Chimney Rock of western Nebraska, a rock column that rises out of a rock base to a height hundreds of feet above the plain. The emigrants had not yet reached true mountains, but they were already much enthralled by the bluffs of western Nebraska.

One of the Bennett family's fellow travelers noted in his diary, the day after seeing Chimney Rock, that they "camped without water or wood in a valley bordered on each side by high Bluffs presenting the most romantic scenery I ever saw."[2] Another of the company waxed even more effusive for the same western Nebraska area:

> The scenery became more and more singular; fallen columns, blocks of massy stone, and broken walls. At intervals, there were collections and groups, having the appearance of ruinous castles, monasteries, towers, and every description of massive building. This was, to the travellers, curious, grand, and picturesque, and entirely dissimilar to any thing they had before witnessed.[3]

By the time the emigrants had reached western Nebraska they were about five weeks into their journey. Necessarily, their wagon train life had evolved into a routine. Because the Bennett family undoubtedly participated in this regime, a good description of this routine allows us to see how the Bennetts lived during their months on the overland trail. Eliza White, a member of their party, wrote a full account of their daily life.

> They traveled all day, steadily onward, till four o'clock in the afternoon, when they halted. As large a circle was made as could be formed by the wagons drawn up, one behind another, and the mules, horses, etc., with ropes of perhaps fifty feet in length, attached to them, turned loose upon the prairie to feed till evening. Each person then built a fire opposite his own wagon, and while this was being done, the females were preparing food for cooking. Two forked sticks were driven into the ground, a pole laid across, and the kettle swung upon it.[4]
>
> Those who had tables, set them out, while others laid the cloth upon the ground, and seated themselves around, after the fashion of older time, partaking of the food before them with appetites not at all wanting in keenness. After the meal, they usually enjoyed a season of recreation, sauntering about at their leisure, and it was really the most delightful portion of the day. At sunset, the horses were caught, and each by his rope fastened to a stake, at suitable distances, and left for the night. Sentinels were then stationed at different points, and in all directions were next heard the blows of the axes and hammers of the men, driving the stakes and preparing the tents. Most of the women and children slept in the comfortable, Pennsylvania covered wagons, and the men on blankets spread under the tents, with coats and saddles for pillows. As day dawned, according to a law, made as in other republics, by a majority of votes, at a given signal, every one rose to prepare for departure. The boys went out in all directions to collect the teams and herds, which often detained them for several hours, as the cattle would sometimes wander off for miles. The first meal being over, the dishes nicely stowed, and everything pronounced in readiness, he who had taken the lead the day previous, went to the rear, while the next in order took his place. This rule was invariably observed, as it prevented any feeling that others were preferred to them.[5]

The grinding monotony of plodding daily along the treeless, burning plains was more characteristic of this first portion of their trip. Harder labor would come later in the mountains, with narrow passageways, exhausted stock, and streams to be forded. Mary Bennett and the other women of the party faced the usual problems encountered with domestic duties along the overland trail: dust and dirt, inadequate time or water for washing, and poor cooking fires fueled by chips of buffalo manure, all that was available in the treeless plains.

Their trip through June had experienced discomforts, controversies, one death, and one family's return, but no true calamities. Around June 28 they arrived at Fort Laramie, located on the North Platte River, approximately sixty miles northeast of the present-day city of Cheyenne, Wyoming, and an even greater distance northeast from the present city of Laramie. In 1842 Laramie was not a proper "fort," but rather a collection of three separate trading posts, often called trading forts because they were armed, located in close proximity to each other. It became a military base in 1851 when the United States Army purchased one of the trading forts and began improvements. By 1842, however, the name Fort Laramie was already used more widely than the specific names given by the traders to their proprietary outposts.

The traders at the posts advised the emigrants that they would not be able to take their wagons over the trail to Oregon. Several overlanders then sold wagons, oxen, and lame cattle, taking pack horses in exchange. According to Winston Bennett, his father, Vardamon, sold one of his wagons at Fort Laramie. They stayed at Laramie for almost a week, allowing for rest, refitting, and repairs. The most significant thing they did at Fort Laramie was to hire Thomas Fitzpatrick, an experienced mountaineer, to guide them across the Rocky Mountains. He was to lead them as far as Fort Hall, located in the southeast corner of present-day Idaho.

Fort Laramie to Fort Hall

Their route continued to take them along the North Platte for a few days. Then they switched to a tributary of the North Platte and followed this new river, the Sweetwater, westward through the middle of Wyoming. They passed and noted Independence Rock and then continued along the Sweetwater through South Pass. This remarkably gentle pass, the most gradual of all the passes across the Rocky Mountains, does not seem like much as the traveler passes through. However, it marks the crossing of the Rocky Mountains, the Continental Divide. The emigrants knew this, and several noted the new direction in which the waters now flowed.

After going through South Pass the emigrants went along several streams: the Little Sandy to the Big Sandy, down it to Green River, about thirty miles north of the Wyoming city of that name. Here, at the Green River, the party divided, some wishing to push on faster with only pack animals and the others not wishing to abandon their wagons. The Bennetts kept their wagons. Although geography required some modest portages, the wagon party continued to follow rivers, picking up the Bear River in the southwest corner of Wyoming, briefly entering present-day Utah, and then traveling along the Bear River up to Soda Springs, Idaho. Several diarists noted the numerous water spouts and boiling springs of this area, one calling it "the greatest Natural Curiosity I ever saw."[6] After a few more days of travel, the emigrants arrived at Fort Hall, in mid-August.

The character of the journey from Fort Laramie to Fort Hall was quite different than it had been from Independence to Fort Laramie. The going was in general much tougher. They gained elevation, and nights became cold. Grass now was sparse and the ground more arid and sandy. Game became less plentiful, and a few days after reaching the Sweetwater River they paused several days to smoke buffalo meat to carry along with them. The terrain required that they ford rivers much more frequently. They had much greater contact with Indians in this portion of the trail. Indians in groups both large and small frequently accosted them, demanding gifts or some trading, in tones that were not quite hostile but which the emigrants might reasonably regard as threatening. Frequently they were obliged to halt, explain their purpose, smoke a peace pipe, and distribute presents.

Three incidents within a few days of each other loomed largest. The first was on July 16, when a gun accidentally discharged, killing its owner. Winston Bennett explains:

> The gun had been thrown carelessly into the wagon and the man had gone up to the rear to get something from the vehicle, while fumbling around the traps in the wagon, the gun went off with a fatal result.

They reached the large mass of feldspar and mica known as Independence Rock in mid-July and remained there for two weeks, curing buffalo meat. Dubbed the "Great Register of the Desert" in 1840 by the great French Jesuit explorer, Fr. Pierre DeSmet, overlanders regarded it as a prime place to carve one's initials or name. Earlier, fur trappers had noted their names and dates of passage, and now the emigrants had begun. Several of the Bennetts' party indulged in this, but Lansford Hastings, the elected captain, and Asa Lovejoy, his lieutenant, decided to linger after the meat was cured to make more artful signatures. The wagon party moved on with no objection from Hastings or Lovejoy, who saw no problem with catching up on horseback, unencumbered with cattle or wagons. Some time after the wagon party had left, Hastings and Lovejoy found themselves surrounded by several hundred Indian braves, some of whom were decidedly hostile, others not so. After a period of rough treatment, the two persuaded the Indians to escort them back to their wagon party. The main body of emigrants realized their leaders were missing and, alarmed at the approach of such a large group of Indians, circled their wagons and prepared to defend themselves. However, the Indians released Hastings and Lovejoy without further incident.

About a week later, in a third major incident on this portion of the trail, the party, including Mary, of course, stumbled on the encampment of a very large war party consisting of several thousand Sioux, Cheyenne, and other tribes' braves unaccompanied by their families, engaged in a campaign against the Snake Indians. They could easily have totally destroyed the emigrants. It must have been a very frightening encounter. However, the chief of this large body sent over an escort of a few hundred braves who safely escorted the emigrants past the encampment. There were no hostilities, although a few emigrants apparently suffered the theft of some horses and cattle.

They traveled along the Sweetwater River for only about two weeks, roughly from July 10 through July 28, but those two weeks must have been the most frightening time of the entire trip for Mary Bennett. Not only did the two Indian incidents and the shooting death occur during that period, but two other events took place in that short time that directly affected her family.

For July 17, 1842, Medorem Crawford noted in his diary that one of Vardamon Bennett's daughters was "slightly wounded by an accidental discharge of a gun."[7] Lansford Hastings provides further details:

> Another accidental discharge of a gun, which produced much alarm, especially among the ladies, yet no injury resulted from it, other than a slight flesh wound in the foot, of a small child, which was sitting in a wagon, through which the ball passed.[8]

We do not know exactly who this was, but from the description of small child and daughter, it would necessarily be either Julia Ann (who was four) or Samantha (who was two). If the ladies generally were alarmed by the incident, we can only imagine the alarm of Mary Bennett, the mother.

Three days later came another incident for the Bennetts that clearly caused intense angst for Mary. It occurred during the time the party had stopped to smoke buffalo meat. Men went out hunting, and occasionally some would run back into camp in terror, stating that they had been chased by Indians. After one of these episodes, Elijah White noted that

> the mother of a lad of eighteen, named Bennett, [i.e., Mary Bennett, mother of Winston Bennett] took it into her head that her boy, who was absent, though in an opposite direction, was in danger. She began running about the camp with immense strides—for she was almost a giantess—screaming and hallooing equal to any wild Indian, wringing and clapping her hands and tearing her hair. "Oh, my Philly[9] is dead! my Philly is dead! Turn out, men! turn out!" It affected all her hearers rather comically, though they sympathized with the distracted woman; for her agony, though drolly acted, was terrible. With all possible despatch, [sic] the men armed, and were just starting out to seek the lost one, when in walked Philly, very quietly, bearing upon his shoulder a huge piece of buffalo, all unconscious that he had liked to become the hero of a tragedy, the effect of which was now spoiled, and turned into farce.[10]

Yet "Mother Bennett," as White called her elsewhere, was telepathic in sensing her son was in trouble, although the danger may have passed by the time she sounded the alarm. Neither White's account nor Bennett's give specific dates, but judging by where they were on the trail when the incidents happened, it is very likely that Mary Bennett's angst coincided with an event that Winston Bennett himself described when he "and another went out hunting. They had killed a couple of buffalos and were on their way to camp with the meat when they were surrounded by Sioux Indians and their horses taken from them." Medorem Crawford mentions the theft of the horses under date of July 20, 1842, only three days after one of the Bennett girls was accidentally shot. He added that Winston and his companion "came back to camp verry [sic] much frightened."

An American trader named Nathaniel Wyeth completed Fort Hall in 1834. He sold the outpost to the Hudson's Bay Company in 1837, and that British firm was still operating it when the emigrants arrived in mid-August. Fort Hall was located approximately fifteen miles north of modern day Pocatello, Idaho. The emigrants stayed there several days, resting themselves and their animals, trading, and making repairs. In general, they were favorably impressed with Fort Hall and noted that the prices were lower than at Fort Laramie. At Fort Hall they were again advised that they would be unable to take their wagons over the Blue Mountains into Oregon. The company determined to switch their transport from wagons to pack horses. The Hudson's Bay Company purchased some of the wagons but only for a trifle as the purchase was really only an accommodation. Others, including the Bennett family, abandoned their remaining wagons. Vardamon surely would never know it, but his abandoned wagon was not totally without further use. An emigrant of the following year noted that his company "found the wagons of the emigrants of 1842." Apparently they had more horses for use in pulling wagons, and "Mr. Keizur got a wagon Vardmond [sic] Bennett had left."[11]

By the end of August, the emigrants were on their way, leaving Fort Hall for their final push over the Blue Mountains of Oregon to Walla Walla, and then westward on the southern side of the Columbia River to The Dalles.

Fort Hall to The Dalles

After Fort Hall was reached, the emigrants supposed—erroneously as events played out in subsequent years for other parties—that all danger from the Indians was behind them. Accordingly, the travel became more informal, single men pushing on ahead of those with families, and occasionally families traveling by themselves. The group with which the Bennetts traveled continued along the Snake River until they reached Salmon Falls, near present-day Twin Falls, Idaho, where the Shoshone Indians were taking their annual supply of salmon. Winston explains:

> The fish were plenty and were taken by the ton. The party halted here for a couple of days and devoted themselves to eating fish. It was quite a relief from jerked buffalo, but their appetites were larger than their discretion and misery resulted.

Shortly after leaving Salmon Falls they needed to cross the Snake, and this was both dangerous and difficult. They had to angle across upriver, making for a long ride before reaching the opposite bank. One of the men, not of the family group, who had gone ahead was careless, then "borne away, and, in the midst of cries and shrieks, drowned, in the sight of his friends. His implorings for help were most touching, but it was impossible to reach him."[12] They reached Fort Boise, a small trading post located in present-day southwest Idaho near the border of Oregon, in very early September. The fort and the modern city are both named after the same river on which they sit but not at the same location. The emigrants continued to follow the Snake River northward until reaching Farewell Bend, located off modern Interstate 84 some twenty-five miles northwest of Ontario, Oregon.

From this point they left the Snake and headed west through the Burnt River Valley. Their next passage, through the Blue Mountains, proved to be difficult travel. The path was precipitous, a lot of up and down, constantly over rocks, crossing several streams, amid lots of fir and spruce. Eventually they descended into a very fertile valley and found some Indians who guided them into the Whitman Mission on the Walla Walla River, a short distance west of the present Washington city of that name. Marcus Whitman was a Presbyterian missionary who, together with his wife, Narcissa, had founded their famous mission in 1836. They received overland emigrants with great hospitality, creating some distrust among the Cayuse Indians to whom they preached.

All was well at the mission in 1842. The emigrants praised Whitman's industry and cultivation, admired his fields and grist mill. They also appreciated his hospitality, with some provisions given gratis and others at a very modest charge. The overlanders had arrived at Whitman's mission in mid-September, four months after leaving Independence. Their return to a modicum of civilization impressed itself upon their minds. One wrote, "I was never more pleased to see a house or white people in my life, we were treated by Dr. and Mrs. Whitman with the utmost kindness."[13] The emigrants all concurred in this and gratefully accepted his invitation to rest there for a few days. Their stay included a Sunday, and the emigrants attended the Presbyterian services. Winston Bennett noted that

> the congregation was composed of Indians who paid the most respectful attention to the sermon. The seemed specially to enjoy the singing, in

which they all joined making excellent music for the kind. There were about 500 Indians in attendance at the service.

In 1847, five years after Mary and her party visited the Whitman mission, a smallpox epidemic swept through the vicinity. Many of the Americans had a natural immunity that the Indians did not, which resulted in a much higher death rate among the Indians than the Americans. This heightened the hostility that already existed, and many Indians believed either that the Americans had intentionally introduced smallpox or that Whitman cured American children but not Indian children. Eventually, a small group of Cayuse Indians slaughtered Marcus and Narcissa Whitman along with other Americans at the mission.

After leaving Whitman's, the emigrants followed the Walla Walla River down to its confluence with the Columbia River, then along its southern side to The Dalles, crossing over barren land and experiencing considerable cold wind and rain. When they reached The Dalles, by the end of September, they could see Mount Hood's high, snowy peak off to the west.

Frenchmen gave the place the name of The Dalles because it is descriptive of the reality that here the Columbia River is forced through narrow gorges. Methodist missionaries established a small mission here in 1838, and it became a pivotal spot in the overland travel to Oregon since further progress seemingly was blocked by the Cascade Mountains. Many emigrant companies built rafts and floated down the Columbia to the area of settlement south of Willamette Falls. However, rafting on the Columbia River was full of danger, and many died as the result of an attempt to use the river. In 1846 a man named Barlow built a toll road along the south flank of Mount Hood that offered a longer but much safer alternative to the river. That was not available to the Bennetts' party in 1842.

From The Dalles to Oregon City and Settling into Oregon

The emigrants chose not to attempt rafting on the Columbia but instead to go overland to their destination, Willamette Falls, site of the present town of Oregon City. This is the head of the large Willamette Valley, the major agricultural region of Oregon and the destination of most American emigrants. At The Dalles, they were only some sixty miles from their destination, but Mount Hood, at 11,239 feet in elevation and the highest point in Oregon, stood in their way. Instead of the river, they chose to follow an old Indian trail at the base of Mount Hood on the north side, not the south side where the Barlow Road would be built in four more years.

They stopped at The Dalles for a day to prepare themselves and to hire an Indian guide. The loads had to be lightened. In the Bennetts' case, Vardamon left behind all their luggage that could not fit on a single pack horse.[14] The casting aside of precious possessions became a common practice on the overland trails. It occurred whenever wagons went into disrepair or otherwise had to be abandoned, or when the numbers of pack horses had to be cut down. We do not know what family heirlooms or treasures Mary Bennett was forced to set aside at The Dalles, but we can be sure that she suffered loss.

The emigrants described the trip across Mount Hood and the Cascade Mountains as the worst single portion of their entire trip. Early on they encountered a snowstorm, and many of the horses stampeded and ran back toward The Dalles. Some horses were recovered, but several horses were lost. Then the emigrants faced days of climbing up and over and down sharp precipices, hills, rocks, rapid streams, and logs, repeated over and over. Their animals additionally suffered from poor grass. One diarist, Medorem Crawford, admired the mountain scenery but also vividly described the treacherous passage:

> We came to a verry [sic] rapid river . . . very difficult crossing on account of large rocks and deep water, almost impossible to get along up the steep hills over the rocks & between the trees . . . road horrible beyond description.[15]

Still another trail injury on this final push across the Cascades must have caused great anxiety in Mary Bennett. One of her younger sons was mounted behind Winston on the same horse. Winston's memoir explains:

> While rounding a turn in the trail his horse slipped and fell a distance of 25 feet. The little boy escaped unhurt, but Mr. Bennett [i.e., Winston] received some severe bruises from which he did not recover for several days. It is a miracle that both the riders were not immediately killed.

They arrived at Willamette Falls in the first week of October, the end of a continental crossing of nearly six months. John McLoughlin, chief factor of the Hudson's Bay Company, had established a settlement here to build a sawmill to utilize the power of the Willamette River's falls. Soon renamed Oregon City, it was the headquarters of the American settlers in Oregon, the place where they filed land claims, and where they congregated. It became the territorial capital of the formal American Oregon Territory, during the years 1848 to 1851. In these early years Oregon City rivaled Portland for importance.

Even earlier, including when the Bennetts arrived, the term "Oregon Territory" was used to describe the present-day Oregon, Washington, and the southern portion of British Columbia. This vast area was under the joint administration of Britain and the United States, the ultimate boundary between British North America, now Canada, and the United States not being fixed until 1846. The most powerful institution in Oregon Territory was the British trading and trapping firm, the Hudson's Bay Company. Because of its power, many emigrants disliked and distrusted it immensely, although the company and especially its local manager, Dr. John McLoughlin, treated one and all fairly and with great kindness.

Although the emigrants of the Bennetts' party were among the first to arrive by the overland trail, other American emigrants had already reached the Oregon Territory by boat. John McLoughlin had adopted a policy of encouraging American emigrants to settle south of the Columbia River, hoping that in the eventual political settlement between England and the United States present-day Washington might remain British, or alternatively that it would remain unsettled sufficiently to remain useable for trapping. The fewer American settlers north of the Columbia the better. Their absence would favor either of his desired outcomes. Although Washington ultimately became American, Britain gained exclusive trapping rights for an additional ten years in the 1846 settlement of the boundaries. Ironically, John McLoughlin, never properly recognized by Britain for his services, later threw his lot in with the intruders and became an American citizen.

In the early 1840s McLoughlin was generous in aiding emigrant farmers, providing credit for seed and farm implements. American settlers already in Oregon showed equal hospitality by giving aid in selecting land, providing food and other provisions, and helping in the construction of homes. Because of McLoughlin's encouragement and the tangible aid given by him and the existing American settlers, most arriving Americans did in fact settle south of the Columbia in the early 1840s. That settlement was concentrated in the wide and long Willamette River Valley, running from Willamette Falls at Oregon City south through modern Salem to Eugene and beyond. However, Americans were not the only settlers. French Canadians had also arrived in some number, and there were scatterings of other nationalities.

After the Bennetts arrived at Willamette Falls, Vardamon went to consult with the missionaries and farmers near present Salem to select a final location for his family. He concluded by settling on a location about sixty miles south of Oregon City, which was south of Salem and just a bit north of present-day Albany, Oregon. The family moved there, and Vardamon built a house. However, his restlessness had not yet abated. In late November he abandoned the house he had built only the month before and returned to Willamette Falls, remaining there during the winter.[16] It is unknown why he removed to Willamette Falls or whether his family accompanied him. Perhaps he found work in the sawmill at the falls.

Lansford Hastings never intended to remain in Oregon. His plan had always been to move on and include a description of California in his projected book. However, a difficult journey and hostile Indians lay between the California and Oregon settlements, and he needed a group to travel with to assure the safety of the enterprise. He visited the various American farms in the Willamette Valley and found sufficient dissatisfaction with Oregon or just plain restlessness to assure a sufficiently large company. The planners designated a point to rendezvous, twenty-five miles from Willamette Falls, then settled in for the winter and awaited the spring to see how many would turn up for the trip to California.[17]

Although Vardamon Bennett eventually stood with the disaffected settlers who left for California, he became an Oregonian in spirit, even if his stay was short. He signed a petition, along with sixty other settlers, addressed to the United States Congress, warmly denouncing the Hudson's Bay Company.[18]

Chapter 4

From Oregon to California

Fifty-three emigrants for California appeared at the spring rendezvous on the Willamette River, including twenty-five armed men. Lansford W. Hastings won the election for captaincy of the company and served as leader of the overland trip to California as he had before, at least for the majority of the journey, on the expedition from Missouri to Oregon.[1]

Included among these discontented emigrants to Oregon was the Bennett family. We cannot know their specific dissatisfactions, but Bennett family lore suggests that excessive rain and too cool a climate drove them to California.[2] Since they were from the southeast region of the country—North Carolina, Georgia, Tennessee, and Arkansas—that seems likely.

The route to California was southward through the Willamette Valley until reaching the Rogue River. The emigrants crossed the Rogue, no small task, and proceeded eastward to Klamath Falls, thence southward into California. They continued south, bearing west until reaching the Sacramento River near the present-day town of Tehama, some twenty miles south of Redding. The lateral movements in their journey, east and then west, were made to avoid the high Siskiyou Mountains, and then to take advantage of the most favorable passes and valleys going back to the Sacramento Valley. Once at the Sacramento River, the Hastings party followed it down to John Sutter's establishment of New Helvetia, the site of the modern city of Sacramento.

The group left their place of rendezvous in Oregon at the end of May, and they encountered no particular difficulties until they reached the Rogue River in southern Oregon. Necessarily, they had to cross the Rogue to move east to Klamath Falls, and that required help from some Indians, even while multitudes of other Indians pestered them. The Indians thronged about them as they awaited the crossing, occasionally rushing toward them. It seemed not a full attack but an effort to cause confusion that would facilitate theft.

Hastings would fire a gunshot or two into the air, the Indians would fall back, then regroup and repeat the tactic. Eventually, the emigrants, including Mary, and their loads of baggage successfully forded the Rogue.

Shortly thereafter, they encountered a party driving 1,500 head of cattle from California to Oregon. The cattle fetched only four to five dollars a head in California, whereas they could be sold in Oregon for forty or fifty dollars apiece. Some settlers traveled with the cattle herders, intent on abandoning California and settling in Oregon. They told terrible stories about California, although Hastings added the further detail that they regarded California itself as delightful but felt they had been oppressed by the Mexican government there and were removing only *for the time being*. In fact, the Mexican California authorities treated American expatriates quite magnanimously, but these tales of woe caused a significant number of the Hastings party to return to the Oregon settlements. Their guide abandoned them as well, and the numbers of armed men dropped to sixteen.

Soon they began to notice Indians watching them from hilltops. Whether the emigrants passed in low, deep valleys or more expansive plains, Indians seemed always on higher grounds watching. While at the Klamath River, still in Oregon, Indians shot an arrow that struck a man named Bellamy while he was standing guard duty. Gunfire dispersed the attack, and Bellamy suffered from a painful but not life-threatening wound. It was a harbinger of more trouble awaiting them in California.

When they reached the Sacramento River on July 4, 1843, Winston Bennett noted the profusion of wild oats with stalks large enough for walking canes. This terrain provided perfect cover for a band of approximately 400 Indians who attacked them two days later on July 6, 1843, along the Sacramento River. Hastings ordered four older men to fall back with the women, children, and horses. The remaining men stood their ground and repulsed several waves of attack. Hastings vividly describes their initial attack:

> They continued to advance, with most terrific and frantic yells, which together with their fiendish gestures, and demonic grins, too clearly indicated their hostile designs. They now, rapidly advanced, with increased yelling, gesticulating, and grinning, as though mere frantic gesticulations, wild noises, and demonic grins, constituted irresistible weapons of warfare.

According to Hastings the battle continued for two hours, leaving perhaps three dozen Indians dead and the emigrants untouched. Winston believed he had killed two Indians in their initial charge with but one bullet. As the smoke of the gunfire following the first attack cleared away, Winston Bennett heard a voice at his side saying

> "Why Winsty you have killed two of those poor creatures!" He looked around and there stood his mother [i.e., Mary Bennett] in the thickest of the fight. She said she couldn't stand it to be in under shelter while her boys were out liable to be killed.

After the Indians were repulsed, the fighting men withdrew to rejoin the remaining party in their rear, the older men, women, children, and freight. Then they moved forward near to where the engagement had taken place. The Indians had regrouped and appeared to be advancing until they reached the point of the initial fighting. Hastings explains that

> upon arriving at this place, and perceiving for the first time, that their companions in arms were actually dead; they commenced a most tremendous howling and yelling, which plainly indicated that this was the first knowledge, which they had, of the desolating ravages, that death had made in their ranks. This was further evinced, from their throwing down their bows and arrows, and falling upon the dead bodies, of their companions, and their most piteous howling and lamentation, with which they now rent the air. They paid no further attention to us, but continued to howl and yell most furiously, falling upon their dead, and pulling and hauling them about, in every direction, evidently, so utterly confused, that they knew not what they did; entirely insensible, of all surrounding circumstances.

The emigrants continued on, unmolested by Indians, following the Sacramento River. Only three or four days later, on July 10, 1843, they arrived at New Helvetia or Sutter's Fort, the headquarters of the baronial estate of John Augustus Sutter, a Swiss immigrant. They arrived, as Winston Bennett put it, "out of provisions and worn down with their journey." They rested for two weeks enjoying Sutter's lavish hospitality. Sutter, Hastings thought, "rendered every one of the party, every assistance in his power; and it really appeared, to afford him the greatest delight, to be thus enabled, to render important aid, to citizens of his former, adopted country" [i.e., the United States]. Sutter did enjoy being host, but the hospitality was for his benefit, as we shall see, as well as that of the emigrants.

The California of 1843 in which the Bennetts had arrived was a land in transition. Although a part of the Republic of Mexico and very much Hispanic, the native Californios thought of themselves as Californios first and as Mexicans second. Loyal to Spain during the eleven-year agony of Mexico's revolution, between independence in 1821 and the year 1843, they had three times expelled Mexican governors by military force and regarded themselves as a cut above Mexicans. Some even used the term "Mexican" as an epithet.

Although united in opposition to outside rule, political harmony stopped there. Mexican California was riddled with petty political feuds, absurd military posturing and bloodless coups, and above all with endless bombastic pronouncements filled with flowery political rhetoric. Personal rivalries for lucrative government jobs formed one root of the controversies. The traditional California sectional rivalries between north and south, Monterey and Los Angeles, constituted an even larger cause for strife. At stake was the location of the capital and with it the customs house, through whose customs duties California obtained the largest share of her revenue.

Foreign merchants held in their own hands most of the commercial trade, both retail and wholesale. They too had a stake in this struggle as every trading ship would be obliged to stop at the port of the capital to pay customs duties. This meant the stimulation of retail trade by sailors and also the operation of warehouses to buy and hold the cattle hides and tallow used by the Californios to exchange for manufactured goods. Thus far history stood on the side of Monterey, the traditional capital of California. However, time favored the Angelinos; already in 1843 Los Angeles was the most populous community in California.

In 1843 California held only some 7,500 *gente de razón*, or people of reason, as white persons of all shades were called. Of these, foreigners constituted perhaps 10 percent, largely Americans but with a solid contingent of British. Additionally, some 4,000 ex-mission Indians lived in various stages of civilization, mostly in towns or on ranches, some still around the missions, with countless others still living in a native state in the great valleys and the mountains.[3]

The once vast and wealthy missionary establishments had declined into mere skeletons of their former selves. Secularized and converted to parish status in the last half of the 1830s, corrupt administrators appointed to succeed the missionary padres had looted them, their lands given to private hands through land grants, their chattels sold, their livestock slaughtered, and their buildings neglected and fallen into decay. Although some of the missions collapsed into absolute ruin, most had somehow survived with padres at least in spiritual charge. Several hundreds of Indians, perhaps more than a thousand in total, still lived in communities around the missions, eking out a miserable existence in the gathering gloom of the old establishments. In March 1843 the departmental government restored control of what slim amount of lands and cattle remained to the friars in twelve of the missionary establishments. Taken as a whole the California missions in 1843 were moribund, living corpses.

Private ranchos had supplanted the role of the missions, physically in that they occupied ex-mission grounds, economically because they now supplied the cattle hide and tallow that were California's largest export commodities, even paternally since they now were the largest employer of Indian labor. The ranchos were vast; a size of two leagues, about 9,000 acres or roughly fourteen square miles, was average, not large. The California government gave them freely, gratis, to any Mexican citizen, by birth or naturalization, who had the means and ambition to stock them and tend to their use. In the 1840s it became sufficient that an applicant give written notice of intent to become a naturalized citizen.

Spanish California, 1769–1821, had also offered land grants. However, Spain was stingy with her grants, and those she gave were almost all in the nature of a license to use land so long as it was ranched. Mexico, on the other hand, and the California government in particular were most generous in grants of the land itself, outright, with only a few perfunctory conditions to be satisfied before the grantee acquired a full, transferable title. Well more than 90 percent of the so-called Spanish land grants in California were derived from the years 1821–1846, the Mexican era.

For most of the Californios life was a matter of relative ease, interspersed with brief periods of hard labor such as at the cattle roundups, brandings, or slaughters. They employed Indians for much of the heavy labor, and for themselves they put much emphasis on parties, dances, picnics, bullfights, and the displays of horsemanship for which California was renowned throughout the Americas. In this sparsely settled society, rancheros always welcomed visitors, even strangers, for a visit of a few days or a week and stoutly rejected remuneration for their hospitality.

Yet to the thoughtful, the delightful California ambience seemed transitory. Anyone with the slightest knowledge of world affairs knew that Britain, France, and the United States all coveted her. Californios had heard rumors and warnings of war between Mexico and her expanding sister republic to the north. Only the year before Commodore Thomas ap Catesby Jones of the United States Navy had seized Monterey, California's capital, under the mistaken belief that war had broken out. America's imperialist designs were impossible to mistake.

For many years Americans had controlled California commerce. However, only in the two years immediately preceding the Bennetts' arrival in 1843 had American farmers shown interest in immigration. Less tolerant of Hispanic ways than the American traders, by 1843 these American farmers already spoke of a takeover. Many no longer bothered with the formality of application for naturalization or even attempted to obtain formal permission to remain. If war did not make California American, they reasoned that there was always the possibility of an emigrants' uprising, an independent republic, and an early American annexation—in short, a repeat of the Texas takeover, California style.

In the face of this threat, the central government in Mexico, although repeatedly warned of the dangers, proved to be utterly unable to act, wracked by repeated revolts and upheavals, plagued by corrupt or incompetent leaders. In consequence, Mexico neither garrisoned, fortified, nor colonized California. Many of the easy-going Californios had no concern about a change of flag, and some of the more thoughtful felt an American administration might increase the value of their lands. In any event, with a corporal's guard of soldiers and a tradition of comic warfare spawned from its bloodless revolutions, California could make little resistance on its own. Unable to govern itself well, unwilling to accept Mexican administration, and with Mexico itself impotent to insist on its sovereign rights, California drifted and wobbled, her political vacuum a magnet to a United States of America caught up in its Manifest Destiny to occupy the continent. Increasingly, California became a ripe plum, low-lying fruit, waiting to be plucked.

In 1843 John Augustus Sutter held only a short connection with California. Swiss by nationality, German by birth, Sutter had fled Europe in 1834, successfully escaping both family and creditors. In 1835–1837 he involved himself with commercial adventure in the Santa Fe trade between Missouri and New Mexico. Abandoning that, he traveled to California by a most indirect route, via Oregon, Alaska, and Hawaii. Sutter arrived in Monterey in July 1838, virtually penniless but with many flattering letters of recommendation and an abundance of ambition and energy.

Sutter applied to the governor of California, Juan Bautista Alvarado, for a large grant of land. Alvarado advised Sutter to announce his intention to become a naturalized Mexican citizen, go into the interior and select an unoccupied tract of land, and then return to Monterey in one year, at which time his naturalization and grant documents would be ready.

Sutter complied, going into California's vast central valley and selecting a tract sixty miles long and twelve miles wide straddling the Sacramento, American, and Feather Rivers. In building his headquarters near the confluence of the Sacramento and American Rivers, he founded California's future capital of California. He returned to Monterey, became naturalized, and received the grant to his enormous tract.

Sutter commenced living in the baronial style of a feudal lord, securing his position by attracting other settlers to his colony and building a well-fortified bastion, often referred to as Sutter's Fort but which he called New Helvetia—or New Switzerland. By creating a class of loyal partisans beholden to him for their own fortunes and building a fortification impregnable to the feeble Californian military, Sutter managed to operate independently of the California government. He regarded himself as a loyal Californian or not, obeyed orders or not, as his own interests dictated. He strengthened his power by the purchase of the Russian possessions at Fort Ross, lands, buildings, cattle, and armaments, when they withdrew from California in 1841, even though by the transaction he also acquired a debt that proved to be a difficult burden.

Sutter's operations were extensive, including cattle ranching, farming, construction, and all the other activities that related to the management of an extensive establishment of 720 square miles. The California government appointed him *alcalde*, combination judge and mayor, so with some color of authority Sutter issued passports, performed marriages, punished criminals, concluded treaties with Indians, and raided hostile tribes. However, Sutter's actions and activities far exceeded the legitimate range and expectations of the authority granted him, and he can best be viewed as a feudal lord, proud and independent, presiding over a central valley fiefdom.

The geographic location of Sutter's Fort astride the two main arteries of immigration, from the north and Oregon, and from the east and Missouri, offered benefits that were mutual and reciprocal. Sutter offered aid to the emigrants, replenishing their supplies and always offering opportunity for rest and nourishment both for the weary emigrants and their even more weary stock. Sutter's Fort as an operating establishment, with mills, repair shops, armament building, construction, ranching, and farming, held other advantages to the emigrants in the form of temporary employment. Additionally, Sutter could be counted on for a passport into the populated coastal areas, although by what authority he issued these was vague at best. Some few might even hope for a letter of recommendation that might be parlayed into a more rapid land grant.

These advantages were not entirely one-sided to the emigrants, since Sutter gained a reliable if temporary work force, at least more reliable than the only alternative laborers, Indians or the few available *kanakas* from Hawaii. The Californios almost to a man refused to engage in any manual labor for hire as beneath their dignity. Still another advantage to Sutter was the opportunity to purchase wagons, very scarce in California, from emigrants anxious to acquire horses so as to see the country more rapidly. Through all his help to the emigrants, Sutter also acquired friends and potential allies. He was, after all, operating in the twilight zone of legality, and from Sutter's point of view, armed and independent American settlers might become extremely useful at any time.

The Bennetts received Sutter's customary hospitality and rested at Sutter's Fort, together with most of their fellow travelers from Oregon, for two weeks. During this time the company was warmed by the stirring culmination of a trail romance. As Winston tells the story,

> While stopping at Sutter's a romantic wedding took place between George Davis and Miss Lizzie Sumner. An attachment had sprung up between the young people who had been thrown together during the long journey, and, on arriving at the Fort they agreed to join their hands and fortunes.

Her mother and sister opposed the match, but George, one evening took Lizzie in a boat, crossed the river and Capt. Sutter, who was then Alcalde, performed the ceremony. They sent their matrimonial compliments to the parents, who, when they saw that the thing was done, relented, sent for the young couple and gave them their blessing.

After their time at Sutter's Fort, the Bennetts, together with three other families, traveled west to the nearby Napa Valley and camped on the ranch of George C. Yount. An American expatriate, Yount arrived in California by sea in 1831. He settled into Napa Valley in 1836, where he worked his two land grants. At the same time that the emigrant families camped on Yount's ranch, he played host to Gorham H. Nye, a sea captain, and his wife, Lydia Rider Nye. Both were natives of Massachusetts. Mrs. Nye had strict religious scruples that included a total abstinence from liquor. She was also an expert horsewoman. During her sojourn in California, Mrs. Nye kept a daily journal, apparently to inform her family as well as for her own amusement, and she describes Mary Bennett in two passages under dates of August 18, 1843, and August 19, 1843. For August 18, she wrote:

> By the way, I heard there was three families of emigrants that had traveled by land from the States to Oregon. Did not like it, so kept on traveling 'til they at least [sic] stopped here. We had a great curiosity to see them. Upon inquiry, found the other two families had not found a resting place yet. In short Mrs. Bennett and daughter soon called upon us, dressed in their best attire, which if I should describe, would cause you to laugh, and that I would not do myself. Meanwhile, Gorham [her husband, Captain Nye] went to see the carpenters who were cutting timber close by, which left us to ourselves. And sure enough they gave me a history of their journey, which seemed to me almost incredible. In the evening we returned the call, saw her husband and eight children—hearty as pine knots. They left with property but their expenses had taken it all. But what is more strange, they were packing to start Sunday morning to go seventy miles further where her daughter was going to marry Mr. Sinclair, and where they too thought of settling.[4]

It is a shame that Mrs. Nye did see her way clear to describe the women's clothing. The tone of condescension, the view that the Bennetts were wearing their best attire but it was still laughable, resulted from a marked difference in social and economic class. Mrs. Nye, with her status as a sea captain's wife, her origins in New England and a reader of books, obviously thought the Bennett women, working-class southerners, to be something akin to what today we would call hillbillies.

In 1843 the Bennett daughters were Catherine, nineteen; Mary Ann or Amanda, twelve; Julia Ann, five; and Samantha, three. Only Catherine would be of marriageable age. One historian suggests that the "Sinclair" reference is to John Sinclair, a one-time business associate of Sutter's and then manager of Rancho del Paso, just north of Sacramento, and someone whom Catherine could possibly have met at Sutter's Fort.[5]

The Nye couple left the Yount ranch the next day, and Mrs. Nye relates,

> When the news reached Mrs. Bennett I was going, she, with her husband and children, came over bringing her horse, which she had rode from the States, and kindly offered it to me, which I very gladly accepted. Having mounted, bade them a final farewell. . . . Found Lady Pansy (the name of my horse) to be very gentle and easy.[6]

Mary Bennett clearly was capable of great acts of kindness. This was one; we shall see others. She was a complex woman, and we must remember these acts of munificence when we also see her engaged in mean-spirited disputes, over-reaching, and litigation.

According to Winston Bennett, they remained camped at Yount's ranch for only three weeks, gathering a supply of provisions and resting their livestock. Then the family moved "to the Sacramento river [sic] and built a house about eight miles from where Sacramento city now stands." This move gives credence to the prospects of a pending marriage between Catherine and John Sinclair. The Ranch del Paso that Sinclair managed was located immediately north of the American River at its confluence with the Sacramento River. That is approximately three miles from Sutter's Fort, which was in the heart of the small settlement of Sacramento. The ranch itself extended northward about four miles, so that a location on the Sacramento River about eight miles from Sacramento itself would be close to where the present Sacramento Airport is located and only a mile or so distant from the ranch that Sinclair managed. It would certainly be close to their daughter's new proposed home on the Rancho del Paso.

The extremely dry winter of 1842–1843 produced a disappointing crop in 1843 at Sutter's Fort. Frustrated by crop failure and the constant pressure of creditors both Californian and Russian (it had been just two years since the ambitious purchase of the Russian American Company's Fort Ross), Sutter was anxious to seize new sources of revenue. By October 1843 the Hudson's Bay Company had not sent their annual contingent of fur trappers from Oregon, and Sutter resolved to try his hand at trapping. His entry into this endeavor resulted in a great surge of local temporary employment.[7] It is quite likely that Vardamon Bennett, his oldest son Winston, and perhaps some of the other Bennett boys became fur trappers for a time.

In December 1843 the Bennett family moved again, this time to Yerba Buena, now San Francisco. The proposed marriage between Catherine Bennett and John Sinclair did not occur, and the failure of these prospects may have furnished cause for departure. Sutter's trapping experiment failed, and that also may have contributed. Probably general restlessness and the lure of greater financial prospects elsewhere contributed the most.

Winston Bennett explains carefully that at this time when the family moved, he did not. He remained in Sacramento and worked that winter for Sutter as a carpenter. Winston was now of age. We will often see him again, sometimes living in his mother's home, often working for his mother, but he will be an adult and a fully independent actor.

Chapter 5

The Bennetts Live in Yerba Buena

Yerba Buena was the youngest of the three separate communities located in what is now the city and county of San Francisco, the very head of the large peninsula lying between the Pacific Ocean and San Francisco Bay. In 1843 these communities were still very much separated and distinct from each other. The padres had founded the Mission of San Francisco de Asís, often called Mission Dolores, in the interior of the head of this peninsula on June 26, 1776.[1] By 1844 the mission had been looted of almost all valuables in the process of change from mission to parish status. Its buildings were largely in decay, although not completely abandoned nor completely destroyed. Somewhat fewer than 100 Indian converts still lived in and about the mission.

Juan Bautista de Anza's expedition began the San Francisco Presidio as a military fort on September 17, 1776. Located by the water, it was at the tip of the peninsula by the entrance to San Francisco Bay, the narrow strait, later called the Golden Gate, that separates San Francisco from the Marin Headlands. Although a military fort, the Presidio always had a large civilian contingent of independent artisans, civilian employees, settlers, and the soldiers' wives and families. General Mariano G. Vallejo had transferred the actual soldiers of the San Francisco Presidio to Sonoma long before 1844, but some Californios remained, living in or near the buildings of the old Presidio.

Yerba Buena, later San Francisco, occupied the same ground as San Francisco's present financial center and North Beach, excepting the portion of the financial center today that is created from filled land. It was to the east or bay side of the peninsula's head. The community traced her origins to 1835 when William Richardson, an English sailor-turned-trader, built a crude, temporary dwelling in the vicinity of the corner of present Grant and Clay Streets. It took a year for Richardson to acquire his first neighbor. So slowly did the future metropolis grow in her early years that by 1840 it possessed a population of only some fifty persons, including sixteen foreigners, or non-Californians. In December 1843 when the Bennetts arrived, Yerba Buena had grown from these humble beginnings but still showed no sign of the major city the Gold Rush was so soon to make of it.

Hudson's Bay Company established a warehouse and trading center in 1841. However by 1845 the future Queen City of the West had only approximately twenty structures, and most of them were crude adobes. A Mexican census held in July 1844 revealed seventy-five men in Yerba Buena liable for military duty, that is from ages sixteen to sixty, of which thirty-six were foreigners. Considering that California had many unmarried adult males but virtually no unmarried adult females, it is inappropriate to merely double the number of adult males to find the total adult population. Then children should be added in. Taken all together, a reasonable estimate of Yerba Buena's population in December 1843, when the Bennetts arrived, would have been around 150. Nonetheless, people regarded Yerba Buena as a growing town; significantly, foreigners, and most of them Americans, comprised the majority of the population.

Because of the natural advantages of San Francisco Bay, Yerba Buena was fast becoming a favored port, notwithstanding its scanty population. Ships called here from many nations, including Russia, Germany, and Scandinavia, although the ships of the United States, Britain, France, and naturally Mexico were the major contributors to the traffic. The purposes of the ships were equally diverse. Exploration parties, whalers, trading ships—these last called Boston Ships by the Californians because so many came from New England—all came into Yerba Buena for rest and repairs and to take on fresh provisions. Some came into port for trading.

Foreign traders, mostly American, came to California to exchange manufactured goods for the hide and tallow of California cattle. This trade was the largest single economic activity in Mexican California, and the high customs duties on the incoming manufactured goods constituted the largest source of the territorial government's revenues. Many whaling vessels regularly called at Yerba Buena and the small community of Sausalito across the bay for rest and repairs, but they were also traders. Most trade was limited to Monterey, the location of the custom house, but the California government permitted the whaling ships to sell a limited amount of manufactured goods elsewhere in exchange for supplies. Because these sales were exempt from the onerous customs and irksome inspection requirements, considerable subterfuge and smuggling grew up around this practice. All this gave Yerba Buena the strange mixture of a sleepy, small pueblo combined with a cosmopolitan trading center.

When the Bennetts arrived in Yerba Buena late in 1843, they found a piece of vacant land in North Beach along the rutted passageway now known as Pacific Street. Probably they just squatted on it, ignoring any question of title in the usual manner of Americans in Mexican California. The alcaldes, or mayors also judges, of Mexican California had the duty to grant town lots to settlers. However, Bennett's name is absent from a schedule of grants made by municipal authorities of San Francisco, including Yerba Buena, between 1835 and July 7, 1846,[2] the later date being when the American government deemed the Mexican government had lost sovereignty due to the American invasion.

Vardamon Bennett received a land grant from an American alcalde for the lot on February 3, 1847,[3] but that merely confirmed his previous occupation. Bennett's lot was indicated by name on the Buckelew Map of Yerba Buena prepared between December 15, 1846, and January 20, 1847, which was itself based on a still-earlier map received from the last Mexican alcalde.[4] The lot lay within the block formed by Broadway to the north, Pacific Street to the south, Grant Avenue (then DuPont Street) to the west, and Kearny Street to the east. The grant measured fifty *varas* wide and went to the center of the block between Broadway and Pacific, this being the standard town lot. The *vara* was a general Mexican unit of measurement, about 33-1/3 inches, so that fifty varas extended about 138 American feet. This constituted the middle third of the south half of the block between Grant and Kearny. The later-constructed Columbus Avenue skewed this entire block, indeed passed through the Bennett lot, but that was a development that did not exist during these years.

The Bennetts enjoyed a reasonably sized lot of a half-block length and a 138-foot width along Pacific Street. It was large enough for them to raise chickens, turkeys, and ducks for their own table and for sale. In addition Mary took in sewing, washing, and ironing.[5] There is no record of it, but undoubtedly Vardamon's first activities on the lot were to build a house, as he had in Oregon and north of Sutter's Fort in Sacramento. He engaged in a fair amount of carpentry and building, three houses within just a few years, and it is not surprising that the Mexican census of 1844, the *padrón*, lists him as a carpenter by trade, age forty, and his son Dennis, age nineteen, similarly.[6] Carpenters alone typically built houses in the mid-nineteenth century, as neither plumbers nor electricians were required. A new bridge and a new customs house for Yerba Buena, built in 1844,[7] may have provided some carpentry employment for Vardamon and Dennis.

In addition to carpentry, Vardamon had a number of other activities. In various ways he catered to the growing numbers of sailors visiting Yerba Buena, mostly American, and utilized the advantages of his location. His lot lay close to the water, only a few blocks from the new wharves at the foot of Clay Street. The waterline and wharves were then mid-block between Montgomery and Sansome Streets. For one of his economic activities, Vardamon operated a horse stable on his lot, from which he rented horses to the visiting sailors on shore leave so that they could tour the countryside. For this business his lot location proved beneficial beyond just its proximity to the wharves. A ride of two short blocks took his customers to the point on Kearny Street where the principal trails within the San Francisco peninsula converged. From that nearby point one trail led northwest over the hills to the presidio and in the other direction went along Kearny for a few more blocks, then southwest over some sand hills, yet generally on a relatively flat surface toward the mission.

A Connecticut whaling ship, the *Benjamin Morgan*, tied up at the wharf in Yerba Buena in the fall of 1844 to obtain fresh water, meats, and vegetables. The captain gave the crew shore liberty, and the reminiscences of one young sailor, W. B. Osborn, illustrate the operation of Bennett's horse rental business:

> We found the town to be nothing more than a few adobe houses on the gently sloping hillside. Off to the N.W. to the right and back of the town a quarter of a mile, there lived a family of emigrants from Arkansas. Their name was Bennett. This place the sailors called the milk ranch. Mr. Bennett had two daughters [actually four girls, the oldest two, Catherine and Amanda, being about twenty and fourteen respectively in 1844; their sisters were several years younger] and lots of California horses. The boys when it was their day on shore or "on liberty" as it was aptly called— would hire horses of Mr. B. for one dollar a day, and spark the Misses

Bennetts, but one of them being cross eyed if two of us went together we were puzzled to know which one received the most attention, and it was too delicate a matter [to] be referred to the lady in question without some explanation which would naturally give offense—but the horses were our hobby and some of us who never rode before mounted the Spanish saddles—the first we had ever seen and started over the sand hills for an excursion to the Mission Dolores.[8]

Vardamon also operated a groggery in which he sold *aguardiente*, a rough California brandy, by the drink and by the bottle.[9] He had competition in the liquor business, but he also operated what were probably the town's only bowling alleys.[10] From time to time he provided room and board to travelers but in a somewhat desultory manner. Although it was not a steady business, at one time during the Gold Rush, the crowds in San Francisco were so pressing that Vardamon had to use his bowling alleys as sleeping compartments.[11]

The Bennetts continued their distinctive characteristics and temperaments. As on the trail, people noticed them, and some were moved to write down their opinions. William Heath Davis, a leading American merchant in Yerba Buena, described the Bennett couple, and Mary Bennett in particular, in considerable detail:

Mrs. Bennett arrived in Yerba Buena from Missouri about 1842 [actually from Arkansas and in 1843], with her husband and a large family of children. I mention her first, as she was unmistakably the head of the family—a large, powerful woman, uncultivated, but well-meaning and very industrious. Her word was law, and her husband stood in becoming awe of her. Their children were respectably brought up. . . . I trusted her for goods frequently, not knowing, or caring much, whether they were ever paid for; but they always were. She was an honest, good woman, and while not regarded as an equal by the better-cultivated and more aristocratic ladies, she was always pleasantly received in their houses, as foreign ladies were scarce and class distinctions not rigidly observed.[12]

This is a remarkable description. It lavishes praise, but with a large element of condescension, regarding her as déclassé. Mary's southern and working-class origins clearly showed. Another contemporary observer, Joseph T. Downey, an enlisted man in the U.S. Navy and perhaps himself a bit déclassé, had a very different take on Vardamon and Mary Bennett. Not inconsistent with Davis's observations, it presents a different viewpoint:

> Bennet [i.e., Vardamon Bennett] is the sole proprietor of the up town bowling alley, and is, in his own way, a diamond of the first water—his house is always open and his face ever on the smile to receive customers, no matter what their size, age, sex, or complexion, and when he laughs, ye Gods! 'tis the explosion of what would appear to be the quintessence of all that is cachinatory; Bennet[t] has a family and they are all family too, one in which is contained most of the *bone* and *muscle* of Yerba Buena. They are rousers, male and female, and can work their way anywhere.[13]

Davis, an affluent merchant, and Downey, an observant sailor, are describing the same people. Their own positions in life give different colorations to the characteristics they each noted.

Of course, whalers, trading ships, and exploring parties arrived at this far-off Pacific port only sporadically. Hence the patronage of Vardamon's groggery and the admiration of sailors for the Bennett girls must also have been sporadic. For the most part Yerba Buena remained a sleepy place. Petty crimes and assaults happen everywhere, but about the only topic of local scandal in 1844 and early 1845 was the suicide of William Rae, the Hudson's Bay Company's local agent, on January 19, 1845. The inquest revealed that Rae had been depressed on account of his own personal financial problems, his having taken the losing side of yet another California revolt, the poor showing of the company's business, and the fact that an affair he had been conducting with a Californio woman had become public. That last fact naturally led to friction with his wife and was complicated by the fact that it was her father who was responsible for Rae's managerial position. Doubtless all this was thoroughly discussed throughout the Yerba Buena community.

Even so, Yerba Buena was a placid, dull place. Vardamon was relieved from the quietness of life by a California-style revolution. It was a typical example of the sort of posturing and bombast that characterized serious political disputes in Mexican California.

The native Californios, although Mexican citizens, held considerable antipathy toward Mexico, preferring to be governed by one of their own, and fiercely wanted to handle their own revenues. Although Los Angeles and

Monterey could never agree and frequently clashed militarily over the location of the capital with its prestige and the customs house with its revenue, Angelino and Montereño could agree alike on opposition to a governor imposed by the central government. The new governor, Manuel Micheltorena, was a gentleman of culture, easygoing and honest, although given at times to pomp and bombast. He was an able administrator, aided the padres, was friendly to all, perhaps overly so to foreigners, and even made strides to reconcile the traditional California regional strife between Los Angeles and Monterey.

The two main problems were first, and unavoidably, that the central Mexican government had appointed him as governor. The second problem, easily avoidable but not considered in advance, was that Micheltorena had brought with him from Mexico an "army" of some 300 soldiers, a large force for California, recruited from convicts and ex-convicts. The year of his arrival, 1842, as well as the next were poor trading years, and the revenues from customs duties were utterly insufficient to pay his men. Money from the central government, racked by upheavals and revolts, was only a theoretical possibility seldom realized in California. Accordingly, his soldiers survived by theft and petty depredations on the California citizenry, who in turned labeled the soldiers *cholos*, coarse half-breeds. The simple epithet that the native Californios often hurled against these soldiers—*mexicanos*—shows the degree of their separatist feeling.

Micheltorena arrived in California in August 1842, and as quickly as twelve months later rumors of revolt began. The uprising finally started in November 1844, with Manuel Castro and Juan Alvarado raising a force of some 220 rebels and Micheltorena marching out of Monterey with an army of 150. After several days of meaningless maneuvering in the vicinity of San José and Santa Clara, negotiations resulted in Micheltorena's promise to send the *cholos* away within three months, while the rebels promised to respect the governor's authority and retire to Mission San José to await the fulfillment of the promise. Curiously, many Americans supported Micheltorena, believing that the native Californios' hostility toward the governor was on account of his friendliness with the foreigners.

Vardamon and his son Winston were engaged, if marching and posturing in the cold, rainy weather without the firing of a single shot can be called engagement, on behalf of Micheltorena during the first phase of the revolution. In fact, Winston and a small party of others achieved some short-lived fame by capturing the original rebel leader, Manuel Castro, who was, nevertheless, promptly exchanged for other prisoners. Winston, and probably his father as well, ceased their role as soldiers during this lull.[14]

Unfortunately, Micheltorena did not keep his promise to send away the *cholos* and instead marched out in January 1845 to engage the rebels. The revolting army marched southward to Los Angeles to marshal support there and in a brilliant stroke of fortune gained the adherence of its own foreign contingent. The "battle" of Cahuenga ensued, February 20–21, 1845, where, after a day and a half of maneuvering and volleying of cannons, the total casualties consisted of two dead mules, balanced evenly one to each faction. Neither side had sufficient munitions for much sustained firing, but that problem was solved by simply firing back the opposition's spent cannon balls. California revolutions were acts in the theater of the absurd. The foreigners at Cahuenga, primarily Americans, upon seeing the comedy of the bluster and posturing and especially after noticing that there were fellow Americans in the opposite camp, decided that this was not their fight and retired from the field. Without his foreign allies Micheltorena had no heart for a fight. He quickly arranged a truce, agreed to leave California with his *cholos*, and in fact did. Pío Pico became governor, headquartered in the south, and José Castro became military commander, headquartered in the north. As events unfolded Pío Pico was the last Mexican governor of California.

Mary, of course, did not participate in this particular break from monotony. She had to manufacture her own excitement, and a festival preceding Lent, probably in 1844, provides an amusing example. The Californians had a quaint custom for the pre-Lenten season involving hollowed egg shells filled with scraps of silver or gold papers, or sometimes filled with cologne water. As William Heath Davis, the affluent merchant, explains:

> It was in the nature of a game or trick played upon one another, the idea being to catch the victim unawares, and gently smash the egg and distribute its contents over the head. A gentleman, for instance, would call upon a lady, and be pleasantly received and entertained. When his attention was attractively occupied, the fair hostess would deftly tap his head with the egg, which, breaking, would cover his head with the bright scraps of paper, or with the cologne; and a good laugh would ensue at

the success of the stratagem. The gentleman, in turn, in calling upon the ladies, would go provided with these pleasant missiles, and would seize opportunities to break them on the heads of the fair entertainers. This custom was observed all through the department [i.e., Alta California]. It has long been practiced in Spanish countries. Much maneuvering and various ingenious devices were resorted to by the ladies to catch the gentlemen off guard in order to accomplish the delicate feat. The gentlemen, at the same time, exercised all their tact and skill to get a similar advantage. When successful, and the lady or gentleman's head received the contents of the egg, whatever company was present joined in the outburst of merriment.[15]

As this activity was in the nature of a carefully controlled practical joke among social equals, it was only rarely performed in public. "The practice of this amusement in the street, however, was entirely confined to those of a humbler position," notes Davis.[16] That, of course, included Mary Bennett. In the festival of 1844, Mary Bennett became the leader of a entire party of men and women crashing eggs on each other in the courtyard, or main plaza, of Yerba Buena. We can be sure that there was nothing "deft" about Mary's behavior. Indeed, probably thinking that crashing eggs was insufficiently physical and insufficiently pugnacious, Mary encouraged a more vigorous engagement in which revelers threw water at one another. The result, something akin to a near riot, took the sport, in Davis's carefully measured words, "beyond its legitimate bounds."[17] Aside from the few opportunities for Mary Bennett to promote her own amusements, life probably rolled on with monotony and boredom for her in sleepy Yerba Buena. Who is to say that this alone may have played at least a minor role in Mary's momentous decision of 1845?

For in 1845 Mary Bennett decided to take her minor children and separate from Vardamon, moving to Santa Clara, a distance far enough so that she would neither see Vardamon nor receive his help with the children on a regular basis. The next chapter will examine how she did this, but here we will examine her motives, why it was she wanted to leave her marriage.

On June 6, 1845, Mary Bennett filed a petition with the Monterey-based American consul and leading merchant Thomas O. Larkin, seeking consular aid for protection "from her husband in her person and the persons of her children that she may be enabled to live separate from said Vardamon Bennett and support herself and family free from molestation on his part." Specifically, Mary asked the consul to write the alcalde of San José and Santa Clara and request this Mexican official to protect her as "she is in fear of her person and life from words and threats that he continually uses toward her." This implies that she had already separated and relocated to the geographic region of San José and Santa Clara and was no longer in Yerba Buena. As a more general statement of the reasons for her separation, she alleged in this petition that "Vardamon Bennett the Father of said children has entirely neglected her and Family, refuses to support and maintain them, and takes from them by force their daily earnings and even their clothes leaving her and said children destitute of living."[18]

Her allegations were essentially those of nonsupport and threatened violence. These accusations are difficult to believe. According to the keeper of family tradition, Mable Born Early, Mary's great-granddaughter, Mary stood over six feet tall and weighed between 300 and 350 pounds.[19] Entirely disinterested observers had noted that Mary Bennett was a "giantess" (Elijah White on the overland trail), "powerful," the "head of the family," and that her husband Vardamon "stood in becoming awe of her" (William Heath Davis in Yerba Buena). We will see additional descriptions of her in the years that follow in a similar tenor. It makes no apparent sense that a gigantic, powerful woman would tolerate the least bit of physical force directed at her. As for nonsupport, that does not fit what we know of Vardamon's activities. While perhaps not a master of commerce, he was nevertheless a hard worker. We have seen him build three houses for his family over the course of just a few years, as well as engaging in the businesses of renting horses and operating a groggery, bowling alley, and occasional boarding house. The allegations probably are Mary's or perhaps the consul's idea of proper "grounds" for a separation that would induce the most positive response from the California authorities. In other words, stock grounds probably were offered in order to obtain help for Mary, not as an expression of their truth.

An alternative explanation from the Bennett family lore suggests that Mary was opposed to Vardamon's operation of his liquor business and thought it would be a bad influence on their children.[20] That one is not easy to disprove yet on analysis seems unlikely. Superficially it might fit. Although we do not know whether Mary had a church affiliation or preference, it is very possible that she was Baptist because she was Southern and working class. The disapproval of Baptists toward drinking alcohol is well known, and we might conclude that this presented a big issue for her. The Baptists, however, were not then so opposed to drink as they are now; the Southern Baptists did not issue their resolution condemning alcohol until 1886. Moreover, it does not seem that Mary Bennett was excessively protective of her children. A woman who has allowed her daughters to travel on long unchaperoned trips with sailors on shore leave is unlikely to be offended by the deleterious influence of an occasional drunk at her husband's bar, especially since she was there to directly supervise the saloon.

Although not objecting to the saloon as such, Mary's real objection may have been to Vardamon's personal consumption of the product he was selling, in other words that he was a drunkard. According to the recollections of the oldest son, Winston, already in his twenties when his parents separated, his father died "in San Francisco in 1849 from the effects of alcoholic stimulants."[21] A husband with a drinking problem may have greatly contributed to Mary's decision. However, it seems under all the circumstances that more was involved.

The most pertinent factor was probably that Mary ultimately decided that Vardamon lacked sufficient ambition. In California she saw all around her examples of other people—Americans not just Californians—getting substantial grants of land for free. Land! The very essence of wealth for every nineteenth-century man or woman, and especially for the Irish. Yet Vardamon seemed content to just sit on his small lot in Yerba Buena and take in minor bits of money from renting horses, selling occasional drinks and bottles of liquor, and running his bowling alley, all dependent on the sporadic arrival of ships. Of course, Vardamon's one-sixth of a block in San Francisco's North Beach would be worth a great amount of money after the Gold Rush. Nobody knew about that in 1845, and as of that time it appeared that Vardamon was content with small potatoes in a small town.

Mary Bennett wanted better. She saw opportunity. Within the next year in Santa Clara, she would receive a substantial land grant of her own and be completely independent of Vardamon. In February 1847 she had a conversation about her land grant with Stephen A. Wright, a recently arrived American immigrant. He testified by deposition before the Land Commission adjudicating her Mexican land grants about that conversation.

She said it would be a valuable tract of land when she got able to cultivate it. She stated also that she had been very poor. She talked a good [deal] about its being her dependence—that it was valuable land and . . . that she depended on that to make her home, when she got able to enclose and cultivate it.[22]

It appears it was the motive to change poverty into prosperity that led Mary Bennett to strike out on her own and abandon her husband.

Chapter 6

Mary Bennett Separates from Vardamon and Moves to Santa Clara

Divorce in the modern sense did not exist in Roman Catholic Mexican California, with the exception of ecclesiastical annulments where grounds existed for the invalidity of the marriage. These were rare but increased after the arrival of California's first bishop, Francisco García Diego y Moreno, in December 1841. California did have judicial procedures for separations. They followed the usual course of litigation before the local judge, in some years known as alcalde, in other years, *juez de paz*.[1]

A complaint would be filed with the town court. Next came a conciliation hearing with the usual *hombres buenos*, or good men. These were persons appointed one by each party to aid the alcalde in proposing a judgment that would resolve the litigation, a step essential to all Mexican litigation at this time.

If a reconciliation were not achieved at the conciliation hearing, or occasionally if emergency compelled it even earlier, as the first procedural step the judge ordered the wife placed in an honorable home other than that of her husband. This deposit into a "safe house," as it was called, was designed to protect the wife from abuse and to prevent the possible scandal of an unchaperoned female in the community. It was also a step that would assuage Latin male suspiciousness and sense of honor and therefore promote subsequent reconciliation. Generally a wife was placed in the home of her father or other adult male relative, such as an uncle or a married brother. Or she might be placed with her *hombre bueno* or with other figures above reproach in the community, such as the American consul and his wife. This procedure was not unique to California and was practiced elsewhere in Mexico.

Then the alcalde or *juez de paz* turned to setting a usually very modest level of support for the wife and made any other necessary protective orders, ranging from a simple order that the husband should behave himself or jailing a husband because of domestic violence, to more creative orders, as when one alcalde directed a husband to take his wife's clothes out of pawn.

The conciliation process of ordinary litigation was designed to achieve harmony, and it worked even more effectively than its usual high rate in the case of marital separations. The alcaldes frequently exhorted spouses to attend to the obligations owed each other and to forget resentments. The rate of reconciliation was extremely high. The judicial records of Mexican California reveal only two or three permanent separations of married couples with a final support order or separation agreement.

These procedures for judicial separation in Mexican California had little attraction for American women who desired to separate from their husbands. Not only was the process slow and cumbersome, but American women took umbrage at being ordered about summarily by the local judges and being confined in a safe house. These women had the drive and mettle that enabled them to cross the plains, and their independence was compromised by confinement in any safe house.

The story of one young American immigrant well illustrates this disdain. Susan Biggerton's stepfather abandoned her in 1845, upon their arrival in California. She married William Lewis, an Englishman, at Sutter's Fort in Sacramento, apparently upon her suitor's representations that he was wealthy and had a good farm and many cattle in Yerba Buena. After a few days the couple traveled to Yerba Buena, where she discovered that he was in fact impoverished and that his inducements were all false. She immediately left him and stayed temporarily with an American couple.

Unfortunately, Lewis was not willing to give her up and enlisted the aid of the local alcalde to institute proceedings to compel her return. Following customary California procedure, the alcalde sought to place the wife in a safe house pending his investigation into the status of the marriage. The alcalde and another man, an Englishman and probably the husband's *hombre bueno*, "came and told me," in a manner obviously resented by the young woman, "I must leave the house I am now in and go to one they may think fit to find me, and if I do not go tomorrow they will take me by force." Writing to William Leidesdorff, the American vice-consul stationed in Yerba Buena, she begged to ask your interference, and wish to know what I have committed that I am to reside where those people think fit to Send me, and being a perfect Stranger in this place and having a great dislike to the idea of living in a Spanish house as a Prisoner I hope you will advise me and assist me with your Protection.[2]

Obviously a woman as stubborn and independent as Mary Bennett would not tolerate this California procedure. When she separated from Vardamon she just took her children and left. However, that does not imply that she did this without thought and planning. The evidence suggests that she had decided on Santa Clara as her new home in the spring of 1845 and had actually moved there well before she appeared before the American consul in June 1845 to sign her petition. Her involvement of Thomas O. Larkin was not in any sense to legalize or legitimate her separation but arose out of needs for protection of both person and property.

In 1845 Santa Clara was a small community that had grown around the decaying Mission Santa Clara. It was located just a few miles north of San José, connected by a road called the Alameda. Santa Clara lies just to the south and west of the very end of San Francisco Bay. Alexander Markoff, a Russian visitor, wrote a sketch of the town as of 1845. Santa Clara, he wrote,

consists of only a few houses, situated not far from the bay. The houses are separated from each other by rather long distances, but the intervals are filled up with gardens full of cabbage, turnips, garlic, cucumbers and mustard. There are also many vacant parcels of land which have never been cultivated in any way. Behind the village there are gardens with apples, pears, peaches, almond, olive trees and grapevines, also Greek nuts and blackberries, squashes and all kinds of melons. The site of the village of San Carlo [Santa Clara] is more beautiful than that of any other settlement around San Francisco Bay. All around it are low green hills with small brush and flowers and occasional dense groves of live-oak and pine, while fertile plains extend beyond as far as the eye can reach, to the foot of the blue-mountains in the dim distance. The blue bay frames and completes the charming picture. The deepest silence reigns in full accord with the general air of listlessness which pervades the inhabitants of this happy clime.[3]

Following supper with his hosts, Markoff went out to view the village of Santa Clara more closely:

> From some of the houses a little smoke was rising, indicating that supper was being prepared within, and as the deepest silence had set in without, I could distinctly hear the sound of something flying. A very few chickens roamed among the houses, sheep were feeding in the grass and in some places cows were being milked and calves were gamboling upon the turf. Not far from the shore boys were running around barefooted over the sand; at one of the houses an Indian was making himself a bed, in the shape of a thick blanket, greasy with tallow and torn in many places; further on there were gardens surrounded with fences or ditches.[4]

Yet Mary Bennett would not have been primarily attracted by the community's charms or location. What prompted her to pick this small settlement over several others? The probable reasons were the availability of land and that she knew two persons in Santa Clara who could help her. George W. Bellomy, who had traveled with the Bennetts overland to Oregon in 1842 and then down to California in 1843, settled in Santa Clara when he arrived in California, married a local California woman, and operated a shop and tanning operation. That must have been some comfort to Mary. However, the greatest reason for Santa Clara is that somehow, there is no evidence of how, she had made the acquaintance and friendship of a woman named Silvería Pacheco, who probably married later to a former English sailor, Thomas Cole, a resident of California since 1833. And the significance of that friendship, for Mary Bennett, depended on Silvería Pacheco's relationship with the padre then in charge of Mission Santa Clara, Fray José María del Real.

José María del Refugio Suárez del Real, to use his full name, was born about 1804 in Mexico. He came to California in 1833 and served as the missionary in charge of Mission San Carlos in Carmel, with additional responsibilities for the parish church in Monterey, in which town he resided in a house he personally owned. In 1844 he was assigned to the Santa Clara Mission, with additional responsibilities for the parish church in San José. He returned to Mexico in 1851.[5]

Father José Real was a complex figure. He certainly had supporters, including the California general Mariano Guadalupe Vallejo, famous for his friendship with the American cause, who thought Real was "one of the most genial and kindly men of the missionaries," informal and friendly with his parishioners.[6] However, for a missionary and priest, he had a rather unusual sexual life.

A fellow cleric filed an indictment in Rome against Fr. Real in 1851, alleging that while he was in Monterey Real "caused a scandal by living almost publicly with three women, two of whom were single, one a widow. They were known as the 'women' of Real and their children by him known as the 'Real' children." When he was sent to Santa Clara Mission he took over the care of the woman and children of the previous priest and then increased her family through the addition of other children. He also sent aid to his women and children in Monterey and visited them occasionally.[7]

Apparently, while at Santa Clara, Fr. Real was able ultimately to focus his sexual energy onto a single concubine. That woman was Mary Bennett's friend, Silvería Pacheco. James Alonzo Forbes, son of the British vice-consul, who lived in Santa Clara and had been baptized by Fr. Real, wrote in 1905:

> At Santa Clara [the] padre [José Real] had the woman he lived with and from who he had several children (I knew two boys and one girl). The woman lived across the street from the Mission Church. . . . The woman the padre kept at Santa Clara was a Silvería Pacheco.[8]

Silvería Pacheco was obviously in a good position to influence Fr. Real, and Fr. Real was in an excellent position to aid Mary Bennett. Santa Clara was included within the missions at which Governor Micheltorena had restored temporal power to the missionaries in 1843. Although there was not much left after the looting by the earlier administrators, many buildings still remained, over which Fr. Real had total authority. More important, his recommendation would matter a great deal regarding a government grant of lands close to the former mission.

Therefore, it was because of Mary Bennett's acquaintance with Silvería Pacheco, of which, again, we have no real detail, that matters moved forward for her land grant from the Mexican government in California. As she, Silvería Pacheco, herself later explained in testimony in the proceedings for confirmation of the Bennett land grant:

> I went to the priest—the curate of the mission, and told him that Mrs.

Bennett wanted a piece of land there, and he told me that he would give her a piece of land anywhere that she wanted it. Mrs. Bennett looked around there for a piece of land, and finally selected the piece which was afterwards given to her.[9]

Before we discuss her selection, we need to go back to her June 1845 meeting with Larkin and its purpose. Marital separations often exhibit familiar patterns where parties attempt to lay their hands on liquid or moveable assets, to harass the other by manipulation of their children, and to keep nonliquid assets, such as real estate, out of their own hands for fear the other may lay claim to it. All this happened in the separation of Mary and Vardamon Bennett, and it was critical that Mary establish the high moral grounds for her leaving Vardamon by her manipulation of the facts and her allegations, as we have seen, of threatened violence and nonsupport. Larkin aided her considerably by repeating her allegations in a letter to the alcalde, or local judge and mayor, of San José and Santa Clara, where she was now living, written on June 6, 1845, the same date as her petition:

> Mrs. Mary Bennett, of the United States of America, has presented to me that she has by her Husband Vardamon Bennet[t] Eight children, and that for more than one year her Husband has refused to support her and her children. She begs of me as Consul of the United States to afford to her assistance and protection, she wishing to live separate from said Vardamon, that she may be enabled to maintain herself and children, which she says she can not do while her Husband is allowed to molist [sic] and deprive her of her earnings. In consideration, I have to beg the favor of you, that you will render to the said Mary all protection within your power, should she apply to you for the same. Mrs. Bennet[t] wishes to settle on land withen [sic] your Jurisdiction and maintain herself and family free from the molistitations [sic] of her Husband. You will oblige the undersigned, should be said Vardamon Bennet[t] make any attempt to break the peace or the law of the land he lives in, to see that Justice is administrated [sic] towards the parties.[10]

This letter had importance beyond the unneeded protection it sought. The local alcalde was required to pass an opinion to the governor on land grants within his jurisdiction, primarily whether the required land was truly unoccupied. He also must walk or ride around the boundaries of the land grant with the grantee and put that party into possession for the grant to become effective. The creation in this local official of a favorable climate of opinion toward Mary Bennett was important.

When Mary traveled to see the consul in Monterey, she took her adult son Winston with her. Vardamon had precipitously taken seven horses which were in Winston's care, according to Mary and Winston. Winston filed his own petition, on the same date as his mother's, alleging the theft of these horses—claimed by him to be his horses—by his own father. Apparently Vardamon had taken the horses back to his stable on Pacific Street in Yerba Buena, and Larkin wrote a second letter to another alcalde, the alcalde of Yerba Buena, asking him to investigate "the case, and act in the same as you in your wisdom may see just and proper."[11]

The Yerba Buena alcalde, José Sánchez, did just as Larkin requested. He summoned both father and son together before witnesses. Winston testified that the horses had been given to him by his father but admitted that the purpose was for the "service and common benefit of the family." The judge determined and reported to Larkin that not only was the violent stealing of the horses falsely imputed to Vardamon but so also "the rest that is asserted in your writing with respect to his ignoring of his obligations to his family." Perhaps Sánchez knew of the grounds alleged for separation from other information because it was not included in Larkin's letter to the Yerba Buena alcalde.

Sánchez's decision implied that Vardamon initially thought he would join his family in Santa Clara. Reasoning that since the gift of the horses was for the maintenance of the family, the alcalde determined that Vardamon had the right to revoke and invalidate the gift in light of the scandalous gossip and "in view of the reproachable conduct with which his wife and children have conducted themselves (as is public and notorious) and as his ungrateful sons have abandoned him." Referring to the entire Bennett matter as one of the most scandalous happenings of Yerba Buena, the judge concluded that Vardamon Bennett's reclamation of the horses was proper and that "they remain taken by right."[12] The alcalde's decision reflects both a distinctly cultural reaction to Mary's separation and forcefulness and also a strong criticism of her manipulation of facts. The judge in Yerba Buena, who presumably knew the Bennett family before Mary's departure, just did not believe Mary's story of threatened violence and nonsupport. Nor should we regard that story as more than grounds that Mary asserted to manipulate events and obtain her land grant.

Vardamon launched a sort of counterattack by seeking to obtain custody of his minor children. He initiated the process by seeking out Larkin. Thomas Larkin may have somewhat tired of the Bennett family's squabbles. However, he did his job and wrote to the Yerba Buena alcalde, without mention of the previous horse stealing matter, that Vardamon Bennett had applied to him for "advice respecting his taking charge of his own children in preferance [sic] to their being with their Mother." Reflecting accurately the general American law of the early nineteenth century that fathers were the primary custodians of minor legitimate children, he wrote the Yerba Buena judge:

> I have only this to say, that by the Laws of the United States, I consider that the Father of minor children should have the care of them when there is no dispute, but he is willing and able to provide for them in a proper manner.[13]

Perhaps the custody "fight" was only an effort to scare Mary. Vardamon made no further attempt to contest her custody of the minor children. Mary Bennett did not scare easily, and there is no evidence that she was affected by this custody threat. She had something more serious to worry about.

If she acquired the proposed land grant she had discussed with Silvería Pacheco and doubtless Padre Real, what would be Vardamon's claim regarding it? She could not have known the details of California's community-property legal regime, but even under the common-law property rules she probably had a vague idea that her spouse would gain rights of curtesy in property she acquired and a life estate following her death. But more important, Vardamon could have claimed common-law rights to manage and control his wife's property while she was alive and during the existence of the marriage. Chief Justice Zephaniah Swift of Connecticut made a succinct statement of the applicable common-law rules, about which Mary Bennett must have worried, in 1818:

> The husband, by marriage, acquires a right to the use of the real estate of his wife, during her life; and if they have a child born alive, then, if he sur-

vives, during his life, as tenant by the curtesey [sic]. . . . As to the property of the wife accruing during coverture [i.e., acquired during the marriage], the same rule is applicable.[14]

The American consul Thomas O. Larkin made the useful suggestion for Mary that she should put the land grant in her son's name. On the same day, June 6, 1845, that he wrote to the Santa Clara alcalde, asking that he protect Mary from Vardamon's probably nonexistent "molistitations," he also wrote to Padre José Real concerning the proposed grant of land:

> The undersigned has been applied to by Mrs Mary Bennet[t] of the United States of America, who inform [sic] him that you have kindly offered to assist her and her family in building a House near the mission now under your charge, and that you request a letter from me, on the subject.
>
> The undersigned would give as his advice, that should you be willing to serve Mrs Bennet[t] as mentioned—and it would be doing a great favor on a poor woman who unaided by her Husband has a large Family to support—that it would be better that any property the family may receive through your kindness should be given in the name of the eldest son Winston, which may prevent the Husband of Mrs Bennet[t] coming forward and claiming it, as it is said he refused to support his Family.

Larkin went on to thank the priest for his "kind offer and attention to his countrywoman."[15] It appears that Mary Bennett had convinced both Padre Real and the American consul of her allegations of threatened violence and Vardamon's refusal to support his family. Mary herself jump-started the process of the land grant's being put in her son's name. Without Winston's knowledge she simply forged her son's name in the Hispanicized form of Narciso onto a petition for Mexican naturalization, a requirement for a land grant, and then onto the petition for the land grant that was sent to the governor together with the recommendations of the local Santa Clara alcalde and Padre Real. A credible witness in the later land claim proceeding testified that Winston Bennett was not in Santa Clara at the time of the petition for the naturalization and grant and that he had heard Winston say that it was done without his knowledge.[16] No reason existed under California practice why a land grant could not be made to a woman. Although not as common as grants to males, women did receive Mexican land grants in California. It was the fear of Vardamon's claim that led to Mary's forgery and petition in Winston's name.

Winston himself was often at the land grant, worked there often, and even lived there for a time. But contemporaries in Santa Clara understood that it was Mary Bennett's grant and her farm.[17] Much speculative writing has centered on Narciso Bennett, including the extreme suggestion that Narciso was actually Mary's estranged husband Vardamon![18] During the land commission proceedings to confirm the Mexican grants, Winston recorded a deed from Narciso Bennett to Mary Bennett with the Recorder's Office of Santa Clara County. The deed described the lands received under the grants, recited a nominal consideration, and acknowledged that the lands to which title was being transferred "have been heretofore in the use and occupancy of my mother the said party of the second part" [i.e., the grantee].[19]

When Mary Bennett and her family first came to Mission Santa Clara, in early 1845, Fr. Real, the priest, allowed her to occupy an old mission adobe that formed a part of the enclosure of the mission vineyard, on the eastern side of the vineyard or to the west of the mission church.[20] From here she petitioned for her grant.

She asked in two petitions dated September 4, 1845, for a grant of two separate parcels, a house lot of 140 varas square, located approximately three-quarters of a mile south of the mission church, together with a larger parcel for farming. This larger parcel was 2,000 varas by 1,000 varas and located a mile or two to the west of the Santa Clara Mission. Since a vara is the approximate equivalent of 33 inches, the dimensions of the farming plot was 5,500 feet by 2,750 feet.

In the mid-nineteenth century the Republic of Mexico had a policy of disposing of its public land to actual occupiers of Mexican nationality in order to build up the country. The United States held similar views during the period. The American preemptive laws granted squatters on the public lands a first option to purchase at low prices when the line of settlement advanced sufficiently to permit survey and settlement. This encouraged pioneer settlement beyond the settled areas. Beginning in 1863, the federal government granted free land, homesteads, on condition that the acreage granted be cultivated and a residence be built.

Mexico was following the same line of thought regarding development and often attached a condition of cultivation or a residence to its grants. In California many people who had an actual need and the capacity to utilize the land could obtain some grant. The amount of land Mary received was actually very modest by California standards, yet it undoubtedly came because both Padre Real and the California authorities, as an American settler in Santa Clara noted, were "disposed to favor Mrs. Bennett because she had a large family and was very poor."[21]

Hispanic practice generally and California practice specifically preferred building lots to be close in a community, with the growing fields lying a short distance away. Farmers of small plots, as distinct from the large *ranchos*, generally lived apart from their farms. For convenience the smaller plot will be referred to as the "house lot," with the larger parcel referred to as the "farm."

Following informal requests or discussions between government officials and applicants, the formal procedure for obtaining California land grants began with a petition stating the reasons for the request, a report from the alcalde, attesting that the land was vacant and under no one else's claim, and a *diseño*, a crude map showing the boundaries of the land requested.

The California governor would then accept or reject the petition, often making a notation on the petition itself. Following an acceptance, a formal title document would be prepared and sent to the applicant. This title document would describe the land granted and list any conditions to the grant, often that a smaller grant within the area of a municipality be subject to any public roads and requiring that within a year the applicant bring portions of the land under cultivation, build a residence, and sometimes adding a requirement that a portion of the land be enclosed. We cannot know the exact conditions to Mary Bennett's grant because the original title papers were lost.[22] Copies of the petitions and Governor Pío Pico's order that the grant be issued were found in the California archives following the American invasion,[23] but the titles themselves were lost and had to be established through secondary evidence.[24]

The last requirement, following the issuance of the title, was the giving of "judicial possession" by the town alcalde. He and the grantee, together with witnesses, including adjoining landowners, rode over the grant's boundaries, noting the described boundaries, any conflicting uses, and settling ambiguous lines or reference calls to the geographical boundaries.

Mary asked for the land, in her son's name, because it was uncultivated and he had "a large family to support," and lacked "tillable land by which to provide the sustenance of the said family."[25] That is the totality of Mary's stated reasons for the grant, but that generality was typical of petitions for land grants in California.

Very little controversy arose over the house lot. That smaller lot, located a short distance to the south of the Mission Santa Clara church, was ultimately confirmed, surveyed, and patented in much the same size and shape as originally contemplated. Its 3.48 acres comprised, in modern terms, the Santa Clara city block bounded by Market and Bellomy Streets to the north and south and Lafayette and Alviso Streets to the west and east.

However, many difficulties and much litigation arose out of the farm grant from the very beginning because even the petition was vague. It described the plot as being 2,000 varas by 1,000 varas, but then stated that the boundaries were the heights (*alta*) of Santa Clara on the north, and the margin of the oak grove on the south. Vague physical descriptions were common to grants in Mexican California, as could be expected in an underdeveloped and sparsely populated region. Mary's *diseño*, or map, attached to the petition is merely a drawing of a strictly rectangular plot surrounded by these named boundaries.

The problem is not just the vagueness, since that was common enough. However, this description has only two boundaries, not the four necessary to complete the rectangle. Moreover, it was clear to every interested person, and never in controversy, that the higher lands, the *alta*, on which the church building and enclosures of the Santa Clara Mission rested, were to the *east* of the grant and could not be its northern boundary. The issue later became how *far* east the grant extended, never that its 2,000-vara measure ran east to west, or that the higher grounds of the mission church itself were to the east.

Along with the two petitions and the maps, the town alcalde prepared a favorable report indicating that the lands were unoccupied, the padre added his recommendation, and the package went on to the California governor. Governor Pío Pico approved the grant on November 28, 1845, a single grant of the two parcels.[26] Dispute later swirled over whether or to what extent the "judicial possession" was actually conducted with Bennett by the alcalde. But the preponderance of the evidence is that the alcalde, Mary Bennett,

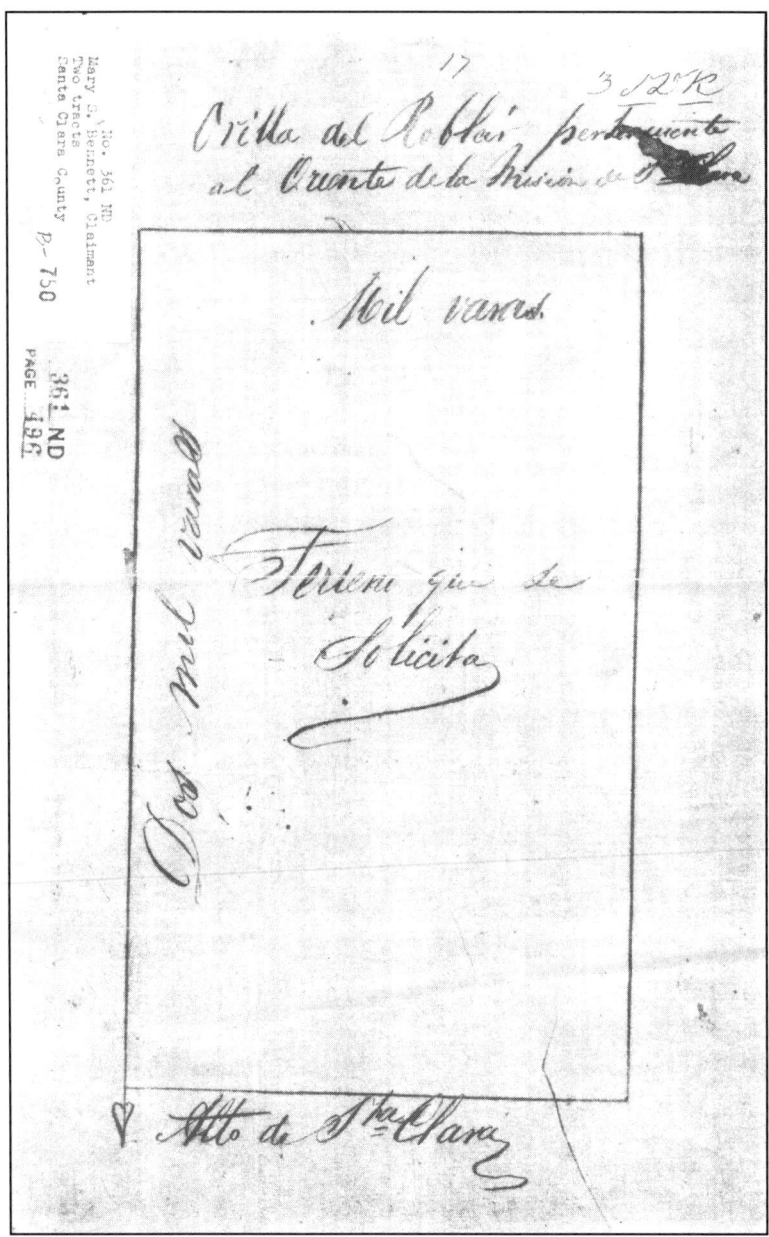

Map, or *diseño*, of Bennett land grant prepared by the Mexican authorities. Note the sharply rectangular boundaries compared with the boundaries later claimed by Mary Bennett Love, as well as the clearly called-out size of 1,000 varas by 2,000 varas. From District Court land claims records, 361 N.D. 496. Courtesy, Bancroft Library, University of California, Berkeley.

Winston Bennett, and a party of witnesses, accompanied by Padre Real, did conduct a formal transfer of possession. The house lot came first, in February 1846, with the farm shortly thereafter. The ceremonial showing of landmarks and boundaries of the farm occupied about a half day.[27]

A plot of land 2,000 varas by 1,000 varas covers an area of approximately 355 acres. The alcalde probably put Mary into possession of all vacant land that seemed in any way bounded by the two physical boundary descriptions. He did not employ measures.[28] And there is no question whatsoever that he put her into possession of a tract considerably larger than 355 acres. The grant corresponded to the petition. However, these "heights of Santa Clara," the higher land surrounding the church and enclosures were themselves quite wide from east to west, in some areas one and a half miles wide. What was the "alta de Santa Clara" and from where should it be measured? From its eastern edge? No, Mary Bennett never contended her grant included all of the mission buildings. But from where then? The middle, or the western edge? Should it be where the alcalde had actually put Mary into possession in 1846? Or, alternatively, should the eastern portion be reduced since the land to the west was more desirable agriculturally and agriculture was the original purpose of the grant? These issues roiled the tract's survey process following its confirmation, and the significance of the argument lay in the fact that the easternmost extent of the grant as claimed by Mary Bennett had meanwhile become developed and constituted much of the town of Santa Clara.

We will leave Mary's real estate activity for now at this juncture. She is in possession of her grant, but her land holdings are soon greatly affected by the American invasion of California in July 1846. However, there was another matter that competed for Mary's attention in 1845, along with her separation and land grant, although in a sense it may have had its origins in her marital discord. The other problem was her daughter Catherine and—in Mary's mind—her great misdoings.

Chapter 7

Catherine Bennett Marries Isaac Graham

When Mary left Vardamon, they each doubtlessly filled their children's ears with slurs about the other. Both forceful people, Mary and Vardamon probably offered threats as well. Children often react negatively to such pressures, and by the summer of 1845 Catherine had had enough of both her parents. She became twenty-one that year and fully ready to make a move of her own.

She fled to Santa Cruz, a small community on the north cusp of Monterey Bay, opposite Monterey on the south cusp and over the coastal mountains from Santa Clara. She stayed temporarily with an American emigrant, Julius Martin, and apparently worked for him. He was about to return to his home and family in Gilroy and wanted to find some place where Catherine could live. Martin wrote to Thomas Larkin, in colorfully spelled English on July 11, 1845:

> I have one of old man Bennetts daughters aliving with me and I shall go back to Gilroys Ranch Ranch [sic] next weeke and have no house sutable for company and she wishes to come to Monterey and live with your wife for a short time as she is determined never to live with her Father nor mother any more. You will find her a very industrious girle for bisness. If she can come let me know by letter the first opportunity and I will come in with her and if not I must looch out a place for her unttill I moove on the other side of the Bay or become more settled some wheare.[1]

Perhaps Catherine did live very briefly with the Larkins in Monterey, since she served as a witness to a marriage that Larkin performed on August 24, 1845.[2] Of course, this does not establish where she was living, but her actual presence in Monterey plus the request made in Martin's letter make it probable. It was a brief sojourn in Monterey because romance was soon to enter her life.

Undoubtedly she was in contact with her older brother Winston, the one

Bennett child who was emancipated and living apart from both parents. Since early 1845 Winston had worked for Isaac Graham, an American expatriate whose California residence dated from the mid-1830s. In 1845 Graham owned the Zayante Rancho in Felton, California. Located in the coastal Santa Cruz Mountains, the ranch was not far from where Catherine had been temporarily staying, in Santa Cruz. Winston was to remain at Zayante until the fall, sowing and harvesting a crop of grain,[3] and it was probably in late July 1845 that he introduced his sister Catherine to his employer.

Isaac Graham was a well-known American in Mexican California, although he was by no means admired or liked by those who knew him. Graham began his life on September 1, 1800, in Fincastle, Botecourt County, Virginia, the son of two British immigrants. Within three years the family moved to Lincoln County, Kentucky, where the father died, leaving two girls and ten boys, Isaac being the youngest child. Isaac had no formal education and never learned to either read or to write at any level beyond his signature.[4]

He was too young to serve in the War of 1812 but did find employment as a jockey. In 1818 he traveled west to Missouri and spent some five years there. He took an interest in the aged pioneer Daniel Boone, then residing in Missouri, and was apparently at Boone's bedside when he died in 1820. A few years thereafter Graham determined to return to Kentucky, but en route he stopped at Jonesville, Tennessee, to work. There he met and married a Miss Jones, with whom he had four children, Isaac Wayne, Jesse Jones, and two daughters. Either he was forced to leave Tennessee for some offense or westward wanderlust returned, but in any event by 1830 he had deserted his family and was engaged as a trapper in Fort Smith, Arkansas.

A group of a few dozen young men, including Graham, organized themselves into a trapping party at Fort Smith, resolved to head west. They moved slowly, engaged in fights with Indians, and then arrived and trapped in the Rocky Mountains. Then they drifted down to Taos, New Mexico. The governor sought to expel the party since they lacked permission to enter Mexican territory, but they remained for the winter of 1830–1831. Graham then continued to trap in the plains, the Rocky Mountains, and in New Mexico, where he appeared to spend considerable time, presumably primarily in the wintertime.

Graham individually or with a group, but not the original Fort Smith trapping party, arrived in California between 1833 and 1836. The evidence conflicts as to when, and there is no consensus of historians. If the earlier time is correct, Graham may have continued to trap sea otters along the California coast for a few years. By 1836 the sea otter was becoming nearly extinct, and whether Graham was a new arrival or had been in California for a few years, he turned to a different trade. With two partners, Henry Naile and William Dickey, he leased some land on the Rancho Natividad, about twenty-five miles east of Monterey, not far from Salinas, and built a whiskey distillery. It quickly became a collection point for assorted American and British expatriates, described by various contemporary observers as "noisy and disreputable," with "runaway drunken sailors" and "ruffians."⁵

The aggregation of these types at Natividad soon gave Graham a new profession, that of mercenary revolutionary. In 1835 and 1836 Mexican California again underwent a period of political instability in which different parties and factions contending for the governorship engaged in the bombastic proclamations and military posturing typical of California revolutions. A young and aspiring politician by the name of Juan Bautista Alvarado had the idea to engage the services of American riflemen. Graham raised an American fighting force of some fifty of the Americans who were hangers-on at his distillery, and Alvarado promised to reward the riflemen with Mexican citizenship and land.

Graham's riflemen marched into Monterey together with Alvarado and his Californio forces on the night of November 3, 1836, with the intent to depose the governor sent up from Mexico, Nicolas Gutiérrez. While Alvarado parleyed with Gutiérrez the next morning, Graham grew impatient and fired off some guns. Gutiérrez immediately capitulated, and Alvarado became the governor. Southern California did not readily accept this result, and Alvarado marched southward, taking Graham's rifle company with him. In the face of Graham's *Los Rifleros Americanos*, the southern opposition collapsed.

Once established as governor, Alvarado saw less need for Graham's services. Along with that new viewpoint, Alvarado failed to honor his earlier promises of land grants. The relationship between the two men turned bitter. Alvarado complained that Graham taunted him in public. The stage was set for a greater confrontation.

In the early morning hours of April 7, 1840, Graham and his Natividad confederates were arrested by Californio authorities under the order of Governor Alvarado, the beginning of a very confusing period known to historians as the "Graham Affair." Several dozen foreigners were rounded up and subjected to interrogation in Monterey by the governor and his assistants. Some were released but forty-seven, including Graham, were sent to Mexico, charged with sedition. They were in the main foreigners of the worst sort, mostly Americans, who had entered California illegally and had proven to be troublemakers. Alvarado may have truly thought that an uprising was imminent, but definite proof was lacking.

An American writer, Thomas Jefferson Farnham, was on hand. He interviewed Graham and wrote extensively about the alleged ill-treatment of the arrestees and the supposed treachery of the Mexicans. He lionized Isaac Graham as an American hero. His book, *Travels in the Californias, and Scenes in the Pacific Ocean,*[6] published in 1844, canonized Graham and further fanned the American enthusiasm for the heady prospect of stealing California from its owners. Once Graham and his fellow prisoners had arrived in Tepic, Mexico, the difficulties of lack of positive proof became apparent. Eustace Barron, the British consul, immediately obtained better treatment for them. Through British and American diplomatic efforts and the fiery spirit of Farnham, after a year in Mexico the local courts tried the prisoners and found them entirely innocent of all offenses charged against them and also entitled to compensation for their losses. Graham and his fellow prisoners returned to Monterey on July 20, 1841, and an American merchant observed that they were "dressed neatly, armed with rifles and swords, and looking in infinitely better condition than when they departed."[7]

Graham did not return to his distillery but instead took on a new occupation of lumberman, called then a "sawyer." He and a few partners bought Rancho Zayante in the Santa Cruz Mountains, located about eight miles east of Santa Cruz. The ranch engaged in agriculture, ran cattle, and later even added a new distillery. Graham being Graham, and any distillery being a draw for questionable characters, authorities continued to think him guilty of harboring deserted sailors, stealing cowhides, plotting sedition, and other crimes, but no affirmative steps were taken against him. However, Zayante was different from Natividad in that its principal activity was quite legitimate. That was cutting trees in Zayante's coastal hills, rich in redwoods, and then sawing the timber into boards. Graham built and operated one of the first, perhaps the actual first, water-powered sawmills in California.

Graham did engage in a bit more mercenary activity, supporting Micheltorena in the same uprising in which Vardamon and Winston Bennett fought. All three supported Governor Micheltorena against the insurgents, but while the Bennetts were engaged only until the lull in fighting that accompanied Micheltorena's unkept promise to expel his convict-soldiers, Graham supported Micheltorena until the Battle of Cahuenga, when all foreigners agreed to retire from the field and remain neutral. Graham's support for Micheltorena was not motivated as before by hopes for reward, but instead by motives of revenge. It was the same Juan Bautista Alvarado who earlier had arrested Graham and shipped him to Mexico in chains, who was now in revolt against Micheltorena.

That brings Graham's life up to mid-1845. Other than Farnham, who eulogized Graham for his role in the "Graham Affair" of 1840, few people who knew Graham had anything good to say about his character. James W. Weeks, an Englishman who jumped ship in San Francisco in 1831, had a widely varied California career as trapper, cook, and ranch hand, among other modest professions. He knew Graham from his work as a trapper and summed him up as "the cause of several deaths and a great deal of humbug." Benjamin D. Wilson spent eight years in New Mexico as a trapper and trader. In 1843 he moved to California and became a rancher and Indian fighter in the southern California frontier. He recalled that Graham had a bad reputation in Taos, New Mexico. "He was noted for being a bummer, a blowhard, and a notorious liar, without an atom of honesty in his composition." Probably Herbert Howe Bancroft, the eminent early California historian who had access to conversations and the dictated recollections of many hundreds of early Californians, wrote the best and most succinct summary of Isaac Graham's character:

> In N[ew] Mex[ico] and on the plains . . . he had the worst of reputations, amply justified by his career in Cal[ifornia]. At the best, he was a loud-mouthed, unprincipled, profligate, and reckless man, whose only good qualities seem to have been the personal bravery and prodigal hospitality of his class, with undoubted skill as a hunter, and a degree of industry.[8]

As for a physical description, probably the most complete is that of United States Second Lieutenant Henry Watson in his journal entry for May 13, 1846:

A most uncouth looking man, which I believe is his character, laying
aside the roughness of his dress . . . he may be thus described. Six feet
high rather stout, about Forty-five years old, Grey eyes, small red nose,
small mouth, high cheek bones somewhat weather beaten, (fair complex-
ion once) but very Florid now, quick spoken, considerably inflated with
self large head with long thick shaggy hair. Armed to the teeth.[9]

Serious troubles are likely to follow if a man of this character becomes
involved with a family having the forcefulness of the Bennetts. And so it was
to be. The very beginnings of the Isaac Graham–Catherine Bennett romance
can be dated rather precisely since the July 11, 1845, letter from Martin to
Larkin recited Catherine's desire to live with the Larkins in Monterey. Obviously she was not yet involved with Graham. Only three weeks later she was.
On August 2 and 3, 1845, Graham had a house guest named James Clyman,
an old fur trapper and mountain man who had recently guided a party to
Oregon. Clyman, one of the few mountain men who was literate, kept a
daily diary. For those two days he recorded, in a style reminiscent of James
Fenimore Cooper, that

if report be correct the hardy vetrian [sic] is fast softning down and he is
about to cast away the deathly rifle and the unerring tomahawk for the
soft smiles of a female companion to nurrish him in his old age.[10]

By September 1845 Catherine Bennett and Isaac Graham had commenced
living together in a common-law marriage. This was not a nineteenth-
century version of a casual sexual relationship. Common-law marriages
were recognized in many states and referred to the situation where a man
and woman intended to be actually married, held themselves out to the
world as being married, and in all other respects acted as though they were
married. All the relationship lacked was a formal ceremony.

The reason why common-law marriages were popular on the frontier was
the relative scarcity of clergymen who could perform a marriage ceremony.
In these circumstances both Roman Catholic and Protestant frontiersmen
resorted to expedients. On the Roman Catholic frontier it was common
that young people wanting to marry commenced living together but posted
bonds to guarantee that they would be married by the priest upon his next
appearance in their village. Protestants tended to invite friends and neigh-

bors to informal ceremonies or, alternatively, engaged in a true common-law marriage whereby the couple would commence living together, dispense with any ceremony, and simply announce to the community that henceforth they were married.

Mexican California had an abundance of priests, but they would not marry Protestants, who comprised the overwhelming majority of the Americans there. Some Americans sought aid from the American consul to perform marriages. Larkin did perform one or two marriages but very reluctantly since he had serious doubts about his authority. In 1844 and 1845 he repeatedly requested instructions from the State Department, and eventually a letter came, just after the American invasion in 1846, announcing that he had no matrimonial powers. Neither did the Californio alcaldes, but a few of the foreigners who had become alcaldes, most notably John A. Sutter, had begun marrying Protestants.

However, Isaac Graham, no respecter of officials, would have loathed to travel to any "authority" to be married. Then, too, there was considerable uncertainty over what specific person they might request to perform a marriage ceremony. So he and Catherine went the route of a common-law marriage. Interestingly, they did not simply enter into a consensual relationship by agreement but attempted to solemnize their status by a reading of the actual marriage ceremony witnessed by two loggers and ranchmen of the Santa Cruz Mountains. Then they signed a simple statement of what they had done:

> Marriage in the year 1845. Isaac Graham, of Santa Cruz, and Catherine Bennet[t], of San Francisco, were married at Lyant [Zayante], by bans, this 26th day of September, in the year 1845, by one who was requested to read the ceremony, Henry Ford. This marriage was solemnized between us, Isaac Graham, Catherine Bennet[t]. In presence of William Wern, Henry Ford. [11]

Apparently, William Ware, a long-time friend of Graham, and Winston Bennett, Catherine's brother, were additional witnesses.[12] Curiously, the marriage angered some of Graham's colleagues. Young American women were such a rarity that they may have resented Graham's good fortune in taking up with Catherine so quickly and so easily.[13] In fact, twenty-one Santa Cruz loggers, Graham's neighbors, petitioned the local Mexican authorities to kick Graham out. The discontented were primarily American and British expatriates, with one or two Frenchmen. Only one had an Hispanic surname. In their petition of late spring 1846, they charged that Isaac Graham

> is perpetually corrupting the peace of our vicinity and for the last six years has not ceased to invite or attempt revolution, challenges for duels, assassination, and disobedience of laws. . . . We have agreed to represent the case to Government asking . . . that he may be dislodged from amongst us that we who are neighbors and inhabitants of this place may live in peace believing as we do that said Graham is the only author of so many aggressions and which may be proved by his dissolute and adulterous way of living which is a scandal to all classes of people.[14]

But the anger of Graham's fellow woodsmen paled in comparison to the rage of Catherine's mother, Mary Bennett. Doubtless she was concerned that Isaac Graham was nearly twice as old as Catherine: Isaac's forty-five years contrasted with Catherine's twenty-five. Mary also appeared to have scruples against common-law marriage and regarded the informal ceremony they had held in the mountains entirely insufficient.

So with forceful personality and righteous rage, she once again turned to Thomas O. Larkin, the American consul. Larkin was most concerned about the status of any future children. Although as a young man Larkin had briefly served as a justice of the peace, he had no formal training in law. His most intense practical experience with legal matters came from his work as a merchant dealing with commercial law and from his work as consul, dealing primarily with admiralty cases and seamen's claims. He had very limited exposure to domestic-relations law. Yet he grasped the sophisticated legal point that the validity of the Graham marriage was not to be judged by whether a common-law marriage would be valid if contracted in the United States. Rather, its invalidity in the United States would result because of its invalidity under the Mexican law of California, the place where it was performed. In other words, American law would look to the law of the place where the marriage was celebrated in order to determine the marriage's validity. On November 19, 1845, Larkin wrote José Antonio Bolcoff, the local Santa Cruz judge:

> I am informed that Mr Isaac Graham and Catherine Bennett both citizens of the United States of North America are living together as married

people, without being legally married, and as this cannot be permitted according to the laws of this country [i.e., California] and their children (in case they have any) are illegitimate according to the laws of their [sic] country [i.e., United States], unless their parents are married by a competent authority, you will confer a favor on the undersigned by causing an immediate separation of these two people without any excuse from either party, and in case Mr Graham cannot on account of sickness, present himself with Catherine Bennett at this consulate, do me the favour to remove her from the house of Mr Graham, and send her to her parents or place her in some respectable family for the present.[15]

José Bolcoff, the *juez de paz* [justice of the peace] at Santa Cruz, wasted no time and interviewed Graham almost immediately. However, on December 4, 1845, he responded to Larkin rather lamely that

Graham said that they were well married and that he would not separate from the side of Bennett, that he would lose a thousand lives before he would give her up, and that Mr. Parrott and other Gentlemen having approved of his Marriage, that nobody could force a separation from Bennett, and that he could not present himself before you account of his infirmities.

You well know the character of Graham. He never likes to obey any authority; I leave it to your judgement. I would have taken from his side Bennett, but to avoid scandal, and I tell you that he talks much against whoever it may be.[16]

Mary Bennett was apparently mollified by the birth of the first Graham/Bennett child, Matilda Jane Graham. As the first child born of two American parents in the Santa Cruz area, she arrived, most appropriately, on July 4, 1846. A second daughter, Amanda Ann Narcissa Graham, came in 1849.[17] However, the marriage was in trouble. Catherine later alleged that Isaac mistreated her, but probably the single most explosive matter was the 1850 arrival of Jesse Graham, Isaac's son by his previous and undissolved marriage in Tennessee. He brought the startling news that Isaac's first wife was still alive. As we will follow in a later chapter, this led to theft, child abductions, a barrage of litigation, and murder.

Chapter 8

Mary Operates Her Grant and Becomes More Acquisitive, 1846–1852

Shortly after the alcalde put her into possession, Mary Bennett began to operate her two tracts, the house lot in February 1846 and the farm shortly thereafter. By the spring of 1846, with the help of her sons, she had built a redwood dwelling on the house lot, dug a well, and built a corral. This corral was constructed from poles and was used for milch cows.[1] Mary personally milked cows there in the corral.[2] The Bennetts began to enclose the entire house lot, and probably by the fall of 1846 that task was partly complete.[3]

In addition to the milk cows, she used the house lot for several other miscellaneous purposes. She stored lumber, threshed wheat hauled there from her farm, and one immigrant thought she had a garden on it.[4] The agricultural uses of the house lot must have been minimal, however, since it was located on the higher grounds of the mission property, the alta, and that was stony and arid land, with many squirrels and much mustard. It was not much good for cultivation.[5]

One thing that Mary did *not* do on her house lot was to live there. She lived elsewhere and never on her house lot. However, two of her sons lived in the redwood house located on the three-acre house lot. The sons kept two servants, undoubtedly Indians.[6]

The record of Mary Bennett's activities on her farm grant, especially for the early period of 1846 and 1847, is far murkier than that of the house lot. That is because the farm grant was caught up with the land grant confirmation proceedings. There were some witnesses who testified that there was no cultivation or improvement of any sort on the farm tract from the time of the grant until the American invasion in July 1846. This testimony was offered in an effort to defeat the entire claim, and it was brought out on cross-examination that a squatter living on the claim had paid the witnesses either expenses or money in addition.[7]

Then, too, there was sharp controversy as to exactly where the early cultivation was, in an effort to move the grant eastward toward the land made more valuable by the growth of the town of Santa Clara or westward to free much developed land from the Bennett claim. The Board of Land Commissioners considered all this conflicting evidence and in the end concluded that it really did not matter for the validity of the grant itself:

> The evidence shows . . . that in the year 1846 they [the Bennetts] enclosed and cultivated in wheat a portion of land supposed to be within the tract of 2000 by 1000 varas granted by the Governor but whether such cultivation was within the boundaries as now claimed or will be contained by them when the location and survey shall be made by proper authority it is impossible from the conflicting evidence to discover—It is clear however that the cultivation and occupation was commenced in good faith to carry out the purposes of the grant and was intended to be on the premises granted.[8]

Many residents recalled seeing Mary and her sons Dennis and Jackson sow and thresh wheat on what they took to be the Bennett farm in 1846 and 1847.[9] Mary herself cleaned the wheat following the threshing.[10] The Bennetts enclosed a large portion of the farm with a brush fence.[11] Mary Bennett contracted with Charles Brown, another expatriate, for her sons to cut wood timber on his land to use in making a post-and-rail fence around the Bennett farm. They began culling the timber in May and June 1846 and distributed the wood around the perimeter of the brush fence. Then in the chaos of the American invasion in July 1846, the post-and-rail fence was not put up.[12]

Mary experienced a lot of thievery of timber and cut wood in the operation of her land grant, even in the early days before the American invasion of July 1846. A United States Marine lieutenant observed Mary in May 1846 and wrote a striking passage in his journal that not only describes her fierce determination to vindicate her rights as she saw them but also demonstrates her keen interest in the legal process to do just that, even before American jurisprudence was available to her. It is remarkable that she had acquired a reputation for being litigious within the first year of her residency in Santa Clara, where resides one of our countrywomen Mrs Bennett, whose height size & pujelistic [pugilistic] powers has completely paralyzed the passive Mexicans [sic] authorities and she rules without the knowledge of a superior. Mrs. Bennett is one of those instable restless beings, who adds all the phlegm of an instable disposition to the most continuing energy and perseverance. I am informed that she frequently has business with [the] Alcalde of the Peubla [pueblo], and either by argument or force always obtains a judgement [sic] in her favor, she boasts that if she had fifty Kentucky women she would take California.[13]

In addition to the wheat, clearly the major activity on the farm tract, Mary had another corral with five horses and eight milch cows[14] and a vegetable patch with corn, watermelons, and vegetables.[15] Clearly the Bennetts were putting a considerable amount of energy and activity into the farm.

Throughout the beginnings of this activity, Mary herself remained a resident of the old adobe building adjoining the mission compound that Padre Real had assigned her in early 1845. And when she did move, it was not to consolidate her position on her land grant but rather to acquire still more land.

Mary Bennett's thirst for land had not been quenched by obtaining her land grant from the Mexican government. In fact, the ease of her gaining possession and title to a reasonably large amount of land only seemed to whet her appetite to obtain more. This must be seen in the context of Mary's being a descendent of Irish immigrants. In the nineteenth century generally, and for the Irish specifically, ownership of land was the very symbol of wealth and social status, and Mary had been poor her entire life.

Another element of context to explain Mary's increasing grasp for land is the tumultuous times of California in 1845 and 1846. We have already seen that the resolution of the revolt against Governor Micheltorena in 1844–1845 resulted in his departure. Pío Pico became governor, headquartered in the south, and José Castro became military commander, headquartered in the north. Persistent rumors of war between Mexico and the United States engaged Californios and American expatriates alike during 1845 and became more and more insistent in 1846. Everyone knew that war with Mexico meant that the United States would seize and hold California. Indeed, the United States had already signaled her designs, having made many fruitless attempts over the years to purchase California. Then, in October 1842 and under a mistaken belief that war had actually broken out between Mexico and the United States, an American naval commodore with two men-of-war, actually invaded and for a few days occupied the Mexican California capital of Monterey.

Mary surely knew that an American takeover was imminent. She additionally knew that this would affect her increasing avarice for California land in two ways: first, Mexican land grants would very soon end, and second, all the vacant land lying about Santa Clara and elsewhere in California would soon become United States public land. Actual squatters would then acquire rights under the American preemption law. Moreover, she was prepared to act upon her understanding of this law.

In the summer of 1846, Mary Bennett was still living in the mission buildings, the adobe structure alongside the vineyard enclosure that Padre Real had permitted her to occupy the previous year. However, Mary had her eye on another parcel of land located some six or seven hundred yards north of the mission buildings, her land grant "house lot" being located in the opposite direction from the mission.

She first approached José Castro, the military commander, for a grant, seeking it under a curious name, "Mrs. Mary McSwain." Probably the use of her maiden name was to give the impression that this was her only request, Castro not having been involved in her earlier grant. If this was her thinking, it worked splendidly, and on June 1, 1846, only a month before the American invasion, José Castro granted her petition:

> Whereas Mrs. Mary McSwain has solicited of the General Commandery (sic) for her personal benefit, and that of her family, a building lot in this place of Santa Clara, and in attention to her known honesty and integrity I have concluded to grant to her provisionally this favor, meanwhile she obtains the corresponding approval of the Superior Governor of the Department, which license is permitted her in consequence of this being at the present time a Military Post, and always subject to the said superior resolution. Santa Clara June 1st 1846. Francisco Arce José Castro[16]

Mary was on her way toward a second land grant, but there is no evidence that she prepared a map, the *diseño*, clarified the boundaries, and submitted this to Governor Pío Pico for his approval. Probably there was not enough time to take these steps before the American takeover that came just the very next month. But losing out on the land grant did not mean losing the land she coveted. It simply brought into play another system for obtaining it, the preemption laws that allowed an actual possessor of public domain the right to buy up to 160 acres per individual at a low price when a survey later took place. These preemption laws began on a temporary basis during the 1830s and became permanent in 1841. They responded to the problem of American settlers outrunning the official surveys and land offices. Individuals might increase their claims by adding family members' claims for adjacent land. In a few years, when Santa Clara became an American town, its newspaper ran numerous articles about the preemption laws. But in 1846, without lawyers or even newspaper articles to guide her, Mary was well aware of these laws.

By October 1846 she lived in a new, still partially uncompleted adobe house, located north of the mission and alongside the road to Alviso, where she kept one Indian servant.[17] Although Mary initially enclosed only a relatively few acres around her house, she had much broader claims to the mission lands surrounding it. Substantial agricultural fields had once been located north of the mission church, near to and irrigated by Mission Creek and almost adjacent to the north and west of the new adobe house that Mary had built. These fields are generally referred to as the mission gardens, but the names given are confusing since that area was sometimes also called a vineyard, sometimes also referred to as an orchard.

There was another very distinctive mission orchard, a large area, approximately 600 by 800 feet, enclosed by adobe walls. This orchard, located a short distance to the east of the mission church, was very fertile, and during the Gold Rush period became extremely valuable because of the scarcity of fruit. An 1845 inventory showed the orchard as 200 varas by 206 varas, with 1200 trees and 250 vines.[18] This area was involved in massive litigation later and is the piece of property usually referred to as *the* Santa Clara Orchard. There is no indication that Mary Bennett ever made any effort to preempt any of this particular land. However, there were other fruits, vegetables, and vines growing in the garden areas adjacent to her new house. When complaint was made, as we will soon see, that Mary Bennett was occupying the orchard or a vineyard, it referred to this area north of the mission church and not the enclosed area to the east of the church. Before Mary could make substantial efforts to occupy these fields, actual military hostilities engulfed California, including the area surrounding Mission Santa Clara.

Hostilities in California began with a June 1846 uprising of American expatriates farming in the region surrounding Sonoma and in the central valley. The emigrants incorrectly believed that the California government was about to launch an attack on them, burn their farms, and force them out of California. The insurgents seized the town of Sonoma, captured the leading California military commander, General Mariano G. Vallejo, seized Californio-owned horses, and marched through the countryside proclaiming the establishment of the Bear Flag Republic. Commodore John D. Sloat, commander of the United States Pacific Fleet, held standing orders that, in the event of war between the United States and Mexico, he was to sail to Monterey and seize California for the United States. He received credible reports of the beginning of hostilities in Texas, sailed to Monterey, and on July 7, 1846, seized the port and proclaimed American dominion over California.

At first the American conquest proceeded very peacefully. However, in September 1846 the Mexican Californios revolted, captured Los Angeles and almost all of southern California, and repulsed efforts of the American troops to settle down the disturbances. An American military officer, Captain John C. Frémont, later to become the first presidential candidate of the new Republican Party, was appointed to lead a battalion of troops to suppress the rebellion. He went about the northern California countryside and seized horses, cattle, and foodstuffs he claimed necessary to support the American forces. Most of the actual fighting was in southern California and not the north, yet there were two major engagements in the north, one just to the north of the Santa Clara Mission that directly involved the Bennett family. This is a sharp condensation of a very complicated story, yet it is enough to set the stage for the Bennett family's involvement in it.

From summer to fall of 1846, confusion reigned in Santa Clara. The local California Mexican population turned their horses on the crops before harvest, presumably to deprive the means of sustenance from the Americans who had come to steal their country. But it also deprived the Bennetts of the wheat crop they had planted on their farm grant, and they were greatly aggrieved.[19] When Mary had less wheat to sell, she turned to selling fruit from her garden. Edwin Bryant, a journalist who came to California to write a book, traveled with a Marine contingent from San José on September 20, 1846. As he passed through the area on his northward journey, he made detailed observations about the Santa Clara Mission grounds that included Mary Bennett.

> The rich lands surrounding the mission [Santa Clara] are entirely neglect-
> ed. I did not notice a foot of ground under cultivation except the garden
> enclosure, which contained a variety of fruits and plants of the temperate
> and tropical climates. From want of care these are fast decaying. Some
> excellent pears were furnished us by Mrs. Bennett, an American lady, of
> amazonian proportions, who with her family of sons, has taken up her
> residence in one of the buildings of the mission.[20]

It appears that Bryant was unaware that crops had been purposely destroyed and the fields abandoned as a defensive measure. If his statement that Mary then resided "in one of the buildings of the mission" is accurate, this rather precisely dates the time of her move to the preemption claim north of the mission as late September to early October, because an immigrant named Joseph Aram dated a conversation with Mary in her new house as October 1846.[21] She sold fruit and other comestibles to others in the party as well.[22]

The American expatriates' Bear Flag insurgency, the official invasion, and subsequent Californio revolt, accompanied by heated squabbles among the military officers that we cannot explore here, offer a rich historical stew. Added to this was the appearance of a large number of overland American immigrants who arrived in fall 1846, just subsequent to the American seizure of California, and for whom no plans had been made. The total non-Indian population of California in the spring of 1846 was about 10,000. New overland arrivals from the United States had increased from 38 in 1843, to 260 in 1845, and then zoomed to approximately 1,500 arriving in the fall of 1846.[23] In addition to these figures of arrivals from the east, and as the Bennett family itself illustrates, Americans also arrived in California from Oregon.

Captain Frémont intercepted many of the incoming immigrants in the Sacramento Valley. Joseph Aram, later the captain of the immigrants' militia in Santa Clara, recorded that Frémont urged them to push forward as fast as possible, as the Spaniards (i.e., the Mexican Californians, or Californios) were unfriendly toward the Americans. He advised us to go to Santa Clara and take possession of the mission buildings. And as soon as a sufficient number of men arrived to organize a company for our own protection, elect officers to whom he would give commissions. . . . We then proceeded to Santa Clara . . . [and] after the menacing of the Spaniards became alarming, the men held a meeting for the purpose of organizing a company for mutual protection. There were about thirty-three men signed the roll. . . . As soon as the organization was complete, it soon became evident that some kind of barricade was necessary to prevent the enemy from charging immediately on the mission buildings. Being in full command of the place, I set the men immediately at work to fortify the place, by cutting and hauling logs about ten feet in length. They were placed in a ditch about three feet deep, forming a breast work seven feet high. We felt that such a fence was sufficient to prevent the ingress of the enemy.[24]

As we have seen, Mary had her sons cut timber for a fence from Charles Brown's land and then pile them up alongside the brush fence around her farm grant. This timber was hauled into the mission and undoubtedly became a part of the immigrants' fort. The new arrivals also stole wood from her preemption lot.[25]

The newly arriving overland immigrants were truly in a difficult position. Frémont had promised the immigrants groceries from the government stores in Yerba Buena,[26] but as Adna A. Hecox, another new overlander at Santa Clara Mission that winter of 1846–1847, recalled it, "Those rations were like angels visits—few and far between."[27] The Californios generally refused to sell foodstuffs or cattle to them, and who can blame them for refusing to assist a hoard of people who thought it their right to steal the Californios' lands? However, a few would sell and this, together with foraging and outright theft, enabled the immigrants to find food enough to prevent starvation, even though they suffered from shortage.

Conditions at Santa Clara were gruesome for the immigrants. Many of the men were away, having volunteered to serve in Frémont's battalion. At Santa Clara eighty women, twenty-five men, and about half a dozen children remained. One of these women, Margaret M. Hecox, described life for the immigrants that winter of 1846–1847 in her memoirs:

We found the old Mission buildings in a wretched and filthy condition. Many of the adobe sheds were occupied by Indians, others by Mexican and half-breeds, while the remaining rooms were devoid of windows or chimneys. There were no floors and the tile roofs leaked badly. . . . We all set to work with a will to clean out the largest building and make it habitable. The place had been used as a stable and literally swarmed with fleas. A room was portioned off for each family by means of calico curtains, bed quilts, and coverings from wagons. Beds were made up on the ground. . . . As there were no windows we had to burn tallow candles. . . . During all those lonely months while we were prisoners in that damp, dark Mission, our candles were kept burning. The winter rains set in early and poured steadily down through the holes in the roof. A large drain was dug through the center of the building. To this channel each family added a smaller drain. The atmosphere was damp and moldy.[28]

Disease became a far greater enemy to the overlanders at Santa Clara than any Californio foe. Many suffered from what the immigrants called camp fever but what was really typhoid fever. The beds and clothing became damp and unhealthy because of the incessant rain, a disagreeable odor pervaded their mission quarters, and the sick suffered miserably.[29] Hecox vividly recalled "the horror of it all! Many were the corpses I helped prepare for their rude burial. Within a few weeks fourteen of our number were sleeping under the sod of the new land."[30]

But where could these fourteen dead immigrants be buried? The overlanders approached Padre Real for permission to bury their dead in the mission graveyard, but the priest refused, presumably because the dead were Protestants. Mary Bennett gave the immigrants the privilege of burying their dead in the alta portion of her land.[31]

The immigrants who were not sick were causing other problems for Mary. Some were squatting on lands she claimed and were staking out their own locations. She complained to James B. Taber, whom Captain Frémont had appointed as a kind of civil authority for the Santa Clara immigrants. An angry Mary Bennett went to him at one point during the winter of 1846–1847 and complained about the new arrivals imposing on her that way. Taber responded that he "could do nothing for her, that if they jumped other peoples land, they would have to get off it after a while, and it could do no harm."[32]

The comment that claim jumping "could do no harm" was substantially true for her land grant, and later Mary was able to evict some squatters. But it was completely untrue for her preemptive claims to the north of the mission because those depended on Bennett's own occupation and possession, not yet accomplished beyond her preemptive house and the relatively small enclosure she built surrounding it. If her actual occupancy was insubstantial, then that could be broken by adverse squatters taking possession.

Following the uprising in southern California in September 1846, a band of Californios under the command of Captain Francisco Sánchez roamed the countryside surrounding Santa Clara and in the Santa Cruz Mountains. Never more than about 100 armed men, the Sánchez group was not coordinated with the Californios struggling in southern California and to a great extent seemed more disturbed over the military's seizures of their crops, cattle, and horses than about any political dispute with the Americanization of California. Still, Sánchez's group took a few travelers prisoner and seized some immigrants' horses, leaving the American overlanders to firmly believe that this was a major uprising and that Sánchez's revolt was a threat to their very existence.[33]

Much of the military action taken against Sánchez was simply to fruitlessly chase him around Santa Clara and in the Santa Cruz Mountains. But the Americans eventually drew him, on January 2, 1847, into a running engagement with the United States forces marching south from Yerba Buena and then into a very short fixed engagement at a battle site two miles west of Mission Santa Clara, on or very near to Bennett's farm tract. Needless to say, the facts are in dispute. Arrayed against Sánchez were the Mission Santa Clara Company, headed by Joseph Aram, and regular United States forces under the command of Captain Ward Marston, U.S.M. Corps, including the San José Volunteers and the Yerba Buena Volunteers. The San José Volunteers under Marston's command included two of Mary's sons, Dennis Bennett and Jackson Bennett. The forces were nearly equal in number, although the Americans had vastly superior weapons.

After a short engagement, the Californios withdrew. This was followed by an armistice and then a surrender by the Sánchez forces. Not a single Californio man was injured, and but two Americans were hurt, including Jackson Bennett, who was slightly wounded in the heel. According to one participant, "a bullet took off the heel of his [Jackson Bennett's] shoe, grazing his heel and making him lame for a few days."[34] Even here there is a dispute as to whether the injury was caused by enemy fire or a cut from thick oak brushes.[35] In any event, Jackson's injury was not serious.

Mary took an active role in the Battle of Santa Clara. As the prospects of an actual engagement became clearer, civilians from outside the mission buildings enclosure came in to seek shelter. This included Mary Bennett. At the mission high grounds, the immigrants had an excellent view of the fighting just two miles away. Margaret Hecox painted a vivid description of Mary:

> There was an American woman, a Mrs. Bennett, who won considerable distinction on that day. She seemed anxious to take part in the fight. She waltzed back and forth in front of the Mission yelling orders to the men at the top of her voice. Growing more excited she ran forward and grabbing up a large bone lying in the yard, rushed up to a man who had refused to fight, saying that he had no gun. Stopping squarely in front of the startled fellow she thrust the bone into his hands and shouted "take that, you puppy, and go out there and bat the brains out of some Mexican or I'll use it on you." This man quickly disappeared.[36]

Calming down, Mary invited several of the officers and privates, four or five in total to dinner that night. One of those invited, John Henry Brown, pronounced it "a good supper."[37] Probably these were men whom she had known from her days in Yerba Buena.

While the new arrivals suffered severely in the mission buildings during that wet winter of 1846–1847, Mary lived in fairly snug and secure housing in her new house north of the mission. She suffered from the food shortage that afflicted the immigrants, but her home was warm. It gave her the comfort to plan her strategy to expand her holdings to the surrounding agricultural lands.

She made big plans and caused a lot of controversy. What did she claim and, more importantly, what did she actually occupy? According to Joseph Aram, an emigrant who talked with her and her son in October 1846, she claimed only 160 acres that she had staked off to the west of her house.[38] A longtime British expatriate, James Alexander Forbes, estimated the land enclosed around the new house was 100 varas square.[39] She expressly stated that she was holding that land by preemption.[40] A man who boarded with her in October 1846 later testified that, in addition to building her house and enclosing the area around it, she "claimed that she cultivated the land [i.e., the preemptive land, not the farm land grant, nor the house lot land grant], and said she would have cultivated more but that her sons had to go to the Redwoods to saw lumber, in order to obtain means for a subsistence."[41]

A year later, in October 1847, William Campbell began the first survey of Santa Clara, on commission of Padre Real, still at the mission. His description of how he handled the survey of Mary Bennett's preemptive claim is helpful:

> I surveyed off until I came down to within one hundred yards to Mrs. Bennett's house. I then left her a block two hundred yards square besides the streets where she was living and then continued making my survey on two sides of her. From that she claimed a mile square northwardly, that she intended to hold by pre-emption from the U.S.[42]

Whether Mary's preemptive claim was for 160 acres westward of her new adobe house, as she told Aram in October 1846, or a mile square, 640 acres northward, as she told Campbell in October 1847, does not really matter. Either would be hugely larger than the amount she actually occupied and enclosed: "a few acres around her house," according to Aram; "100 varas square" mentioned by Forbes; or probably most accurate, the "200 yards square" mentioned by the surveyor, William Campbell.

What was the evidence of Mary's actual occupancy of these agricultural lands surrounding her homestead to the north of the mission? Mary's sons apparently had done some plowing that winter[43] but then became soldiers during the California uprising. Later in that difficult winter they left for the Santa Cruz Mountains to cut timber as a matter of survival. Mary soldiered on, working herself and probably gathering what temporary laborers she could find. Her activity drew attention and criticism.

These were lands that had actually been of utility to Mission Santa Clara, and Padre Real complained in January 1847 to the local town judge, the office still called alcalde, but now occupied by an American, John Burton. The judge apparently ordered both Padre Real and Mary Bennett to provide additional information, and Padre Real promptly replied, claiming damages from Mary's pruning the vines too early, thereby destroying them, and also complaining about the planks in the vineyard, apparently an unclear reference to the fencing alongside one of these fields. Real presented the judge's order to Mary, who rather brazenly told Real that the judge "had nothing to do with this matter and that she would continue her work."[44]

In response to this, Judge John Burton issued an order and on February 15, 1847, advised Padre Real:

> You will now take charge of the orchards. Should there be any other property belonging to said Mission which you wish to receive, and which appertains to you, be pleased to advise me of it. I have sent an order to Mrs. Bennett directing her to deliver over the said property.[45]

It was about at this time that Stephen A. Wright and some other American immigrants purchased wood from Mary Bennett that consisted of former mission fencing, undoubtedly taken from these lands that she was trying to occupy and Padre Real was trying to repossess. Wright and other immigrants were brought to appear before Judge Burton to answer for this.[46] But Mary Bennett remained recalcitrant. Real presented Burton's February 15 order that Real be allowed to retake possession of "the irrigated lands of this mission," but as he later explained to Judge Burton, "she persistently insists in not vacating the mission gardens by offering a thousand falsehoods and subterfuges." Real called Bennett "ungrateful," doubtless remembering his aid to Mary in obtaining her land grant, and asked for a "new complaint" to be drawn up.[47]

Ultimately, in June 1847, United States Military Governor Richard B. Mason sent troops to Santa Clara to remove squatters from the mission properties.[48] It does not appear that the evictions extended to Mary's homestead itself and the small enclosed acreage immediately surrounding it. This squatter removal doubtless set Mary's efforts back; yet once the soldiers left, squatting resumed. The failure of Mary's plan to extend her acreage into the mission gardens came about primarily because she failed to physically occupy the land sufficiently.

A squatter's right depends on exactly that—squatting, that is to say, physically occupying and possessing. But Mary Bennett was busy with her land grants and, as we will examine in a later chapter, also distracted by the economic opportunities of sawmilling in the Santa Cruz Mountains. Her sons were busy soldiering or cutting timber. She was never able to do enough physical occupying and possessing of her larger claim in the north of the mission, personally or through agents, to qualify it as a valid preemptive claim. Of course, after the American occupation and especially after the Gold Rush, many, many others rushed in, only too happy to plant their own boots on the ground—together with houses, gardens, fences—and make their own squatters' claims to the land that Mary desired.

In the end Mary was able to lay successful claim to only the homestead and the enclosed small acreage that surrounded it. That yielded four small city blocks for her preemption activity, an area, with streets excluded, of approximately eleven acres. This was, of course, in addition to her two-parcel land grant. The preemption claim was bounded by the streets of Harrison to the south, Alviso to the west, and Sherman to the east. Clay Street was the original northern boundary, now the curve of highway 82, El Camino Real, just to the north after its intersection with De La Cruz Boulevard. These two highways, together with the Larry J. Marshall Park, now consume the northernmost of Bennett's two lots and almost half of the southeastern lot as well. Eleven acres is not the large claim Mary aspired to, but it is not bad for a successful claim arising out of a quick move to occupy. Nor did it have the hassles and litigation that would accompany the settlement of the land grant. We will return to the final resolution of this preemptive claim in the chapter on Mary's final years.

Curiously Mary bungled one opportunity to gain a steadfast employee who could have provided sufficient labor on the ground to facilitate the larger preemptive claim she desired. An interesting account of this appears in a much-later biographical sketch of Robert F. Peckham, sire to one of the most prestigious legal families in California history. But in the fall of 1846, Peckham was just a very poor overland immigrant, so destitute that he lacked even shoes. He accompanied Dennis and Jackson Bennett to their mother's house in Santa Clara. For her, Peckham performed his first day's work for wages in California, washing wheat at a small lake near Santa Clara. Mary provided him with a pair of shoes she valued at four dollars, and he was to work it out by washing wheat at the rate of one dollar per day. Apparently that employment went well, and he traveled to "Mother Bennett's, as she was called" again on January 28, 1847, a short time after the Battle of Santa Clara. A later biographical sketch explains that

> she was glad he had come. The military officers had told her that the
> Mission orchard was government property, and subject to pre-emption,

and she was alone with her girls; her three sons were away, Winston with Frémont's Battalion; Dennis a soldier in the pueblo; and Jackson was laid up with a wound received in the battle of Santa Clara. She wanted a worker to take possession of the orchard for her; plow it up and put in a crop of wheat. A bargain was made and the next morning the Judge [i.e., Peckham], for the second time entered the employ of this lady, his wages being thirty dollars a month. This day he got a gun, went out, shot some geese and in the evening returned to the house, where he was given a back room, a candle, and an Indian as room-mate; no bed, no blanket, no floor, neither chair nor stool, and no fire. While here enveloped in reflection Peckham heard the eldest daughter say: "Mother, let us ask that man in to sit with us by the fire," to which generous appeal she received the bluff reply: "No! Let him stay out there with the Indian. It is good enough for him." After a spell his supper was sent in. It consisted of a little Indian corn, roasted on the cob before the fire, shelled off, ground up in a coffee mill and saturated with water. The Judge says: "This was all right for it was all she had for herself and family, but the warm fire was a different consideration." He therefore thought soldiering was preferable, so the next morning he [left Mrs. Bennett's employment].[49]

By such shoddy treatment of her employee, Mary Bennett lost her best opportunity to seriously expand her preemptive claim to include the agricultural lands. The incident also gives us an opportunity to speculate about her character. We have seen acts of generosity such as giving a good horse to the sea captain's wife near Sacramento, providing dinner to four or five soldiers after battle, setting aside part of her land as a graveyard for the immigrants who died during their ordeal in the late fall of 1846, and now this truly rough and inconsiderate treatment of her employee. How can this be reconciled?

Perhaps an understanding comes from Mary's southern background. In the antebellum south, and for years thereafter, poor lower-class whites were socialized into treating upper-class whites with extreme deference, almost homage. Not only was this a social duty but a practicality as the higher class might someday be of help. The tradeoff was that the lower-class whites were allowed, perhaps encouraged, to treat the classes beneath them with callous contempt. This tradeoff permitted the narrow band of upper-class whites to effectively control the entire society. In the south the class below the poor whites was slave prior to 1865 and thereafter was the emancipated Negro.

There were very few black persons in California during these years, so the experience of the South does not fit perfectly. But there is an analogy here. Mary Bennett undoubtedly regarded the immigrants as of her own social class; indeed, she had herself immigrated overland from the United States, first to Oregon and then to California. She probably regarded the soldiers from Yerba Buena whom she invited to dinner following the battle as her equals. Both the new immigrants and the old acquaintances from Yerba Buena might someday be of help to her. Mary probably regarded the finely dressed wife of the sea captain as a social superior; certainly that woman regarded Mary as a mere hillbilly, in modern terms. But this very young boy (who had just turned twenty the day he agreed to plow up the orchard for Mary), too poor to even have shoes on when he arrived at her doorstep, was, for all she could tell, clearly déclassé, of a lower social order than she, and of no more potential help to her than what she could command by her wages. From that southern perspective it was proper that he "stay out there with the Indian," because, just as she stated, "It is good enough for him." This attitude toward the young man hurt Mary just at the time that his employment was critical.

Even the most miserable winter eventually turns to spring, and in the spring of 1847, the immigrants had more food and less illness. With that improvement, entertainment and frivolity returned, and interestingly the immigrants at first adopted the existing amusements of the Californios, including bullfights. One memorable bullfight was held on the feast day of Santa Clara, August 12, 1847. The plaza adjoining the church was enclosed with a strong fence, and seats were constructed for the ladies. Then the unexpected happened:

> One of the ladies "assisted" literally in the spectacle. She got over the fence, walked into the middle of the corral and waved a red shawl. When the bull . . . caught sight of the bright color, he made a rush for her, then a man stepped in between and succeeded in diverting his attention, and the lady withdrew amid great applause.[50]

The woman involved was unidentified in this account, but bearing in mind what we know of her penchant for public spectacle, could we doubt that it was Mary Bennett? The Town of Santa Clara incorporated on July 24, 1852, and at their very first meeting the town trustees outlawed bull and bear fighting.[51] Perhaps it was just too much spectacle.

During the war Captain Frémont and other officers, together with settler volunteers commissioned by the military, had seized horses, cattle, food-stuffs, and other materials to aid their military forces. When the war with Mexico ended and matters settled down in California, attention turned to the question of compensation for the ranchers and residents who had suffered loss. A cumbersome procedure was established for these "California Claims," as they came to be called.[52] Frémont advised Congress that the value of horses in California at the time varied between twenty-five and thirty-five dollars, with an average of thirty dollars, and cattle varied between eight and twelve dollars, with an average of ten dollars.[53]

Mary Bennett submitted an initial claim of $120 for horses. That seems about right, as it would indicate the taking of three or four head, and we have seen testimony in the land claim proceedings that Mary had about five head of horses as of 1846. The "Board for Examination of Claims Contracted in California Under Lt. Col Frémont" disbanded in April 1855 and issued its final report dated April 18, 1855. That report acknowledged the Bennett claim for $120 for horses but relegated it, along with approximately one-third of all claims submitted, to the status of "suspended for want of testimony or explanation."[54]

Mary Bennett was not likely to take this sort of presumed insult without response. She filed a new claim, alleging the government's taking of thirty horses (the evidence is she had five), twelve milch cows (the evidence is she had eight), and 300 head of beef cattle (there is no evidence she had any). Other large alleged losses of foodstuffs included 1,000 gallons of molasses and 1,200 pounds of coffee. She claimed $2,000 compensation for a fence of boards surrounding her house lot grant, $3,000 for fencing "adjoining the mission and enclosing a lot of land of about one hundred acres" (the preemption claim?), and a whopping $5,000 for timber stored at the mission that she claimed had cost her that sum. The grand total was $15,983, a truly enormous sum in those days. At the time she executed this new claim, the Board for the "California Claims" had already disbanded, but perhaps she thought a private congressional bill for compensation might be possible. She was able to obtain an attorney to press her claim in Washington on a one-third contingency fee.[55] The entire new claim was ludicrous, went nowhere, and probably was merely a vent for Mary's anger that her earlier, reasonable claim had been denied for lack of evidence.

Mary in a sense became involved again with Vardamon Bennett in 1849, although there is some slight evidence they had attempted a reconciliation a couple years earlier.[56] Vardamon lived on in San Francisco, formerly Yerba Buena, until his death in 1849.[57] According to his son Winston, he died "from the effects of alcoholic stimulants."[58] He had continued on with his saloon, bowling alley, and hotel and became involved in a dispute over a new San Francisco survey and the boundary line to his property on Pacific Street.[59] He perfected his title to the lot he had occupied since late 1843, the middle one-third of the southern half of the block bounded by Grant (then DuPont), Kearny, Pacific, and Broadway streets, by obtaining a title grant from the American magistrate in San Francisco in early 1847.[60] He considered buying lots in Thomas Larkin's new Benicia development, then decided against it.[61] Throughout these years he and Mary had never divorced, and therefore Mary and her children were his heirs.

Vardamon's lot in San Francisco had become more and more valuable. Even before the Gold Rush real estate prices in San Francisco had risen because of land speculation. The lot was worth around $300 in March 1848.[62] Then with the Gold Rush, San Francisco became a metropolis almost overnight, and property prices soared. When Vardamon died in 1849 his lot had an enormous value.

Ten years later this lot was involved in litigation, the result of a faulty 1839 survey, a "swinging" of the streets surrounding the lot to "correct" the earlier survey, which "correction" Vardamon did not accept. This led to allegations of misdescriptions of land in later deeds. It is a complicated matter best left untouched because it does not involve the Bennetts, none of whom were involved in the subsequent litigation. However, the opinions in that subsequent litigation do provide a few details of Vardamon's activities after Mary's departure.

Vardamon continued living on his lot in San Francisco, in his adobe house on the western side of the lot, and also continued to operate his wooden bowling alley and a saloon. Before he died in August 1849, he sold a part of his lot, roughly a divided one-third portion, in March of that year. Mary filed a petition in the Probate Court of San Francisco, which had jurisdiction over decedents' property, but declined the position of administrator in favor of John Thompson. Sam Brannan became a successor administrator, and he made some boundary adjustments with neighbors approved by the Probate Court in January 1850, paid the debts of the estate, and turned the property over to the widow, Mary Bennett.[63]

This Sam Brannan was himself an interesting character, a Mormon who came to California by sea, expecting to meet up with large Mormon immigration parties and colonize California for the Mormons. When this plan did not work out, in large part because the United States had already seized California, Brannan renounced Mormonism and settled into California business, aided by some ill-gotten tithes taken from some Mormons who had actually arrived.

We know that Mary leased the property at some point before 1854 because she did so in her own name and not that of her second husband, Harry Love. The lease called for quarterly payments of rent. The tenant failed to pay the quarterly rent sometime in 1855. After their marriage Harry Love was substituted as administrator, a normal nineteenth-century procedure, and he brought a lawsuit for the rent in San Francisco. The tenant failed to appear, and Love obtained a judgment by default. Only then did the defendant attempt to reopen the case, and upon the denial of the court to do so, brought an appeal. The appeal was denied.[64]

Then the tenant failed to pay a subsequent quarterly rent. Harry Love sued and obtained judgment. The tenant again appealed, and Harry's (and Mary's) judgment was affirmed in the fall of 1856. Yet again the tenant defaulted, and this time, after demand for payment, the Loves sued to retake possession. Evidence was offered to which the defendant-tenant objected. A judgment for defendant followed, and the Loves, the landlords, appealed. The Loves contended that the arguments of the tenant were "frivolous and vexatious, and made with the intent to delay, hinder, and defraud the estate of Bennett out of an honest and just debt." The California Supreme Court, the highest California court, agreed and reversed the judgment obtained by the tenant.[65]

Mary must have been finding that leasing the lot in San Francisco was too much of a headache to bear for long. In 1855 she filed a petition in the San Francisco Probate Court, essentially asking for partition of the property, claiming a one-half interest in Vardamon's property as surviving spouse and also an additional one-eighth of the remaining half as the mother of a deceased child, Dennis Bennett. She asked that the property be divided.[66] On June 20, 1855, the Probate Court appointed neutral commissioners to make the division. They recommended, with the Probate Court's approval, that Mary receive a portion of the remaining lot, 137-1/2 feet by 60 feet, 5-5/8 inches, and that the seven surviving children receive a portion of 137-1/2 feet by 47 feet, 3/8 inches.[67] That unequal division between mother and children allows for the additional one-eighth interest on behalf of her deceased son Dennis that Mary had demanded.

Almost as soon as the Bennett mother and children recovered possession of their property from the litigious tenant, they sold the property, at some point prior to June 1858.[68] We do not know the price, but it must have been substantial. Winston Bennett remembered in 1888 that his father's estate was worth $15,000, a large sum for those days, but that his mother had managed it so badly that it went into debt.[69] The newspaper printed his recollection of the value as $150,000, but that must surely be a typographical error, with $15,000 intended.[70] Winston's remembrance is certainly misleading as to the debt. Perhaps pending the sale of the only substantial asset in the estate, the lot between Pacific and Broadway, the estate may have had to borrow money. However, the fact that the Probate Court appointed neutral commissioners to apportion the lot, or the proceeds of a sale, between Mary and her children, indicates clearly that there was an actual asset to be divided. That the estate had to undergo litigation with a vexatious tenant necessitated some debt and was not evidence of bad management as Winston thought. In short, through Vardamon's death Mary came into a flood of litigation, but she also received a substantial asset that was ultimately liquidated.

Chapter 9

Santa Cruz County Land Speculations

The Santa Cruz Mountains are coastal hills filled with live oak, pine, and redwood trees, intermixed with grassy mountain meadows, and lying west of Santa Clara and San José. The leading town in the region was and still is the town of Santa Cruz, the seat of the modern Santa Cruz County. The area had certain early advantages. The town of Santa Cruz sat at the northern tip of Monterey Bay and therefore was easily accessible to Monterey, the Spanish and Mexican capital. The settlement of Santa Cruz hosted a mission from early days, and Branciforte, a small community to the immediate south of the town of Santa Cruz and the mission, achieved villa status within the Spanish period. A few land grants lay along the ledges of land above the Pacific Ocean north of the town of Santa Cruz, and more were located in the flatter region south of Santa Cruz, near modern Watsonville.

However, during both the Spanish and Mexican eras the Santa Cruz region never experienced much development, particularly in the very hilly, timbered area northeast of the town of Santa Cruz. A modest amount of timbering and milling during the late Mexican period of the early 1840s was carried on both by the local citizens and also by American expatriates such as Isaac Graham.[1]

Even after the American takeover of California, Santa Cruz County was slow to develop, certainly compared with the steady growth of Santa Clara County and the explosive growth of San Francisco. The 1852 California state census revealed a Santa Cruz County population of only 1,219 persons, compared with Santa Clara County's population of 6,664. As late as 1860 the town of Santa Cruz held only 800 persons.[2] The large stands of redwoods invited further commercial exploitation.

Mary Bennett speculated in Santa Cruz County land and owned a sawmill, but it is a tangled story, difficult to follow. Some problems arise from the fact that several of her sons, especially David Jackson and Mansel, also speculated in Santa Cruz land. Mansel complicated the records by marrying a woman whose first name was Mary, thereby creating a new "Mary Bennett." Then our Mary remarried in 1854, and her real estate and contractual activities appear under her new name of "Mary Love." The family members often sold land among themselves—for unclear reasons but most probably to avoid creditors.

These are problems that can be overcome by diligent research. But three additional problems are intractable. The first is that almost all of Mary's claims in Santa Cruz County depend on someone's preemptive rights. If these were later denied by the government, or if the claim were simply abandoned—and California preemptive claims were sometimes abandoned since land was not nearly as valuable as it is today—then there would be no outgoing record of the land's disposal by an owner. The chain of title would simply disappear. The second major problem is that a 1955 flood in the Santa Cruz County Recorder's Office destroyed many older documents. The third and most significant difficulty is that the very early documents, especially those before 1850, were not indexed by the recorder. The difficulty of finding older

Santa Cruz Mountains on or near Isaac Graham's Zayante Rancho. From Edward Vischer, *Pictorial of California Landscape,* Courtesy of the California State Library.

documents due to lack of indexing was noted as early as 1857.[3] Therefore, we cannot know for sure even what was lost for the period before 1850. This will force us to make a few assumptions in order to explain what would otherwise be inexplicable statements or actions. All such assumptions, and they are not numerous, will be explicitly identified.

Mary's speculations into Santa Cruz real estate did not result in much gain to her. But the fact that she made them illustrates the extent to which ownership of land was available to those of the working class who were willing and able to seize these opportunities. The land grants that existed in Santa Cruz County were along the coast, and therefore the more forested lands of the hills were public, owned by the United States federal government, and subject to preemption claims. It was relatively easy in the 1850s for anyone of little means to claim land in Santa Cruz County. Since land could be bought and sold based merely on these claims, all who had such claims could then engage in the active market for buying and selling.

The first foray of the Bennett family into the Santa Cruz area was in early 1845 when Mary's eldest son Winston worked for Isaac Graham. He sowed, harvested, and marketed a crop of grain on Graham's Rancho Zayante, located on the San Lorenzo River in the Santa Cruz Mountains. Winston returned for the first five months of 1848 to assist his own brother in building a sawmill on the San Lorenzo River at a location only a short distance from Zayante. Then he returned in January 1851, and until spring 1852 "he operated the saw mill which he had helped to build several years before."[4]

Over the years the sawmill would be rebuilt or repaired several times; perhaps there were two different but nearby locations. Winston Bennett recalled that his father, Vardamon Bennett, helped Jackson and Dennis build a mill.[5] Most probably that was in 1847. In April 1850 a Lansing Haight was working with a crew of seven or eight men, building a dam at Bennett's Mill.[6] It was not a large-scale sawmill. A Santa Cruz newspaper much later described the 1850 version as a tiny affair, "operated by an overshot wheel, and of little more capacity than two men and a whipsaw."[7] This operation became appropriately known as "Bennett's Sawmill," and was located at the confluence of the San Lorenzo River and what is now known as Love Creek, within the modern community of Ben Lomand.[8] After Mary's marriage to Harry Love, the sawmill was called "Love's Sawmill."

An individual was entitled to claim 160 acres under the Pre-Emption

Sawmill in Santa Cruz Mountains. An overshot mill similar in style to Mary Bennett's, the Bennett/Love sawmill was probably smaller. Courtesy of the Santa Cruz Public Library, Santa Cruz, California.

Act of 1841, but often family members individually claimed land so that the total aggregated more than 160 acres. We will assume that the brother whom Winston helped was David Jackson Bennett, often known as simply Jackson, and that they both claimed preemptively 160 acres surrounding the sawmill, for a total claim of 320 acres. We can further assume that at some point in the late 1840s Winston conveyed his squatter's rights, his half interest along with Jackson, and not a specifically defined piece of land, to his mother Mary Bennett.

Yet Jackson still had an interest in the sawmill and the land surrounding it—or so he thought. He became involved in other unrelated speculations and soon had creditors hounding him. One creditor by the name of Willard Buzzell obtained a judgment against Jackson Bennett in November 1851,[9] and the sheriff sold Jackson's interest in the property on December 21, 1851, to a William Fogg.[10] At that point David Jackson Bennett took two inconsistent, probably fraudulent, actions. First he sold his interest in the sawmill to Thomas Byrd. The conveyance included the surrounding quarter section (160 acres) of "Government land" (clearly implying that he had a preemptive claim). He mentioned in the deed that this mill was that "known as the Bennett Mill being the same as was built [by himself]." The consideration was $2,000.[11] The very next day he released his right to redeem the property from the execution sale, usually a period of one year, but not to the man to whom he had sold the property, but to William Fogg, the buyer at the sheriff's sale, for a separate and additional consideration of $100.[12] That is a matter of selling what you no longer own.

Throughout the 1850s this mill had become known as Bennett's Mill, and ads for the mill's lumber often appeared in the Santa Cruz *Sentinel* newspaper. But which Bennett actually controlled the mill? It appears that, following the assumed transfer of Winston's interest to his mother, Mary, she assumed more and more control, not in the sense of actually operating the mill but in finding sawyers who would rent the mill from her. Undoubtedly, she came to feel that it was her own mill. But Thomas Byrd, to whom Jackson had sold the property, did not just drift away. He must have attempted to operate the sawmill, relying on the deed from David Jackson Bennett. Mary Bennett then filed a lawsuit against him.[13]

In June 1852 Mary furiously wrote her lawyer, noting that she had leased out the mill in 1850 and 1851 and that "Jackson had nothing [to] do with it in any way." She had paid the taxes. She urged her lawyer to call various former tenants as witnesses and insisted that "the mill, sir, is my own property. I have never said the mill was my son Jackson's nor intimated anything of the kind."[14]

There must have been a truce of some sort, but it did not last long. For six days, beginning October 7, 1852, Mary ran an advertisement in the *Daily Alta California* of San Francisco, stating that her tenant of the sawmill refused to pay rent and seeking a man to act as a receiver, a neutral party to take charge of the property.[15] Within a day or two of the beginning of the advertising, she personally presented papers to the judge in Santa Cruz for an injunction, presumably to compel Byrd from operating the sawmill himself. The judge refused the injunction but did issue an order to show cause why an injunction should not issue in the future, in other words he would not grant Mary's request without a hearing, a perfectly sensible course for a judge to take. Mary was so upset and disturbed by her failure to obtain an immediate order that she became ill and, at least for a day, could not correspond with her attorney.[16]

Byrd ultimately prevailed and ousted Mary's tenant, Fitzpatrick.[17] But Byrd must have tired of running the mill because by November 1852 he wished to find a tenant, and Mary Bennett, his former adversary no less, found him one.[18] Eventually Mary must have prevailed, or paid a settlement to Byrd, since by 1856 she was firmly in charge of the sawmill as shown by her lease to Maury W. Smith dated December 8, 1856.[19] This lease is very revealing in a number of ways.

The prior conveyances from David Jackson Bennett had defined the land very simply, either as Bennett's Sawmill and adjoining 160 acres about two and a half miles northeast from the house of Isaac Graham (the Fogg deed) or as Bennett's Sawmill and the quarter section of government land located about two miles northeast from Isaac Graham's sawmill (the Byrd deed). The Smith lease attempts a more sophisticated description, beginning eight miles from the town of Santa Cruz on the San Lorenzo River, "commencing at a cluster of redwood trees near the bridge on the south side of the creek called Bridge Creek thence in northerly direction to a large oak tree located upon the west side thence in a direction due west from each of the said points between parallel lines so as to take in three hundred and twenty acres of land provided the government of the United States does not interfere with the claim."

This 320-acre parcel was probably the original joint preemptive claim of David Jackson Bennett and his brother, Winston Bennett, although Dennis may have had an interest as well. The rent Mary charged in this 1856 lease was considerable, $2,400 per year for three years, payable $200 each month. The 1856 lease expressly provided that if the government did not honor the claim, the Loves would protect, that is warrant or guaranty, their tenant in respect to the 160 acres situated on the west side of the San Lorenzo River, located within the larger 320-acre parcel and on which was located Bennett's Mill and all its buildings. Obviously, this was the quarter section most actively worked and on which Mary thought she had the stronger claim. Interestingly, the lease excluded "one small log building and one small frame building standing side by side at the edge of the plain." This was the location of the homes that Mary had maintained for several years. She stayed there temporarily when attending to her land or litigation business in Santa Cruz County. She also at times resided in this housing as her home. For example, in the early 1850s she brought along the younger children still residing with her and as a family resided near her sawmill.[20] The proximity of the Bennett family to the Isaac Graham residence only about two miles distant would soon play an important role.

The mill must not have been a very profitable business, for its operators at least. Just as we saw Byrd leave, so the new tenant, Maury Smith, left before the end of his three-year lease. By November 1858, less than two years into the three-year lease, Mary was pleading with her lawyer to "please remember a sawyer to run my mill."[21] She lived on this property later, in 1856 through 1858, with her second husband, Harry Love. Thereafter, as we will examine in more detail in a later chapter, Harry Love lived and farmed on the land, at times operating the sawmill. A flood swept the mill away in 1862,[22] although Harry continued farming there for several more years. With the mill gone, the land substantially lumbered out, and even farming operations unprofitable, Mary and Harry may well have abandoned the claim at that point. If so, that would not result in any public record. The Bennett family tradition is that she sold the sawmill to a son-in-law, Daniel McCusker.[23] There is, however, no extant evidence to support that.

Mary's son Dennis Bennett was murdered in late April 1850, an incident we will return to in the next chapter. Mary petitioned the Santa Cruz Probate Court for letters of administration, alleging that he died intestate, and that she was entitled to appointment to handle Dennis's estate. Mary was appointed administrator on May 13, 1850, upon posting bond for $6,000. That level of bonding might indicate that Dennis had some property, but his probate file stops at exactly that point. There is no inventory, nor any indication that Mary took any steps in the administration of his estate.[24] Property descriptions can be found in the Santa Cruz County public records that refer to "land owned by Dennis Bennett" as a measurement for other property. He undoubtedly once owned real estate in Santa Cruz County, and that probably explains Mary's alacrity in petitioning for letters of administration. Dennis may have had an interest in the mill property, since Lansing Haight, who built the dam in 1850, stated that he was doing so "for Jackson and Dennis Bennett,"[25] and Winston Bennett summarized his father's 1847 participation as "my father helped Jack and Dennis build a mill."[26] However, any property records concerning land during his lifetime would be unindexed and perhaps lost in that 1955 flood. In any event, Mary was Dennis's heir, so that any interest he had passed to Mary upon his 1850 death. Certainly with the death of Dennis in 1850, Mary had complete ownership of the sawmill.

There are some other miscellaneous pieces of land that Mary may have owned or claimed to have owned. Winston Bennett quitclaimed four lots in the town of Santa Cruz, two being on the beach, to his mother for the modest consideration of fifty dollars in 1860.[27] His brother, David Jackson Bennett, quitclaimed to her for $400 a larger plot of land on the west side of the town of Santa Cruz, 300 varas square.[28] A quitclaim deed, unlike a warranty or grant deed, conveys only what interest the seller actually has and the seller does not warrant or promise that he has any interest in the property at all. The seller under a quitclaim deed does not promise he will defend the correctness of the ownership interest he has conveyed if a third party attacks it.

Then there is the mysterious parcel known as the "six acre Bennett lot." It first appears in a warranty deed, not a quitclaim, and with the substantial consideration of $1,000, from Lambert B. Clements to David Jackson Bennett. Dated April 1, 1850, the property is described as situated in the town of Santa Cruz and "commencing at the south corner of my lot and running westerly three hundred varas (being bounded on the south partly by land owned by an Indian named Ricardo and partly by land of A. A. Hecox) thence running northerly one hundred varas, thence southerly three hundred varas thence southwesterly one hundred varas to the place of beginning." That description does not come back to the point of beginning, but there it is.[29] Then David Jackson Bennett, on October 20, 1851, and for the consideration of $500, conveyed the "western part of the lot on which I now live," giving more specificity, and undoubtedly a portion of the previously purchased property.[30]

It is unclear when Mary acquired an interest in this property, but in 1854 she, her new husband, Harry Love, David Jackson Bennett, Mary's daughter and Jackson's sister, Mary Ann Amanda, joined in a conveyance of the land for $600 to a B. C. Whiting, "the same six acre lot originally purchased by Dennis Bennett [sic] of Lambert Clements."[31] The following year Whiting conveyed it back for $500, but to Harry Love, presumably taking title for himself and his wife, Mary. The deed specifically refers to the property as the "six acre Bennett lot."[32] But what was this back and forth of title all about? In 1856 Harry and Mary Love joined in a conveyance for $400 of the property to a Jonathan Guild,[33] and that is the end of the story of the "six acre Bennett lot," at least so far as the Bennett family is concerned.

David Jackson Bennett died in Nicaragua in 1856, probably of natural causes, while engaged in "filibustering," that is illegally invading and colonizing, with William Walker. Walker was one of the most prominent of Americans who gathered small, armed forces to attempt the overthrow of Latin American countries in the nineteenth century. He invaded and was repulsed in Baja California in 1853, in Nicaragua in 1855, again in Nicaragua in 1857, and eventually in Honduras in 1860, where he was executed.

Harry Love filed a petition with the Santa Cruz County probate judge, alleging that Jackson had never married, had no children, and that Mary (Bennett) Love was his only heir. The petition, filed November 20, 1857, claimed that David Jackson Bennett had sold a tract of land in Santa Cruz County, had taken a yet-unpaid mortgage for the property, and that this mortgage was the only property he owned in the state of California. John T. Porter was appointed as administrator, and the court also appointed appraisers to report on and appraise any property owned by David Jackson Bennett.[34]

The records reveal yet another probably fraudulent transaction by David Jackson Bennett, in addition to the earlier one involving the double sale of his interest in the Bennett sawmill. A certain James Williams quitclaimed a five-sixths interest in the Mexican land grant Arroyo de la Laguna to Jackson on August 23, 1855.[35] This tract of land consisted of approximately 2,400 acres west of the town of Santa Cruz, located along the Pacific Ocean to the south and Bonny Doon Road to the west. A few months later, on October 13, 1855, Jackson conveyed the land to Adeline Matilda McHenry. James and Pauline Williams joined in the conveyance to pass title to the remaining one-sixth portion.[36] As a part of that transaction, McHenry gave a mortgage to Jackson for $3,000, the balance of the purchase price, securing three notes of $1,000, with interest at 2 percent per month.[37] So far, this was a straightforward transaction.

However, Jackson then assigned and sold those notes to two different persons, once to Joseph Dinet on November 2, 1855, and then again to David and Mary Jones on January 2, 1856,[38] once again a matter of selling the same property—here the mortgage—twice. James P. Treadwell, a subsequent holder of the mortgage as assigned to Jones, brought suit on January 30, 1857, against all concerned to foreclose on the mortgage and "to set aside and dissolve as void a fraudulent pretended assignment," that from Bennett to Dinet.[39]

Mary was still hopeful and desired to obtain the large tract of land for herself. She was Jackson's sole heir. At least one of the three $1,000 installments of the notes was delinquent. Harry Love wrote their lawyer optimistically that he "must do what you think best in the matter. If we can't get the land the thousand dollars will be very acceptable."[40] The administrator of David Jackson Bennett's estate filed an inventory on August 2, 1858. He stated that the only property he had knowledge of belonging to Jackson at his death was his interest in the Arroyo de la Laguna land, but that was in litigation in San Francisco, being claimed by two adverse parties.[41]

Still, Mary's amazing pluck and determination did not fail her. There were two claimants holding mortgages then fighting away in a San Francisco courtroom, presumably both having claims superior to any of those of Mary (Bennett) Love. Yet in November 1858 she leased the 2,400 acres to a George Liddell for one year. The deed recited the facts of Jackson's purchase, his death, the death of his father, and claimed that Mary was his sole heir. It said nothing about the sale that Bennett had made and nothing about the disputed mortgages.[42] George Liddell probably was in physical possession of the property before this, either as a squatter or a tenant of somebody, since he was a named defendant in Treadwell's January 1857 lawsuit.

Probably the lease was merely an effort by Mary to improve her claim. The lease was only for one dollar, and Liddell was authorized to cultivate as much of the land as he thought proper. There was advantage in this because the man in actual possession of the tract recognized her, Mary Love, as the owner. She wrote triumphantly to John Wilson, her lawyer, within a few days of the lease that Liddell "was glad to take a lease of me. So he is now my tenant. He says that the other parties have not tried to dispossess him yet."[43] So far as the Bennett family is concerned, the records and other extant information concerning Arroyo de la Laguna cease at this interesting point.

For all of these parcels of land that came to be in Mary's hands, the only outward conveyance whereby Mary Bennett or Mary Love conveyed to someone else was the six-acre Bennett lot. Mary never conveyed any title outward to these Santa Cruz properties at any time prior to her death. Even if we exclude the very dubious claim on Arroyo de la Laguna that probably never passed to Mary and exclude the two beach lots quitclaimed to her by Winston and that were probably subject to a prior preemption claim by other parties,[44] several parcels remain in Santa Cruz County as to which she should have been "in title" at the time of her death. Yet no real estate in Santa Cruz County appears in the inventory of her estate, a matter to be examined in more detail later.

Why the disconnect? What happened to the title if there were no outward grants and yet none of the Santa Cruz properties were included in her estate? The answer is that almost all titles in Santa Cruz County, excepting those derived from the ten or so land grants within the county, were built upon squatter's rights, which might or might not prove justified and honored by the federal government. That is why so many of these early conveyances were made by quitclaim deed, a device that conveys whatever interest the seller has but without promising his buyer that he has any interest at all in the land conveyed.

Some of the preemption claims may have been subsequently dishonored by the federal government, and that would pull the rug out from under any sales and subsequent resales of the property claimed by the squatter. That may explain why several of Mary's titles in Santa Cruz simply disappeared. Another explanation is that Mary herself may have abandoned her claim altogether, and that would leave no record. This may have been true especially for the Bennett sawmill and the house on it. Mary was forever searching for tenants, and those tenants seemed often to leave before the end of their leases, clear signs of unprofitability. Thereafter, her second husband lived there and was plagued by fire and flood. To modern eyes it seems nearly incredible that a house might be abandoned. However, we should remember that houses as such were not as valuable in the mid-nineteenth century because they lacked plumbing and electricity—and generally in California had no basement. Labor costs for construction were much lower. Nor was land itself worth very much in the mountainous regions of Santa Cruz County. Abandonment was very probably the cause of the disappearance of Mary's Santa Cruz County properties.

Except for the rent sometimes received from the lease of the sawmill, Mary does not seem to have received much for her efforts in Santa Cruz County. However, she was busy at her work there. The indexes of the Santa Cruz District Court, the name then given to the county court of general jurisdiction, indicate that for the years 1851 through 1861 she was a defendant in six lawsuits respecting property or contracts and a plaintiff in four. However, she was only spinning her wheels. Her attempts to acquire and defend land titles in Santa Cruz County went nowhere, only serving as more evidence of Mary's acquisitiveness and her ambition to accumulate as large an estate of land as possible.

Chapter 10

Catherine Leaves Isaac amid
Massive Litigation

When we last saw Catherine Bennett, she had just married Isaac Graham by "contract," and they were living as husband and wife in Graham's Zayante Ranch, in the Santa Cruz Mountains, just two miles from the Bennett Sawmill. Her mother Mary's angry objections to this irregular marriage had been fruitless, but Mary seemed mollified by the birth of her first grandchild, Matilda Jane Graham, on July 4, 1846. A second daughter came in 1849. Seemingly all was well, yet the fuses to several explosions were already lit.

Jesse Graham, Isaac's son by the earlier marriage from which he had deserted, was en route to California via the Southern Trail. On September 15, 1849, he arrived at Rancho Santa Ana del Chino, near modern Pomona. Isaac Williams, the owner of the ranch, told Jesse that his father was alive and living in the Santa Cruz Mountains. Jesse decided to visit his dad.[1] He arrived in Zayante around the beginning of March 1850 and informed his father and Catherine that Isaac's first wife was very much alive. That meant, of course, that Isaac's marriage to Catherine was bigamous and void.

Catherine was pregnant again when she heard this unwelcome news. She delivered a premature baby on March 24, 1850, either stillborn or one who died almost immediately after birth. Isaac Graham and son Jesse left early the next morning to attend a horse race in San José and perhaps do some business.[2] At this point Catherine felt that she had had enough. Perhaps it was Isaac's deception regarding his previous marriage. Perhaps it was the birth of a stillborn child coupled with Isaac's callousness in leaving her the very next morning. Perhaps it was even more. But Catherine wanted out.

Undoubtedly her mother, Mary Bennett, must have seen the matter through a practical, monetary lens. With the previous wife still alive and Catherine's marriage void, their children might well be illegitimate and therefore not heirs of Isaac Graham and inheritors of his ranch. Still, it is curious that with all the claims of anger and agitation expressed by the parties in their later litigation, adultery and bigamy were not the highest on their lists of grievances. Looking back to the loggers' petition against Isaac Graham in 1845, discussed in chapter 7, the protestors had specifically referred to Graham's "dissolute and *adulterous* way of living" (emphasis supplied). Perhaps learning of the previous wife was not itself the shock to Catherine we might otherwise assume.

Her sister Mary Ann had been visiting with Catherine that week, and Catherine sent her home to their mother, Mary Bennett, with a box containing the dead baby.[3] Then on March 31, 1850, Catherine gathered up the two living children she had had with Isaac, Matilda Jane and Amanda Ann, and fled, taking with her a significant amount of Isaac Graham's gold that he kept hidden in the house. The newspapers subsequently pumped the value of the gold up to $20,000–$30,000, but Catherine later stated it was $8,000, and Graham himself later testified that $7,000 worth of gold was taken. Taking either Catherine's or Isaac's figure, it was a significant amount—$150,000 or more in today's dollars and purchasing power.

Her brother David Jackson Bennett and a handyman named John Palmer aided her flight. Dressed as a man, Catherine took a ship from Santa Cruz to San Francisco—sharing a cabin with a future mayor of San José, Thomas Fallon—perhaps indiscreetly yet innocently, as she claimed. From San Francisco she continued her flight to Hawaii, then an independent kingdom.

Meanwhile, by April 3, 1850, Isaac had returned to Zayante and began furiously searching for his wife, his children, and his gold. On that day he publicized his loss, requesting the public's aid in tracking Catherine down.[4] He claimed that Catherine had a lover, implying that it was for that reason she had left.[5] In a newspaper letter Mary quickly denied that her daughter had a lover.[6] Another letter to the editor from "Many Citizens of Santa Cruz" attested that they had "never heard a word of slander against the wife of Capt. Graham until she disappeared. Since then we have had nothing but vague conjectures, but in no case has anything been said against her private character."[7]

At this point Catherine herself weighed in with a letter to her mother, dated September 27, 1850, and clearly intended for subsequent publication. She vigorously denied having a lover:

I see by the *Daily Pacific News* of the 16th of May, that I have been accused of having a lover with me, which you and the citizens of Santa Cruz pronounce to be false, and which is absolutely false. I did not nor never will degrade myself so far as that.

In this letter Catherine offered a different version of why she had left Isaac Graham:

I was so tired of being beat and having bowie knives drawn over me, (for twice that old brute Graham drew his bowie knife across my throat till the blood ran down my breast, and I expected every day he would kill me.) and finding it impossible to please the old tyrant, I believed that my only chance was to leave him or be murdered by his hand. So I thought it would be better for me to go to a foreign country, where I would not be troubled with him anymore.[8]

She always kept to this position, repeating in 1888 under oath that she had left Isaac because she was afraid for her life and offering an additional incident that at dinner Isaac "pulled a revolver, pointed to my face and said, 'God Damn you, I'll blow your brains out if you put poison in my food.'"[9] Regarding the dead baby, Catherine thought Graham himself was the murderer. "I say he murdered it, because it was abuse that I received from him. His hands was (sic) its death."[10]

Meanwhile, Graham was frantically searching for gold, wife, and kids. He was convinced, of course, that Mary Bennett was behind it all. In early April 1850 he obtained a search warrant and together with the sheriff searched Mary's home near the Bennett Sawmill. They found nothing directly relevant, but Isaac became excited about the box that Catherine had used to convey the dead baby. He claimed that the box came from a locked trunk in which he had kept his gold, and he had Mary Ann, the sister who had been visiting Catherine just before her departure, arrested for aiding and abetting the robbery of his gold. However, Mary Ann was almost immediately released, either for want of proof or—depending on whom one believes—after being "honorably acquitted." Mary claimed the box did not come from Graham's trunk but rather from a box of Catherine's clothing.[11]

Notwithstanding that the search revealed no incriminating evidence in the Bennett house, Isaac continued to blame Mary and the Bennetts generally for the flight of his wife, the kidnapping of his children, and the theft of his gold. The family continued to deny they had anything to do with it, and Catherine in her September letter expressly stated that she "left without the assistance or knowledge of any of you."[12] The small Santa Cruz community "had been thrown into great excitement," according to one contemporary observer, and "strong sides were taken by the friends of the husband and wife."[13] Jesse had naturally taken his father's side in the affair, and he was every bit the hothead that Isaac was. After the search Jesse returned to the Bennett house on several occasions and threatened their lives if they did not disclose where Catherine was hiding, at one point training his shotgun on Mary for long periods of time and threatening other members of the Bennett family, including the girls. The Bennett family remained adamant in denying involvement in the escape and knowledge of her hideout. On one occasion, Jesse actually pulled the lock on his gun as he confronted Mary Bennett:

> On Friday afternoon he came to the garden where I was at work. I was alone with my three little children, some four or five hundred yards from the house. He rode right up to the fence and said "Good morning." I answered him. He then said, "I have come this morning, Mrs. Bennett, to have a private conversation with you; come, get over the fence and go with me." I replied, "No sir-e-e! I can do nothing of the kind." He said I must and should go, and that he came with the intention of having a private conversation with me in the woods. I said, "No, Jesse, whatever you want to say, say it in the presence of my children." He then pulled the lock of his gun about half way, and said, "Come, you must come; with me death is nothing." I said, "Jesse, I can't go; what would it profit you to kill me." He asked "Where is Catherine? You and Mary know where she is, and you both have to die." I argued with him to drop it.[14]

By April 22, 1850, the harassment from Jesse had become so great that Mary Bennett and her son David Jackson appeared before Adna A. Hecox, the town judge in Santa Cruz, an equivalent to a justice of the peace, to ask for a restraining order. The sheriff summoned Jesse Graham, and they all appeared before Hecox, each making their case. After a hearing Judge Hecox ordered Jesse "to give bonds for keeping the peace towards Mrs. Mary Bennett and her family in the sum of one thousand dollars for the term of one year."[15] This technique of forcing a disturber of the peace to post a "peace bond" was a common nineteenth-century technique of policing. One problem with its application was that troublemakers often, as with Jesse in this case, had no money. Nor could they easily find people willing to be guarantors on their bond. Since to this point it was a matter of "he said, she said," and only threats had been made, Hecox took the route that many nineteenth-century lower court judges were forced to take: he increased the amount of the bond but allowed Jesse to stand in effect as his own surety. He released Jesse on his own recognizance, upon Jesse's promise of good behavior. That promise stood good for about an hour.

On the road back into the mountains from Santa Cruz, Jesse followed the Bennetts, mother and son, and overtook them about a mile from the mission. Jesse then fired one shot from his double-barreled buckshot shotgun at Jackson, but missed. He then fired the second barrel at Mary Bennett, and five pellets hit her, two in the hip and three in her legs. A man named O. K. Stampley, the acting sheriff, who happened to be working nearby, took Mary to the nearest house and summoned a doctor.[16] A Dr. Stevenson attended her while she resided with Mrs. John Woods, and for the two weeks she was there Mary was disabled.[17]

Although Jesse had missed with his first shot, Jackson's horse became frightened and threw him to the ground. He was unable to stop Jesse who rode to his father's home and then on to the two Bennett houses, where he called Dennis out from his house, then shot him dead.[18] Jesse fled, and a reward of $3,000 was offered for his apprehension, $2,000 from Jackson Bennett and $1,000 from Santa Cruz County.[19] This affray is presented according to the Bennett interpretation. The world would not learn of Jesse's view of these events for thirty-eight years.

Meanwhile, Isaac Graham continued to search for his children and his gold. For reasons unknown, Catherine became nervous about her hideout ⌐ Hawaii, fearful that Isaac would find her there. She removed herself to Oregon and took up residence in Oregon City at the northern head of the Willamette Valley. Catherine's flight had lasted only a little over one year before Isaac learned of her residence in Oregon City. John Cox, an Oregonian and perhaps the source of Graham's knowledge that his wife, children, and perhaps his gold were in Oregon City, joined Graham in tracking Catherine to a Mrs. Williams's house in Oregon City in May 1851. Isaac threatened to break down the door to her room, but she opened it herself. Once he was inside, Isaac seized the children and demanded the gold. He persuaded young Matilda Jane to reveal that the gold was hidden in the room's stove, where he found $3,000. Graham took the remaining gold and his two children and left in triumph for California and his Zayante ranch. Catherine followed him to begin a massive offensive of litigation.

At this point the reader might appreciate a very brief description of the California state judicial system and a portion of her domestic-relations law, as they stood in 1851. Each town had its own judge, but that was no longer the old Hispanic alcalde but was a probate court or probate judge. Appeal from his judgments went to the various district courts—in the case of appeals from Santa Cruz to the Third District Court, presided over by Judge Craven P. Hester. Further appeal was to the California Supreme Court. Cases were heard and appeals considered with an alacrity that would astonish lawyers in present-day California. In nineteenth-century America, including California, the father of legitimate children had the primary right to custody when the parents separated. A mother could prevail only by showing that the father was unfit. However, a father had no rights in respect to his own illegitimate children.

Catherine fired the opening shot of the litigation in a suit for the children's custody filed in the Santa Cruz Probate Court. Hers was the initial victory, and the judge ordered Isaac Graham to return his little girls to their mother. Then on July 22, 1851, Isaac petitioned Judge Hester for a writ of habeas corpus, demanding the children and alleging that Catherine had been "living in a state of adult[e]ry with one B. B. Rogers in the State of Oregon" and that she had also lived with a man named Daniel Stewart. He had retaken his children, he claimed, "for the purpose of educating an[d] raising them as useful members of society and withdrawing them from the pernicious example of an abandoned mother."

The day after Graham filed the writ, Judge Hester gave temporary custody to Catherine, and continued the case until the fall term at Graham's request so that he could obtain evidence concerning Catherine's conduct in Oregon. He prohibited Isaac from removing the children from Catherine's custody, forbade Catherine from taking the children from the court's jurisdiction, and ordered her to put up a $5,000 bond and give Isaac "undisrupted access to visit said children without interference or hindrance." The girls went back to their mother.

Catherine Tillatha Bennett Graham McCusker, ca. 1865. Courtesy of the Conrado Family Archives.

The following month, August 1851, Catherine left the children in her mother's hands while she took a business trip to San Francisco. Soon thereafter Mary Bennett decided to join her daughter in San Francisco and placed the children in charge of someone named Thomas W. Wright. Isaac Graham became suspicious of this movement of the children and thought it might be a scheme to remove them from Santa Cruz County. He made an emergency application to the Probate Court, and the sheriff seized the children and gave them to Graham, much to the consternation of Mary Bennett, who was just about to go aboard the vessel bound for San Francisco. An immediate cross-complaint to the Third District Court was to no avail, and for the moment custody was back with Isaac.

Two months later, on October 9, 1851, Catherine filed a new case against Isaac, not for custody but for money damages of $20,000. It was brought on the theory that because of Graham's undisclosed previous marriage, the marriage by contract between Catherine Bennett and Isaac Graham was void and the children illegitimate. It further alleged that when Isaac arrived in Oregon City he "brutally assaulted" Catherine and then, by abducting her children and carrying them off to California, he had caused her expense to travel to California to search for them and then recover them.[20]

A modern scholar has written that "one suspects the point of this cause of action was to establish the illegitimacy of the children. As a result, Catherine, as mother, would establish her sole legal right to custody."[21] That does not seem correct, because she could just as easily have raised the illegitimacy in the custody case itself. It seems more likely that Catherine filed this additional lawsuit because the custody case did not provide a route to a judgment for money damages, whereas a case alleging wrongful abduction and assault did. The damages suit did raise the issue of illegitimacy because with illegitimacy Catherine had a clear right to custody, making Isaac's actions in Oregon City a "wrongful abduction." On the other hand, if the children were legitimate then Isaac had primary custody and what she characterized as a "wrongful abduction" would be merely a "rightful retaking" of custody. In any event there were now two separate lawsuits, the custody lawsuit in which both sought custody and the damages lawsuit in which Catherine sought money damages of $20,000.

In the custody case Graham filed a subsequent petition before the Probate Court, spelling out why he thought Catherine was an unfit mother. She was, he alleged,

> a woman of bad reputation entirely wanting in moral character and destitute of every quality of a mother, with bad associations, loose and abandoned in her mode & habits of life, unfit and injurious in every way as a guardian or example and especially so to female minors.

He charged that she had acknowledged to him that she had committed grand larceny (the stolen gold), and he believed that she bragged about that to others. Isaac further alleged that she had lived in Oregon in open adultery and under the assumed names of Mrs. Rogers and Mrs. Stewart. Catherine denied the charges. She admitted taking some money that she felt rightfully belonged to her but insisted that she had led a blameless life in Oregon. The probate judge was unimpressed by Catherine, and on November 13, 1851, he awarded custody to Isaac. Nine days later Catherine posted a $300 appeal bond, but the Probate Court nevertheless gave Isaac custody pending the outcome. The children stayed with their father.

The next month, on December 13, 1851, Judge Hester on the Third District Court returned the children's custody back to Catherine but carried the case over because Catherine's damages suit was on the docket for trial. The children returned to the mother. In late February 1852 Judge Hester presided over Catherine's damages suit. The testimony in the trial centered on the marriage and whether Graham had married Catherine in good faith. She claimed that she was led to believe that Isaac had never married before and did not know differently until Jesse Graham appeared in March 1850. Isaac testified that at the time of his marriage with Catherine he believed that his first wife was dead, having been massacred by Indians. There was also testimony that under Texas law a separation for seven years invalidated the marriage.

The then-standard six-man jury heard testimony over three days and on February 26, 1852, delivered a split verdict. They found Graham not liable for assault but liable for wrongful abduction with damages set at $2,500. Catherine obtained a judgment for $2,500 plus court costs. Isaac was quite upset, largely because of the cloud over the children. Since they were now regarded as bastards, that strengthened Catherine's position to obtain full

Isaac Graham. Photograph of oil portrait. In light of so many negative comments on Mr. Graham's demeanor and uncouth appearance, it seems certain that the artist has exercised considerable artistic license. Courtesy of the California State Library, Sacramento.

custody in the other case. He moved for a new trial, and after that was denied, he appealed to the California Supreme Court.

Before that appeal was heard Isaac and Catherine were back before Judge Hester in June 1852 for a hearing on the custody case. The judge ordered all the documents from the trial before the Probate Court into evidence before him. Catherine testified that she had worked with Graham on behalf of the mill business, had taken only $5,000 in gold, and that she thought it a small amount that was rightfully hers. She admitted sharing the cabin on board the ship from Santa Cruz to San Francisco but insisted that there was no wrongdoing. In fact she denied any adultery at all. In answer to a direct question about her present condition, she responded "I am not now pregnant," an answer she surely knew was incorrect when she said it. In June 1852, after reading all the prior testimony and taking additional testimony from several witnesses, Judge Hester ruled in Catherine's favor. He granted custody of Matilda Jane and Amanda Ann to Catherine, their mother. Isaac had already appealed to the California Supreme Court on the damages case but did not appeal the custody case.

In the rapid manner then characteristic of litigation in California, the Supreme Court issued its opinion in October 1852. It reasoned that because marriage was a civil contract, no particular ceremony was required for its creation. The ceremony that the parties had undertaken and the written paper they signed were sufficient to create a marriage, assuming there was no legal disability to enter into the contract. Because Graham was already married there was a disability, and therefore the supposed marriage of Catherine and Isaac was void, a nullity. However, a California statute provided that "the issue of all marriages deemed null in law, or dissolved by divorce, shall be legitimate." It therefore followed that Isaac Graham's children were legitimate even though the marriage itself was void:

> They are, therefore, in relation to their father, the inheritors of his name, his heirs-apparent, and entitled to look for, and demand from him, his care, maintenance and protection. On the other hand, he has the unquestioned right to their custody, control, and obedience, to the same extent as if they were the issue of a valid marriage.[22]

The court did not spell it out, but the clear implication of its reasoning was that because Isaac was entitled to the children's custody, his removal of them from Catherine in Oregon City was a "rightful retaking" rather than a "wrongful abduction." It reversed the $2,500 judgment that Catherine had received from the jury.

The California Supreme Court's decision did not in itself give custody of the children to Graham. After all, it was merely a lawsuit for damages. And the custody case, in which custody was awarded to Catherine, was not itself appealed. There does not appear to have been any further litigation. Perhaps Catherine simply bowed to the inevitable and handed the children over to Isaac voluntarily after the Supreme Court decision showed the clear likelihood of her losing any further court battles. Perhaps that was not so bad. Isaac Graham clearly loved his two girls. He never sued Catherine for the loss of his gold. It was only the children for which he litigated, and if he had not loved them, he surely would have been scared off by the massive extent of the legal battles. He had signed an affidavit acknowledging his paternity and attempting to legitimate them months before the California Supreme Court's decision.[23] In the end the winner was clear. The 1860 census shows that the two girls, Jane and Anna Graham, ages fourteen and eleven—by then each had adopted her middle name as her first—were living with their father in Santa Cruz.[24]

In December 1852 Catherine Bennett gave birth to a son out-of-wedlock. She claimed in a subsequent 1888 trial that she and Isaac had a reconciliation back in Oregon City and that he had subsequently deserted her on their way to California. However, they had been actively litigating from June 1851. Any reconciliation prior to that would not have affected a birth in December 1852. Additionally, in both the damages trial and the custody trial she had testified that she had had no reconciliation with Isaac Graham after her March 31, 1850, departure. She directly denied being pregnant in her June 1852 trial, although giving birth six months later. It is very clear that Isaac Graham was not the father of the boy she named Frank, born in December 1852.

In the nineteenth century this illegitimate birth could have been a significant problem for Catherine, involving lifelong disgrace. However, she was very lucky, and all turned out well. In February 1853 she married Daniel McCusker, a Santa Clara resident and native of Ireland. He adopted Frank, and the newlywed couple went on to have six children of their own union and lived long and apparently contented lives. Daniel McCusker may have had some slight prior involvement with the Bennetts. As we saw in the last chapter, there is no evidence to support the Bennett family tradition that McCusker bought the Bennett sawmill from Mary. However, he may have been associated with her erstwhile tenant, William Fitzpatrick, and thereby suffered the same ouster executed on January 13, 1853, by Thomas Byrd, a previous grantee of the Bennett sawmill by David Jackson Bennett.[25]

Mary Bennett's first grandchild, Matilda Jane Graham, whose name was reordered into Jane Matilda Graham, lived a long life, was very partial to her father, and had less regard for her Bennett relatives. She married a man named David M. Rice in 1862, and in 1918 she personally filled out a "pioneer card" for the California State Library. Describing her simple life she wrote that she had "married at 16 a poor man and always had my own work to do and a family of six children (plus 2 adopted)." These were the simple annals of the poor. The form asked for her father's profession or occupation, to which she replied "distiller, rancher and gentleman." In the space asking where her father, Isaac Graham, had been educated, she wrote tersely "the world."[26] We shall meet Mrs. Rice again in the epilogue.

Chapter 11

Mary Bennett Marries Harry Love

On May 31, 1854, Mary McSwain Bennett remarried—to a man named Harry Love. It is unclear when and where they met. It is even unclear where they married. Love's biographer states that it was in Monterey, California.[1] In subsequent litigation Mary claimed that it was in San Francisco.[2] These factoids matter very little. What does matter is that the marriage was a disaster. This was an era in which newspapers took sides, and made no pretense at objectivity. Nevertheless, the comments of the San José *Patriot*, a newspaper that was clearly Love's champion, tells us a great deal about the turmoil in their marriage, and the very public nature of it:

> Ever since the marriage of Harry Love, the Texas Ranger, with the widow Bennett, eight or ten years ago or more, there has been from time to time turmoil in the family—quarrels—separations, lawsuits, reunions and a separation again. In fact there has been no harmony in the family, and their domestic affairs have too often been the subject of ventilation by courts and gossips. The woman has never borne an enviable reputation, and there are persons who know them both well, who maintain that Harry Love, with all his faults, was the best of the two, and the least to blame in the troubles of their married life.[3]

When they married, in May 1854, Harry Love was extremely well known throughout California, and that itself may have been an attraction for Mary. He had just come into a fair amount of money, and that may also have helped Mary to decide.

Born in 1810, Love spent some years at sea as a young man, then drifted down to the American South. When the Mexican War broke out, he enlisted in a group of Alabama volunteers. After that war had ended, he reenlisted and served in Texas as an express rider for the army. Then he piloted a keelboat down the Rio Grande River. Attracted by the discovery of gold, Love

Harry Love, Mary Bennett's second husband. Courtesy of the Bancroft Library, University of California, Berkeley.

arrived in California at the end of 1850. After a year and a half of a desultory search for gold, Harry hit upon the idea of hunting robbers and murderers, plenteously supplied in California, for their rewards. He enjoyed real success in this.

One of the most notorious of the so-called "social bandits"—defeated Californios who had taken to robbery—was a mysterious man named Joaquín, later identified as Joaquín Murrieta, who had murdered and robbed many Anglo settlers. There was a clamor for action, and in May 1853 Harry Love persuaded the legislature to organize a group of twenty California Rangers under Love's direction who were authorized to search for Joaquín Murrieta for three months at a salary of $150 per person, with an additional reward of $1,000 to share upon Murrieta's death or capture.

The California Rangers spent about a month in organization and gathering of information, but by July 1853 they were in active search in the San Joaquín Valley. On July 25, 1853, they came upon Murrieta, and when he attempted to flee, they shot him dead.[4] Thereupon, as Love wrote to a pleased Governor John Bigler, "We beheaded Joaquín and one of his principal men and I dispatched [two of his officers] to Fort Miller (being the nearest point) with the heads in order to be put in Liquor for preservation."[5] Quite prudently, Love also gathered many statements from those who had known Murrieta as to the authenticity of the head now preserved in a glass jar. A grateful legislature awarded Love an additional $5,000 reward in mid-May 1854, and it is unclear how or whether he shared that with his colleagues. That may have been a factor in Mary's interest in Harry. After Murrieta's death, his head was displayed throughout California, with Harry Love's name mentioned in the display legend. That, plus the numerous articles in newspapers, meant that Harry was indeed prominent throughout the state.

In any event the factors leading to their marriage were essentially practical rather than romantic. Harry left for a trip to the east coast within a day after their marriage, presumably arranged beforehand, and did not return until the end of September 1854, allowing no time for a honeymoon.[6] On the personal side, superficially they were well suited. Both were plain, hard-working individualists. Both were large people, over 250 pounds— Mary probably already closer to 300 pounds—and both slightly over six feet in height. They were of the same approximate age, Mary in 1854 being about fifty, and Harry in 1854 about forty-four. Mary had some other practical considerations. Her sons were now grown and had moved out of the house. Harry could be of help with the farming on her grant in Santa Clara. She was having problems with squatters, as we will see more closely in the following chapter. Harry, with his size and fame as a gunslinger, might intimidate them into leaving.

Harry might also, she must have thought, be of help with her litigation. First, it was still very much a man's world, and women were not always respected by lawyers, litigants, or judges. Harry being a front man in litigation might alleviate that problem. Then too Mary was involved in such a massive amount of litigation that she could use help to contact witnesses, arrange depositions, meet lawyers, go to court to make filings, and so forth.

Additionally, a more strictly "legal" matter may have entered her thinking. The rules of coverture, the legal disabilities that attended married women, were quite complex. After achieving statehood, California followed the general rules of women's disabilities during marriage, with the sole exception being that a married woman could own separate property. Property acquired after marriage, even if it were technically the wife's separate property, was effectively under the control of the husband. Married women were unable to enter into general contracts and could enter into agreements, conveyances, or mortgages involving their own separate property only if the husband agreed by himself signing the contract, mortgage, or conveyance and if the transaction were acknowledged before a notary. That was not all. The notary also had to append a verification that he had examined the wife separately, away from her husband, and confirmed that the transaction was of her own will.

Mary was able to turn these marital "disabilities" into a positive sword by asserting them to defeat what almost anyone would see as a perfectly proper debt she had incurred and, in a moral sense, ought to have paid. She frequently asserted these marital disabilities as technicalities in order to defeat just claims. She made litigation against her a legal minefield.

An example of this is the lawsuit of Charles Maclay against Harry Love and Mary Love, brought in Santa Clara County. In 1857 both Harry and Mary signed a promissory note for $200 payable to H. S. Washburne as consideration for his surveying Mary's land grant property. Then in 1860 Washburne assigned the unpaid note to Maclay, who became thereafter the owner of the note. In that same year Mr. Maclay sold Mary various goods to the value of $27.40. Since no payment was forthcoming from either Mary or Harry Love, Maclay sued them both for the $200 plus the $27.40.

Mary claimed the complaint was no good as against her. The trial court agreed and threw it out. Mary's argument was that since under California law a married woman had no power to enter into contracts, the lawsuit in effect was to charge this separate property. In other words, since neither community property nor Harry's separate property would be liable for her obligations, any judgment given against her would in effect be a charge against her separate property, that is, her lands. However, although she could encumber or sell her separate property, the only way she was permitted to do so was following the form mandated by the Act of April 17, 1850. This provided in regard to the wife's separate property that "no sale or other alienation of any part of such property can be made, nor any lien or incumbrance created thereon, unless by an instrument in writing, signed by the husband and wife, *and acknowledged by her upon examination separate and apart from her husband*"[7] (emphasis supplied).

That provision was designed to protect wives from spousal imposition, by questioning them apart from their husbands to ascertain that a sale or encumbrance was their own true will. But here that purpose was turned on its head, by Mary's using it as a shield to protect herself from a just debt she had incurred for her own benefit. The signed note was just that, a promissory note, and did not have an attached certification from a notary that he had examined her separate from Harry and that it was her true desire to encumber her property. It would necessarily do that because she could not create a personal debt of her own since that would involve her making a contract which she could not do as a married woman, only a conveyance or encumbrance on her own separate property. So it was only as an encumbrance on her grant that it could be enforced, but for that it needed the statutory form.

The plaintiff appealed the dismissal of the lawsuit to the California Supreme Court. That court acknowledged that Mary had "a right by contracts not imposing liabilities against her personally, to create a charge upon [her separate property] . . . yet such charge must be created in some mode not prohibited by statute. . . . She has no power to create [a charge on separate property] in any other mode than the one prescribed by the express provisions of the statute."[8]

Since the simple signed note did not have the required separate examination, it was void as against Mary. The California Supreme Court affirmed the dismissal of the lawsuit. Of course, had Mary Love been unmarried, it would have been a simple matter of debt, and the judgment could have been enforced against any of her properties. This convoluted case is just an example of how Mary was able to manipulate her marital status to avoid debts. There were other such cases.

It is more difficult to understand why Harry was attracted to Mary Bennett. Perhaps it was because she held some of the same qualities he had: she was hardworking, large, and tough. Then too, she held significant property interests. Mary also could be charming on occasion. Perhaps after so many years alone and on the go, Harry simply wanted to settle down.

The couple lived together in Mary's home in Santa Clara for the first two years of their marriage and then moved to the cabin on their "government land" in the Santa Cruz Mountains, the preemptive claim along the San Lorenzo River on which their cabins were located.[9] Harry Love probably intensely disliked living in Santa Clara. He was accustomed to working out of doors and being on the go from his serving in the army, galloping on fast horses around Texas as a dispatch rider, piloting a keelboat, and hunting down bandits in California. True, he could work outdoors on Mary's farm in Santa Clara, but he was stuck in one place. And that one place, Santa Clara, was a fixed community that itself was becoming a town. These were probably some of the considerations that induced Harry to move up to the mill in the Santa Cruz Mountains in late 1856 or early 1857, bringing Mary with him.

According to Mary, in December 1858 Harry ordered her to return by herself to Santa Clara. Harry denied that he had forced or ordered her to leave, but it is true that at about that time the couple separated,[10] although Harry would intermittently visit Mary in Santa Clara over the next ten years. The marriage was not going well. In addition to both being hard working, plain, and large, Harry and Mary also shared the character trait of being extremely strongly-willed people with domineering personalities. Love's biographer attributes the basic underlying problem to Mary's possessiveness concerning her property. He writes that "in all of these dealings, Harry noticed his wife was very manipulative and controlling. He had expected to share in her property holdings, but . . . she always insisted on sole control of her property."[11]

There is also a tradition in Mary's descendants that "Mary, as well known for her sharp tongue as for her warm heart, was used to running her own business and family and objected to Harry having anything to say about either. They battled continuously and spent most of the time separating and making up."[12] In fact, Mary truly was controlling, sometimes grasping in her acquisitiveness, and not likely to allow another to come close to her economic interests. Yet, in various correspondence with her lawyers in the late 1850s and early 1860s, there are letters written by her husband requesting various actions by the attorneys, and there is some evidence of his meeting with and interviewing witnesses in her cases.

Moreover, there is reason to believe that Harry Love's expectations were not unfounded. Of course, California was a community property state, and Mary's property owned by her prior to marriage remained her separate property. However, California law still allowed the husband control over the wife's separate property, in the sense that she could do nothing with it by contract, conveyance, or mortgage unless he consented. Over the course of time, the sawmill once called "Bennett's Mill" became known as "Love's

Mill." There are assertions, but no evidence, that Harry bought a mill from Jackson Bennett or even from Mary. Instead, probably the name of the sawmill simply changed to "Love" in accord with the fact that her new husband now had effective control over it, more physically than just legally.

Harry did make substantial improvements to the milling operation, however. He built a road along the San Lorenzo River known as the "Love Grade" to more easily move timber to Santa Cruz.[13] The mill had difficulties. With improved shipping, competing lumber from the eastern United States had arrived, and even within the Santa Cruz Mountains there were increasing numbers of lumbering operations. It was difficult to find sawyers. He increasingly relied on his agricultural endeavors, but those were relatively insignificant because of the mountainous terrain. The 1860 Santa Cruz agricultural census showed Harry to have only $200 in machinery, plus two cows, one horse, twelve oxen (for pulling logs), twenty-five hogs, and forty acres in hay. Not a large operation, but he was getting by. He was proud enough of his agricultural prowess that he sometimes brought a prize specimen to Santa Cruz, displaying a huge radish to the newspaper in 1859 and displaying a fourteen-foot-tall cornstalk in 1865. However, he was really not doing well, and he was drinking more and more.

Love had his share of squatter problems, became ensnarled in his own and Mary's litigation over her land claims, and even had some lawsuits from his creditors, but his primary foes were fire and flood. The first fire came in October 1861 when a neighbor lost control over brush he was burning. The fire spread and destroyed some fencing and 150 acres of grass on the Love/Bennett land in the mountains. Love brought suit against the neighbor for $1,500 in damages but was awarded a mere pittance of $60. A second and much larger fire, also in October 1861, did not damage the Love/Bennett property directly, but it created the basis for a future disaster for the sawmill. This larger fire spread through the Santa Cruz Mountains, destroying thousands of acres of timberland, including much of the standing timber along the rim of the mountains surrounding the San Lorenzo Valley.

Lumbering in the San Lorenzo Valley had enjoyed an almost unrestricted run for the twenty years prior to 1862. Much of the tree cover, and therefore the capacity for absorption of rainwater and the prevention of erosion, had disappeared. The cutting was by clear cut, and there had been no replanting. Now in 1861 fires had destroyed additional acreage. If that were not enough to create a serious danger of flooding, the timber men had themselves completed the danger by building skid roads, small passages for cut logs to slide down to the mills. Over the years deed ruts formed in these skid roads, creating a perfect conduit for flood waters to be blown like water through a straw aimed directly at the sawmills.

And then came the storm. Heavy rains pelted all of California in December 1861 and January 1862, but until the second week of January, Santa Cruz County escaped the flood waters that collected in the Sacramento and San Joaquín Valleys. But the rains did fill the creek beds, and the coastal settlers anxiously awaited their fate. Then in the second week of January 1862, a heavy and steady rain pelted the San Lorenzo Valley, and with no further warning flash floods from higher in the mountains came down the already filled creeks and especially down the skid roads directly aimed at the sawmills. Most of the sawmills along the San Lorenzo River were simply swept away. The local newspaper totaled up the damages in the San Lorenzo Valley. The tannery was a total loss, the paper mills had major damage. "Graham's, Hicks', Love's and Bryant's sawmills were all swept off, as well as every dam on the river,"[14] and two other sawmills were significantly damaged.

The Bennett/Love sawmill was gone. Love reacted poorly to the loss, and while he kept on farming, he also kept on drinking. Then in early 1864 came even more disaster; Love's dwelling and tool houses were burned to the ground. The newspaper reported:

> Capt. Love is sure that the fire was the work of an incendiary, as it originated in a tool house, several feet from his dwelling house, in which there had been no fire for some time. The entire contents of the two buildings were also burned and Capt. Love himself narrowly escaped.[15]

Some friends helped him build a new cabin, and Love returned to his farming. In 1865, local citizens asked him to ride in the annual Fourth of July parade in Santa Cruz. That must have boosted his ego. It is unknown how he felt about his common moniker in Santa Cruz, the "Black Knight of the Zayante." He had friends from earlier times and distant places who occasionally visited him, and once a week Harry would go down to Santa Cruz to have dinner with a friend.[16] Still, it was a lonely existence, he was barely making ends meet, and he continued to drink. Freak summer rains again caused damage in 1866, "breaking down standing grain—especially early sown wheat and barley and volunteer oats and grass. The hay crop, which was mown, is probably injured twenty per cent."[17] The specific damage to Love's farm is unknown, but there must have been some and it must have been discouraging to Harry. He continued to have squatter problems, critical to him since actual possession was essential to the preemptive claim. He spent much time in court. In May 1867 Harry Love either mortgaged or sold his interest in the sawmill property to a lumberman named Charles Brown for $300. The transaction is unclear, but Love continued to farm.[18]

In June 1867, the very next month, in the last of his series of disasters on the San Lorenzo, another fire struck Harry. He lost his entire crop of hay:

> FIRE BY AN INCENDIARY—Harry Love informs us that on last Sunday, about 12 o'clock, he was apprised of the fact that his entire crop of newly cut and partly cocked hay, some hundred tons, valued at six hundred dollars, was on fire. Harry is having trouble about his land, and it is supposed this has something to do with the burning of his hay. Whoever the incendiary may be, he ought to be brought to punishment, as there is no safety in the community where such villains are allowed to circulate.[19]

In what must be only a small coda to the body of his previous problems, in July 1867 about a mile from his property, some bee hunters lost control of a fire designed to drive wild bees from their hives. The fire spread, and Harry lost 100 cords of stacked tanbark. Love was nearly at the end of his rope, and in the midst of all this chaos from floods and fires, on August 28, 1866, the sheriff of Santa Cruz County served him with a summons to answer the divorce complaint of his wife, Mary.[20]

Harry had one last chance to stay in Santa Cruz, one last hurrah. In the fall of 1867, he stood for election to the office of justice of the peace for his township. Although there was no salary, the fees were lucrative enough to offer a good living that would be untouched by fires and floods. The newspaper ran a kindly notice of his candidacy and drew attention to Love's exiguous circumstances. He was, the *Sentinel* noted, "a pioneer citizen of this county, and probably as well known as any other man in it," who has "suffered from flood and fire, in the washing away of his mill and the incendiary burning of his hay—the entire earnings of a year of toil—last hay-cutting."[21] Unfortunately for Harry Love, he came in fourth of a field of seven candidates. The farm was lost, and the possible political position of justice of the peace had eluded him. Now he had only one remaining option. He had to deal with Mary, and at this point Mary held all the high cards. Or so Mary might have thought.

Mary Love issued her complaint for divorce on August 9, 1866, signing in a firm hand, not the mark she had formerly used. In it she alleged, essentially, that Harry Love in December 1858 ordered her to leave their house in the Santa Cruz Mountains and return to Santa Clara. She charged that although he had visited her in Santa Clara and furnished her provisions until June 1864, since that time he had neglected her and remained in Santa Cruz County. By reason of this Harry had deserted her, had failed to provide for her, and had refused to live with her and treat her as his wife. There was, so she said, no cause for this alienation since she herself had been "a dutiful wife and has faithfully tried to discharge her duties as such."[22]

Mary filed her lawsuit in Santa Clara County District Court, the court of general jurisdiction for both legal matters and equitable actions, divorce being a case of equity. Harry almost immediately moved for a change in venue, where the case should be heard, to Santa Cruz County since he was a resident there. The lawsuit was transferred to Santa Cruz, and Harry filed his answer, denying specifically the various allegations of his wife. He did not order Mary out of their Santa Cruz County home, he had not failed to visit since June 1864, he had not deserted Mary, he had not failed to support her, and Mary had not requested him to live with her since June 1864. More generally, he claimed that "he has always treated Plaintiff as his wife, and discharged the duties of a kind and faithful husband to her, and is still and always has been, ready and willing so to do." He did not ask for a divorce but rather that her action be dismissed, in other words that the divorce be denied.[23]

Depositions were taken by commissioners a year later, on November 5 and 12, 1867, on the eve of trial. The following are summaries of the witnesses' testimony.[24]

Samantha Bennett, Mary's daughter, testified to some uncontested matters as to where and when Harry and Mary had lived together before their late-1858 breakup, and then she refused to testify further. Mansel Bennett, Mary's son, failed to obey the subpoena to appear before the commission and was arrested and physically taken to testify. He testified as to his identification and then refused to answer any further questions, saying "he will not give any testimony in this case." Julia A. Adams, another of Mary's daughters, testified as to her knowledge of where the couple had lived and when, that she had heard her mother say that Harry Love refused to live with her or support her, and that from the years 1864 until early 1867 Mary was quite impoverished. "She had a few hens. My brother furnished her two cows. She told me that was all she had. What she made off from the eggs." She was not able to derive any rent from her land claim until July 1867 but after that was able to support herself from her land rentals. This raises the question of what happened to the substantial proceeds from the sale of Vardamon's lot in San Francisco in the 1850s. That is a complete mystery.

Catherine McCusker, formerly Catherine Bennett Graham, yet another of Mary's daughters, also testified. She was present at Mary's house in May 1864 when Harry was visiting. She heard Harry say "he wouldn't live with her nor provide for her, that she might provide for herself. . . . It was pretty rough and I didn't want to hear it and tried to avoid it. Mother was complaining about his not providing for her. She was destitute and had scarcely anything to keep house with or to eat. . . . She had nothing scarcely in the house. . . . I heard her ask him to buy some flour and he said he hadn't any money. She gave him the money herself and he bought 50 lbs of flour." Thomas N. Wright was at Mary's house in 1865, employed by her to do some work. As to her means of subsistence then, in the summer of 1865, "I don't think she had much means. She had no money to pay me for my work. I think she was hard run."

Daniel McCusker, the husband of Catherine and therefore Mary's son-in-law, also testified that he had been present at Mary's house in Santa Clara in May 1864. Harry "said he would neither live with her (i.e., Mary) nor provide for her." McCusker saw Harry the next day, after they both had crossed over the mountains. Harry "said he neither would provide for her nor come back again." McCusker visited Harry's cabin on the San Lorenzo River in the fall of 1865. Sitting together on the porch "he told me he never had been back since the time we had been there together. That he had never given her anything to live on and did not intend to and that he did not intend to go back. He told me to sit down and brought on the conversation himself."

"He asked me here in Santa Cruz if I had let the old lady have any money. Said he understood I had. He advised me not to let her have any. That she had plenty of property then to support herself and that I had enough to do to support my own family. He said he had never given her anything and didn't intend to, that he had enough to do to support himself. . . . [However, McCusker knew] she had no means at that time. I was there a week in 1864 and she was in a starving condition. She had no support for a year after that. Since that time she has had a ranch confirmed and has had her support from that. I let her have money several times that year. . . . It might have been two years from that time before she got any support from her ranch."

In May 1864 "she asked him at the time we were in Santa Clara to live with her and provide for her and to behave himself. He said he would be damned if he would do it. He never would live with her or be about the ranch or house where she lives in Santa Clara again. A little while before he left he got very mad and got up and threw a bucket of milk out in the yard. It was milk that was milked that morning. . . . I believe he wanted her to come over in Zayante, and live with him. . . . I suppose that was the substance of it then there was other things with it. There was pretty rough talk amongst them generally. . . . I think she said she wouldn't go, that that was her home and the place where he had married her and that she didn't want to go into those mountains to live that that was no place for a woman to live."

The depositions were supposed to continue on November 18, 1867, and Joseph H. Mein, a witness called by Harry Love, appeared, as did Love's attorney, but not the lawyer for Mary Love. Depositions were continued until November 19, 1867, and on that next day, neither party appeared. Clearly, something was happening. On December 14, 1867, the lawsuit was called for trial. Harry and Mary were both in court when Mary's attorney moved for dismissal. Because the plaintiff who brought the lawsuit now wanted it dismissed, and since the defendant had sought nothing except that dismissal, the court was happy to oblige. The divorce petition was dismissed upon the plaintiff's request, and Harry Love was given judgment against Mary for court costs he had incurred.[25]

But why? Why would Mary want to dismiss her lawsuit, especially since the depositions showed a case for nonsupport? Clearly, something strange was going on, but to understand we must back up a bit and understand Mary's probable motivation for the divorce lawsuit and the probable dangers that presented themselves through the depositions.

Even though 1864 may have been a terrible year for Mary according to the depositions, still it brought a glimmer of hope. It was in 1864 that the survey of her ranch grant was finally approved. Mr. McCusker was wrong in thinking that confirmation of her grant around 1866 meant that Mary was suddenly able to rent out portions of her grant and thereby derive an income from it. The farm grant was confirmed by the land commissioners in 1855 and affirmed by the U.S. District Court in 1857, long before the controversies involved in the divorce. The survey approval was delayed because Mary herself objected to the survey, a matter considered in a subsequent chapter. But even though Mary received far less in the survey than she had hoped for, by 1865 there was increasing certainty of what she had. Then by August 1866, from that certainty and also from the pressures of increasing population around Santa Clara, her income from the ranch grant had increased to the point that rentals from it provided her support. The income from her property rentals was $1095 (at least) in 1868; $1271 in 1869; and $1958 in 1870.[26] The land grant was leased out in parcels to probably four or five separate tenants, with each of whom Mary had to negotiate. She probably also leased out several portions of her preemption property.[27] In those years one could live quite comfortably on this income, especially if one had, as Mary did, her own home, a good garden, and a large supply of chickens. The average per capita income in the United States was then approximately $200 per annum. In her later years Mary was in quite comfortable economic circumstances.

The marriage itself was dead, and that would be one factor for Mary to seek a divorce. But another equally important factor probably was that she was unwilling to share this newly established substantial income with a man who would not (albeit he probably could not) support her in her need as recently as two years back. But if that might explain the timing of the divorce, what can explain her decision at the moment of trial to dismiss her divorce?

We can never know for certain, but Mary may well have had a well-grounded fear that the court might order her to pay support to her husband, Harry Love. Harry had become destitute by December 1867, and Mary had acquired a good income from her farm grant, a far cry from their previous circumstances. Although Harry Love had only asked that the divorce petition be dismissed and had never asked for support, his lawyer may have intimated that this request would be made if the lawsuit were not dismissed. An order that she support Harry might have resulted not only because Mary now held the upper economic hand but also because under the then-existing California law, Mary herself may have been regarded as having deserted Harry.

We must remember the male-oriented state of California law. This can be seen clearly in certain provisions of the Civil Code of 1872. Although this came five years later, it simply codifies in clear statement what was already the existing law. Let us look at a few of its provisions:[28]

> California Civil Code Sec. 156. The husband is the head of the family. He may choose any reasonable place or mode of living, and the wife must conform thereto.

> California Civil Code Sec. 103. The husband may choose any reasonable place or mode of living, and if the wife does not conform thereto, it is desertion.

Within the depositions there was evidence that Harry asked Mary to live with him in the Santa Cruz Mountains and that she had refused. If that were believed, then it was Mary's desertion of Harry, and not the other way around. Mary could hardly convince a court that living in the mountains was unreasonable because she had lived there herself with her children in 1850, and that at a time when she was unmarried and had complete control over where to live. If this were the way their affairs were interpreted—that she had deserted Harry and not the other way around—then another legal provision came into play.

> Civil Code Sec. 176. The wife must support the husband, when he has not deserted her, out of her separate property, when he has no separate property, and there is no community property and he is unable, from infirmity, to support himself.

Here was the danger, Mary may well have thought. Harry Love clearly was impoverished. The mill was gone, his crops were gone, he was older and somewhat wasted through drink. She might well be ordered to support him. Better, perhaps, to offer some sort of reconciliation, out of which she could control what she paid out on his behalf and perhaps get some work out of him in the bargain.

In the event, Harry told his friends and neighbors in mid-December that he was moving to his wife's place in Santa Clara. The *Santa Cruz Sentinel* noted his departure on December 21, 1867. From his perspective he had little choice, although that must have humiliated him. Love gathered up his very few possessions, two horses, a wagon, gun, harness, trunk of clothing, and a few dollars in cash,[29] and went to Mary's home in Santa Clara. Love's biographer writes that Harry stored his belongings in Mary's barn and prepared to bunk there as well.[30] It was an uneasy situation. A San José newspaper later, in July 1868, described the situation between Harry and Mary:

> It seems that of late there was a sort of a reconciliation between the parties, a kind of a half reconciliation, whereby they were for a time enabled to live together under the same roof—but there was no sympathy, no unity of feeling—no disposition, on the part of the woman at least, to forget the past—no yearning for a happier commingling of thought and affection.[31]

It was, quite literally, an armed truce, out of which would come no good.

Chapter 12

Land Claims Litigation and Other Lawsuits, 1851–1864

In February 1848, through the Treaty of Guadalupe Hidalgo that ended the war between Mexico and the United States, America made solemn promises to Mexico regarding the treatment of her citizens in the lands, including California, that America was acquiring. "Property of every kind," among other promises the treaty made, "shall be inviolately respected." The present owners, their heirs, or assigns "shall enjoy with respect to it [i.e., property] guaranties equally ample as if the same belonged to citizens of the United States."[1]

Several factors made it very difficult for the United States to keep its word regarding land in California. One was the great uncertainty regarding titles in California. The Mexican California authorities had made approximately eight hundred land grants with the object of settling the country and fostering agriculture—and in some cases to simply feather the nests of political cronies. No surveys were made, and the crude maps employed to request and make grants, called *diseños*, used sometimes vague or ambiguous reference points. Many grants overlapped, only the very smallest were fenced, and many were of dubious legality under Mexican law.

The discovery of gold at Sutter's Mill in spring 1848 indirectly created the most severe problem for fair dealing with California titles. The Gold Rush seemed to bring the entire world into California; it certainly brought exponential population growth. Just before the American invasion in July 1846, perhaps 10,000 persons of European extraction and 7,000 Indians living a somewhat assimilated life in towns or on ranches lived in California.[2] By 1850 the population grew to 92,597, reflecting the onslaught of the Gold Rush. The state census of 1852 shows a population of about 250,000, although this is questionable since some counties were not included and some people were counted twice, including the Bennett family in both Santa Clara and Santa Cruz Counties. The more reliable federal census of 1860 shows a California population of 379,994.[3]

These figures demonstrate that people stayed on, and more arrived, even after the flush years of the Gold Rush were over. Some disappointed miners may have returned home, but they were more than replaced by newer arrivals seeking opportunities to practice their professions in cities and their agricultural skills on farms. The sheer growth of population put tremendous pressure on California land.

That pressure was exacerbated by the American system of preemption and the nonintensive nature of the existing California agriculture. Americans were accustomed to intensive agriculture in which a 160-acre or perhaps a 320-acre plot of land could support arable fields and pasture for cattle. California agriculture, however, was far less intensive and far more devoted to grazing. The ranches had very few fields, and the slaughter of cattle for their hides and tallow was the basis of the economy. The climate was more arid and the land less lush than in the eastern United States. California cattle raisers needed large expanses of land to support a decent-sized herd of cattle. Accordingly, ranches of about 4,400 or 8,800 square acres, one or two Mexican leagues, were common, and many ranches were even larger.

To a farmer coming from a society with 160- or 320-acre farms, the California countryside appeared to be unoccupied. And Americans of that day clearly understood that unoccupied land belonging to the government meant they could preempt it if they wished. That is to say they could squat on it, improve it, and after it was ultimately surveyed by the government, they would have the first opportunity to buy it from the government at low prices.

The combination of vague titles, population pressure, vast expanses of seemingly unused land, and the American culture of preemption created havoc in California. Squatting became endemic, violence began to increase, state courts attempted to adjudicate property rights in a legal vacuum, and pressure mounted for a legislative solution. An act of Congress, approved March 3, 1851, popularly called the Land Claims Act of 1851, could have provided a solution had it not been so ineptly administered by the federal government. This act required *everyone* "claiming lands in California by virtue of any right or title derived from the Spanish or Mexican government" to present to a board of land commissioners "such documentary evidence and testimony of witnesses as the said claimant relies upon in support of such claims."[4] The United States was an interested party in every claim because the statute made it clear that the default position, in the event the grant was rejected, was that the property involved would be public land.

The United States could therefore present evidence as well, and then the board would "decide upon the validity of the said claim," with appeal possible to the federal district court, not to be confused with the state district courts, and then to the Supreme Court of the United States. Following confirmation of the claim, the applicant would survey the property before obtaining approval from the government's surveyor general. If the claimant's survey was thought to be off the mark, the government could order its own survey. Ultimately, after the final judicial approval of a survey, the government would issue a patent, and this would become a muniment of title, a foundation good against all other persons.

No lawyer could miss the ambiguity in the charge to the Board of Land Commissioners that it "decide upon the validity" of claims. Who has the burden of proof? Does the claimant? That might have been a significant violation of at least the spirit of the treaty. After all, the federal government has never swooped down on a state or two and demanded that every landowner therein prove his title to be good, that he in fact owns his own property. Or, alternatively, did the government have the affirmative burden of disproving the validity of a claimed grant? In the end it mattered very little since the board and the courts displayed a liberal attitude toward the claims. A leading California land historian explains:

> Few grants complied one hundred per cent with the letter of the law. . . .
> The United States Land Commission, functioning in the 1850's, and the
> courts to which appeals were taken displayed a liberal and fair attitude to-
> ward claimants and ordinarily confirmed the titles of persons who could
> prove possession and actual occupancy by themselves or predecessors in
> the Mexican period—regardless of whether or not the provisions of Mex-
> ican laws were followed religiously in obtaining Mexican grants.[5]

The problem for land claimants and squatters alike was that the process took so long. Seventeen years was the average time between the filing of a petition to the board and issuance of the final government patent. Most of that delay came from the surveying and the seemingly interminable time it took for the government bureaucracy to grind out the patent even after a survey was finally approved. During this time it was impossible to sell land with a clear title, so prices were depressed except in settled cities where town lots had a long series of occupancy. During the time between petition to the board and the final approval of the survey, squatters continued to swarm over the land. If a claim were disapproved, then the land would be public and subject to their preemption claims. However, squatters could not easily ascertain whether their improvements were on a grant or the public domain. The act made evictions expensive and difficult because the state court that controlled evictions would be troubled by the question of who had title.

After the confirmation of a land grant, evictions became easier, but squatting continued, particularly on the edges of a grant where the lines of the grant remained indeterminate until the survey was complete. The squatter could still hope he was located on public land outside the grant. All these circumstances bedeviled every California landowner whose title was based on a land grant. Mary Bennett's title to her house lot and the larger farming plot of 1,000 by 2,000 varas of course depended on the validity of the land grant she had received from Governor Pío Pico. On the other hand, her actual residence and the eleven or so acres surrounding it, north of Mission Santa Clara, depended on her own squatting on public land and was not involved in the land confirmation process.

Mary Bennett filed her petition with the Board of Land Commissioners on March 2, 1853. She asked for confirmation of her house grant, the description of which was never in doubt, and also the larger farming tract. In the petition to the board, she was specific about the boundaries she claimed for the grant. It was bounded on the east, she claimed, by the high ground of the mission, on the north by the sowing ground of the Indians, on the west by the land of Ignacio Alviso, and on the south by the land now occupied by Galindo.[6] Contradicting this, both the original petition to the Mexican Governor Pío Pico and the *diseño* that supported it described the tract requested as bounded by the heights of Santa Clara to the north and the margin of the oak grove to the south. The description of the northern boundary must certainly have been a draftsman's error, since the "alta," heights or higher ground, certainly lies to the east or northeast of the tract.

Thus the original petition to the governor did not specify boundaries in two of its directions, north (because the north shown on the map is truly east) and south. Both the *diseño* and Mary's petition to the board do agree that the size is 1,000 by 2,000 varas. The vara is approximately 33 inches, and the amount of land encompassed by 1,000 by 2,000 is approximately 355 acres.

Bennett was originally represented by John Wilson, a San Francisco attorney who had represented her on several prior occasions. Probably because he had developed a conflict of interest, Mary switched lawyers in November 1854, and she and her new husband, Harry Love, signed a contingency fee contract with the firm of Howard & Perley. The firm agreed to represent them through the confirmation stage of the process. If the tracts were not confirmed, there would be no fee. If they were confirmed, Mary and Harry agreed "to pay to said Howard and Perley as their fee" one-tenth of all the lands confirmed.[7] Land claimants and their lawyers generally employed some form of contingency fee agreement in the California land confirmation process. Very few landholders had the funds to pay outright for their attorneys' time. As an additional matter of tidying up the record, Mary's son, Winston, in whose Hispanicized name of Narciso or Narcisso the grant was made, conveyed the tracts to Mary in April 1854 and acknowledged that the tracts "have been heretofore in the use and occupancy of my mother."[8]

The board generally proceeded on the basis of evidence taken by depositions, and after those were submitted a hearing was held, giving opportunity for arguments pro and con by the attorneys. In the Bennett case depositions were held primarily in the months of January, February, and June 1855. Witnesses testified as to Bennett's being put into possession by the alcalde and her occupancy and use, or lack thereof, before the American invasion. Mary's affidavit described the loss or destruction of the actual grant and naturalization papers of her son, and the board allowed her to proceed on the basis of witness recollections of their contents. The petitions to the governor and his favorable response were found in and copies made from the Mexican archives. On July 10, 1855, the board issued its opinion. The board saw conflicting evidence as to whether the Bennett occupation and use of land was within the actual grant but found that really irrelevant. The test was good faith, and it was clear to the board that the Bennett cultivation of wheat and other occupation was made "in good faith to carry out the purposes of the grant and was intended to be on the premises granted." That was enough, and the board ordered the two tracts confirmed "as described in the *expediente*."⁹ The expediente was a bundle of Mexican documents concerning the grant and included Narciso Bennett's petition for the grant and the map or *diseño*. In other words the decree confirmed Mary Bennett Love's title to the land as described on two sides of her grant, *not* the more elaborate boundary description she used in her petition to the board. The board left it to the surveying process to determine the actual boundaries.

The United States appealed the board's confirmation to the Federal District Court for Northern California on February 11, 1856. When the case was called on February 28, 1857, the district attorney for the government informed the court that the attorney general had determined that no further appeal would be taken and that a final order affirming the board's action could be entered by agreement. Now came what appears to have been a legal machination to extend the size of the Bennett grant. Presumably, Bennett's counsel graciously offered to prepare the formal order, something often done by the prevailing party's lawyer, and the harried government lawyer accepted that offer subject to submission of the draft order for his approval. The district attorney did approve the order and submitted it to Judge Ogden Hoffman, the U.S. district judge, for signature. As is customary, the order having been approved by all sides, Judge Hoffman signed it without review. Thereafter, the district attorney discovered that "the description of the land contained in the decree of this Court was widely different from that contained in the decree of the Board; and that the land confirmed by this Court is of larger extent and different situation from that confirmed to the claimants by the Board." Probably Mary had sneaked into the decree her more favorable description of her petition to the board, with its four dimensions and much wider north and south boundaries. In other words she was trying to obtain the land she contended the alcalde had settled on her in the judicial possession, rather than the more limited amount that she, or her son, had asked for originally in the petition to the governor and the map that accompanied that request.

The district attorney moved to amend the court's decree to correct this error, and Mary's lawyers opposed the motion on the basis that because the court term had expired the court lacked jurisdiction. In other words, too much time had gone by. Judge Hoffman ruled that the court did have jurisdiction to correct an error and to amend its decree to conform to that of the board. Judge Hoffman rejected the claim by Mary's attorneys that there was not much difference between the unamended decree and the board's order, writing that "it is enough to say that the description of the land is entirely different, and designates boundaries not mentioned either in the original petition of the claimant [i.e., to the Mexican governor], or in any of the documents presented by her."[10]

Mary's first attempt to expand the boundaries of her grant was to make up different boundaries than those specified on the grant for her petition to the Land Claims Commission Board. That failed when the board verified her grant as described in the Mexican papers themselves, the *expediente*. Then her second attempt to expand the grant failed when the district attorney noticed the inaccurate description of the land in the order presumably prepared by her lawyers and actually signed by the court. Now she moved to a different arena to expand her grant—the survey that would complete the confirmation process.

Under the confirmation process, after the grant was confirmed the claimant prepared a survey. That survey might be approved by the surveyor general, and then valuable time would be saved. Even if not approved, a survey submitted by the claimant would show the furthest extent of the claim and thereby release at least some lands, for which eager settlers awaited, into the public domain. In 1857 Mary hired a surveyor named H. S. Washburne to survey her grant.[11] This survey is apparently not still extant, but it must have given an enormous amount of land to Mary Bennett. The Washburne survey was rejected by the federal Office of Surveyor General, which noted that it included a part of the actual town of Santa Clara, and gave Mary 1,591 acres,[12] in contrast to the 355 acres that a description of 2,000 by 1,000 varas would yield.

Santa Clara had not escaped the population pressures that were affecting the entire state. Incorporated in 1852, Santa Clara grew from the few hundred people of the 1840s village to a population of 2,559 in 1860.[13] By 1860 the town had sold building lots on what it thought were public lands. Many of these lots were on land now claimed by Mary Bennett. Considerable political agitation in California arose against the land claims. Settler leagues, as they were called, representing the interests of squatters, developed all over the state to oppose the confirmation of grants. They formed a political party that nominated candidates for statewide and local races.

These groups attracted farmers who had squatted on the ranches, since to the extent that land claims were disallowed, the land would be public and their own preemption claims would be superior. The Settler's League in Santa Clara primarily opposed the larger *rancho* claims, but it also took aim on Mary Bennett's claim. For example both Peleg Rush and J. H. Morgan owned houses on lots sold to them by the town of Santa Clara that were located on lands that Mary Bennett claimed, and Morgan was actually a member of the Settler's League and had contributed money to defeat her claim.[14]

Protest meetings denounced the Bennett claim. The Santa Cruz *Sentinel* reported on May 9, 1859:

> From a private letter, we learn that the ordinarily quiet town of Santa Clara is now the scene of excitement caused by the survey [Bennett's Washburne survey] of the Mary S. Bennett claim, which covers most of Santa Clara, the line running north and south . . . embracing all the protestant [sic] churches, school houses and colleges, and, in fact, all the business portion of the town. The citizens have been holding meetings every day since the making of the survey.[15]

It was very clear that Mary claimed much of the already-developed land within the city of Santa Clara. She and Harry entered into a supplemental attorney agreement with their same lawyers, now Howard, Perley and Gould, for the legal work needed for the survey portion of the confirmation process. This supplemental fee agreement of January 1861 was also contingent on success, but the payment bargained for was fifteen blocks of land, 300 feet square, located within the survey, selected in alternation with the Loves. The agreement specified that these would include the buildings and improvements on these lots, in other words what the town of Santa Clara had already surveyed and sold off and on which buildings had been erected by others.[16]

One solution to this conundrum caused by uncertainty of location, for those who had purchased lots from the town and perhaps erected buildings, was to buy a quitclaim deed from Mary. That way if the grant were ultimately found to include their lot, their title would be saved by her quitclaim; if it did not, then they would take through the sale by the town. There would be no liability for Mary even if it were found that her grant did not extend to these lots since Mary would make no promise of title through a quitclaim deed, but only convey whatever title she had, if she had any. Mary Love was able to sell some of these quitclaims. For example, in October 1857 she quitclaimed four city lots located on Washington and Franklin Streets to John Darmeyer, for $200.[17] In February 1856 she had sold her house grant, the *solar*, to Elijah T. Fitts, for $750.[18] The description was called out in the names of the modern streets and also by reference to the town's survey, which was complete at that point. That was an enormous price, considering that the average per capita income in the United States was then around $200 and also that the grant, although just approved by the board, had yet to pass its judicial review.

Mary had several squatters who occupied the farming portion of her grant, not merely the town lots. A fellow named Hiram Shartzer had seized sixty-five acres on her farm plot in 1850, built a house, and farmed the property. In April 1861 he took over an additional thirty-five acres.[19] Before her plot was surveyed with at least tentative approval, there was little she could do to evict him. Of course, she did complain. While negotiating with Elijah Fitts over the sale of her three-acre house grant, Mary told him that three or four squatters were causing her considerable trouble in getting her grant. "She said she would get it eventually, and live on Shartzer's place. She said he had a fine orchard there."[20] On December 11, 1865, after both her title had been confirmed and the boundaries set by the government's survey, she sued in state court to eject Shartzer. He defended on various theories and also asked that the court offset the value of the improvements he had made. The trial court gave judgment to Mary for recovery of possession, rental value while he was wrongfully in possession, and refused to allow Shartzer any credit for his improvements. Shartzer appealed, but the California Supreme Court affirmed the decision in Mary Love's favor.[21]

B. F. Watkins trespassed and then squatted on a different twelve-and-a-half-acre portion of Mary's farm lot in January 1855. He was more clever than Shartzer because he purchased attorney Howard's interest in the Loves' attorney fee contract in February 1863, at a time when the lawyers had fully performed since Mary Love's grant had been confirmed. Although the survey was still unsettled, her attorneys were entitled to be paid 10 percent of the land confirmed. When Mary sued Watkins to eject him from her land on December 13, 1865, she won a judgment at trial. She lost on Watkins's appeal to the California Supreme Court. The appellate court reasoned, in effect, that Watkins, through his purchase of the contract right to receive land as earned attorney's fees, had become a co-tenant with Mary. As such he was entitled to possess the land he had originally entered illegally.[22]

Mary was continuously involved in litigation, not necessarily directly concerned with her land. For example, she signed a note for $500 just months before she married Harry Love. When she did not pay and a lawsuit was brought against her, she played the married-woman defense, as she did in almost every lawsuit against her. This time it did not work. The trial court found against her; she appealed to the California Supreme Court and lost again on appeal.[23]

In another case Thomas Hart, a Santa Cruz resident, apparently had loaned Mary Love some money from time to time. Hart claimed $1,000 from her for these loans, but she claimed the note was a forgery and somehow induced the prosecutor to prosecute him, which resulted in his acquittal. The San José *Mercury* reported in early August 1861:

> The testimony of witnesses proved the good character of the plaintiff [Hart], and that of the defendant bad [Mary Love, defendant in Hart's suit on the note]. . . . It is believed by many that it [the criminal indictment] was a concerted movement on the part of Ditmar and Mrs. Love to ruin Mr. Hart by incarceration in prison, thereby making it easier for Mrs. L. to sustain her charge of forgery, and to avoid paying the note, all of which, we are pleased to chronicle, has been happily frustrated.[24]

Of course, these lawsuits were more complicated than these brief summaries. There were at least a dozen lawsuits in which Mary Love was a party in Santa Clara County. Then too, she had several in Santa Cruz County. All of them must have been very vexing for Mary. She even had a second lawsuit with Hiram Shartzer, a man who, it seemed, would never give up. Harry and Mary Love signed a note for $1,500 in favor of William M. Lent on June 27, 1859, secured by a mortgage on a portion of Mary's land grant tract, together with an agreement that a portion of this loan might be paid by the parcel that was mortgaged plus $350. The note only became due sixty days after the patent for the land was issued by the United States.[25] Lent then assigned his rights to Hiram Shartzer in February 1865 for $3,540,[26] an increase that surely demonstrates the rise in property values. Shortly thereafter, Shartzer sued Harry and Mary Love in state court on the theory that they had a duty to move the patent along and had delayed. The Loves asked the lower court to dismiss the case—on the basis that they had no legal duty or even ability to make the government process their patent more quickly. The trial court did throw the case out, Shartzer appealed, and the California Supreme Court affirmed the lower court's ruling in favor of the Loves, pointing out that the cause of the delay was the responsibility of the government and not the Loves.[27]

On April 16, 1861, J. W. Mandeville, the United States Surveyor General for California, approved a survey of the Bennett tracts made by William J. Lewis of his office. The Lewis survey strictly limited the extent of the farm grant to 2,000 by 1,000 varas, 355 acres, and located the western boundary on the margin of the oak grove. This removed it entirely from the town's lots and indeed from all of the then-existing urban development. The Santa Clara citizenry was jubilant. The neighboring city newspaper, the San José *Mercury* reported:

> The claim of Mrs. Mary S. Love, better known as the Mary S. Bennett claim, which has caused much feeling in consequence of the claimants attempting to drift the same over the town of Santa Clara, has been located under the personal superintendence of Surveyor Mandeville, placing it outside of the town, and in the place where it rightfully belongs, if it belongs anywhere, of which there is considerable doubt. The land thus yielded to her is valued at $10,000. If located where she desired, her claim would have been worth $200,000.[28]

Mary Love filed exceptions to the official survey on May 16, 1861,[29] and then her specification of reasons on August 23, 1861. She claimed that the survey (1) "is not made according to the original title papers of claimant," (2) "is not made according to the decrees of the court," (3) "was made in error, and to suit private interests of owners of adjoining land, in disregard of the rights of claimant," and (4) "does not include the land granted the claimant by the Mexican Government, but includes another and different tract of land."[30] U.S. District Judge Ogden Hoffman denied her motion to set aside the government's survey on January 10, 1862,[31] and the formal process for trial began.

This further contest of her tract's description and size resulted in a series of additional depositions and affidavits taken in 1862 and 1863. Mary Love submitted a map prepared by James Stratton that purports to show the tract as it was put into Mary's possession by the alcalde in 1845. It shows dramatically what was at stake. The claimed eastern boundary went east nearly to the mission buildings, with an eastern terminus approximately where the modern municipal court is located. The claimed northern boundary extended past El Camino Real that runs in the direction of San Francisco, more or less where it is located today. The northern limit of her claim ran through the approximate location of the present Santa Clara city hall. It extended from north of El Camino Real southward, well past Saratoga Avenue. Stratton showed dramatically the difference between the government's approved survey and Mary's claims by superimposing the government survey onto his maps.

Perhaps because with the growth and development of Santa Clara it was now very clear how much was at stake, the government did a better job in producing witnesses adverse to Mary's contentions in the survey phase than had been the case in the confirmation proceedings. Sharply conflicting testimony defined the "alta" specified in the *diseño* and grant as, alternatively, a sharp point very near to and just west of the mission buildings where the rising hill came to a head, or a broad line much further west that separated the more arid upland from the more fertile and moist lowland, or "bahia." If the "alta" were more eastward, then Mary's grant would be greater and would encompass much of developed Santa Clara. If the "alta" were lower, then her grant would be more limited. It would then be bounded, as the government survey showed, by the modern-day roads, approximately, of Forbes Avenue to the south, Kiely Boulevard to the west, Scott Boulevard to the east, and a line to the east formed by extending Frémont Street further to the west. The modern-day Santa Clara Central Park is the very approximate northwest corner of the tract as approved by the government.

Although not technically relevant to the survey stage of this drawn-out process, a few witnesses questioned whether there was ever actually a procedure where Mary was put into possession at all. A neighbor to the land and an official testified that they should have been notified of such an event, and they were not. Had the intensity of opposition at the survey stage been brought forth at the confirmation stage, Mary may possibly not have received confirmation of anything. However, at this late stage the only issue remaining was that of the size and boundaries of her grant.

The hearing came on in the summer of 1863. The U.S. district court judge

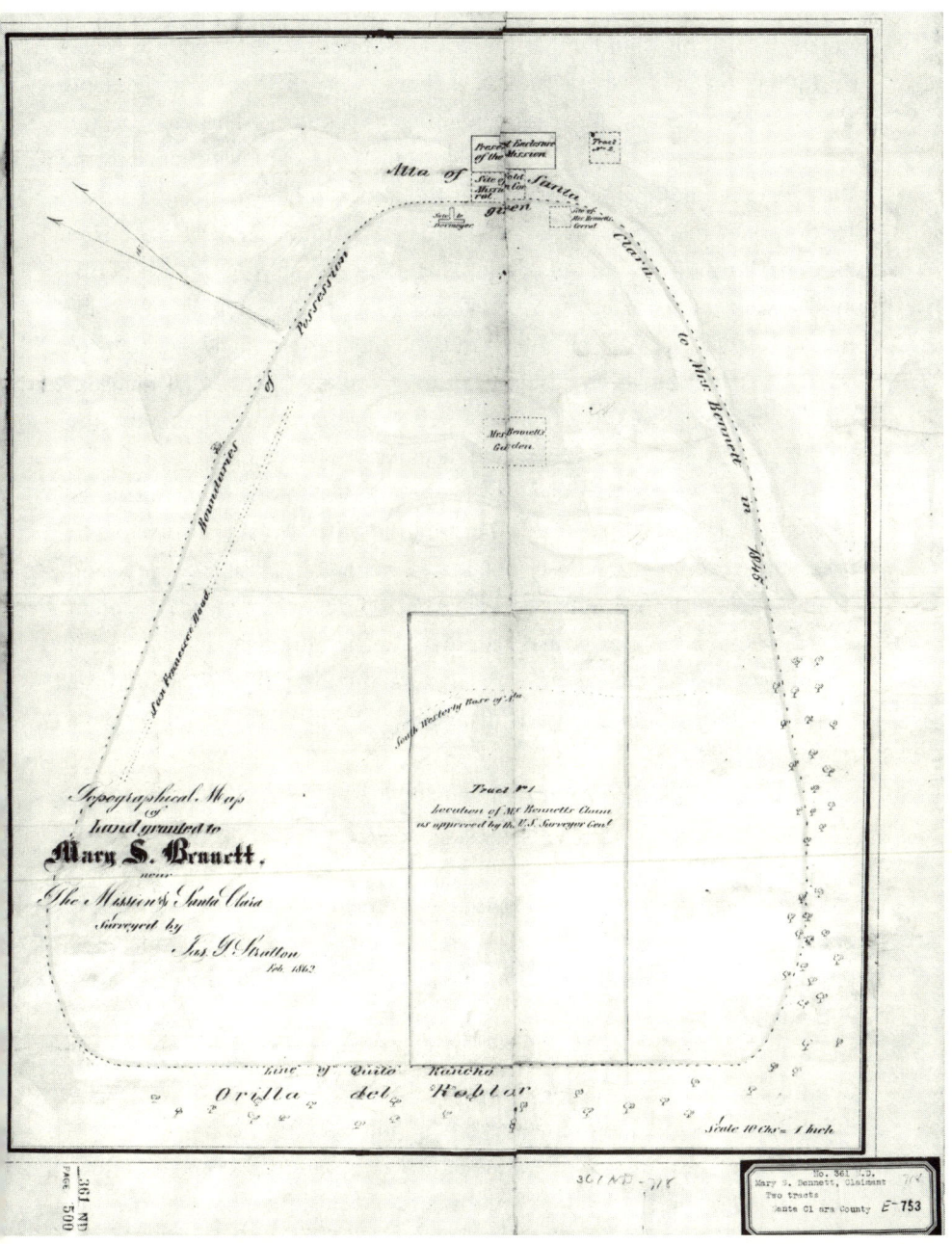

Drawing of the Bennett land claim as surveyed by the United States government within the area that Mary Bennett Love claimed. From district court land claims records, 361 N.D. 500. Courtesy of the Bancroft Library, University of California, Berkeley.

noted early in his opinion that the principal question before him was the location of the "alta," whether it was "a short and narrow piece of high land immediately adjoining the mission buildings," as contended by Mary, or "the whole tract of high land . . . which extends to a considerable distance [from the mission buildings] until it reaches the low land known as the 'Bahia.'" He dismissed the first of Mary's arguments, based on the judicial possession given her in 1845, almost out of hand. Not only was no record made of this judicial possession, and such a formal procedure usually resulted in a voluminous record, but additionally no measurements were made by chains or otherwise. Here, however, it is only fair to record one historian's conclusion that "instruments were seldom employed in laying out the grant, and the alcalde usually guessed at course and distance."[32]

The judge seemed almost to believe that judicial possession was never given at all and pointed, among other things, to the "limits as sworn to embrace a tract some 4 or 5 times as large as the quantity granted." He found it "incredible that an alcalde could have been induced to give possession of a tract so much more extensive than that to which the claimant claimed to be entitled," that is the 2,000- by 1,000-vara amount of the *diseño* and the petition to the governor. Thus he dismissed the judicial possession process from consideration.

Two interesting things must be said about Dolores Pacheco, the alcalde who, according to witnesses and Mary's claim, judicially put her into possession. The first is that he was not a young, inexperienced man. He was about forty-eight years of age in 1846 and had held a number of government offices. Most significantly, he had previously served as an alcalde from 1838 through 1841.[33] He well knew about the process to be followed and the sizes of grants. The second interesting thing is that he did not himself submit an affidavit nor was his deposition taken during Mary Bennett Love's confirmation process. His secretary and others testified as to what Dolores Pacheco did to put Mary into possession, yet he did not testify himself.

The judge also dismissed evidence of Mary Bennett's occupation and cultivation as a basis for showing the extent of her grant. The evidence was confused, he wrote, and not very significant. Even if she had built a corral or grazed some cattle on the higher plane of the alta, further east of the line for which the government contended, the land was then open and her temporary use was not necessarily evidence of her ownership or even a claim of ownership. The judge rejected the conflicting testimony of witnesses and looked to documentary evidence and reasonable inferences from the surrounding circumstances.

The land was solicited to support the Bennett family, and for those purposes the upper land to the east was much less desirable than the moist and arable lower land, the "bahia." The *diseño* itself suggests that the "alta" is not a sharp point but rather a line. The words "alta de Santa Clara" run along nearly the entire of the narrow side of the rectangle that describes the grant, rather than indicating a short and narrow line as Mary contended formed the alta. The *diseño* is reproduced in chapter 6.

The judge looked to the map made by Mary's witness James Stratton. Toward the eastern edge of the tract shown on the government-approved Lewis map, and superimposed on Stratton's map, Stratton, not Lewis, had written the words "South Westernly Base of Alta" and put that legend near the eastern boundary of the grant as shown by Lewis for the government. The judge reasoned that all these factors confirmed the conclusion that the "alta" was a "belt of high land of considerable width" on which the mission was located and that extended westward. "The highest part of the upland is perhaps that adjoining the mission buildings," he wrote, "but there seems to be no topographical reason for restricting the term alta to a small piece of land in that immediate vicinity." Therefore the "edge of that upland constitutes the true northeasterly boundary of the grant."

Mary Love had one final objection to the survey proceedings. She had not been given the opportunity to make an election of the precise location of the tract within the exterior boundaries she claimed. The imprecise nature of the Mexican land grant descriptions was the basis for this right of election given to many claimants. The court noted that the "orilla del Roblar," margin of the oaks that formed her western boundary extended much further than would be necessary to accommodate a tract of 1,000 varas wide. The eastern line was settled by its present order, and there never was a dispute as to the western boundary of the margin of the oaks. However, she would be allowed to slide her grant to the north or south, "but not so as to pass the external boundaries in those directions which she has acknowledged and asserted in her own petition to the Board."[34] Presumably those limits would be the north and south lines on the Stratton map.

At a further hearing on May 4, 1864, Mary waived her right to an election. Should the court still be of the opinion it had expressed before as to the location of the eastern boundary, Mary was content that the tract could conform to the official survey. On that basis, the court approved the Lewis survey.[35] That carefully hedged position preserved her ability to appeal to the U.S. Supreme Court on the issue of the "alta" and her eastern boundary.

The court waited, presumably until after Mary's time to appeal to the U.S. Supreme Court had passed. Then on December 7, 1864, Judge Ogden Hoffman signed his approval onto the official survey. It had been a long process, filled with much contention. Even with total finality by December 1864, it required years before the federal bureaucracy issued a patent, or government deed, to the grant. The patent was issued on July 19, 1871, eighteen years after Mary lodged her petition with the Board of Land Commissioners. Since historian W. W. Robinson found that seventeen years was the average length of time from filing with the board to ultimate patent,[36] the delay on Mary's process seems within the range of normal.

In the end Mary received a plot of land 2,000 by 1,000 varas, precisely the amount requested in the petition to Governor Pío Pico and precisely what the map, the *diseño*, accompanying that petition showed. This was in addition to the house lot that was never in controversy. She ultimately ejected the trespassers, save only Watkins who was entitled to stay because he had become a co-tenant. She was not treated badly at all. The only land she lost to squatters was that near her own preemption claim, north of the mission. She lost some of that acreage only because others were doing to her what she was doing herself. She was squatting on her preemptive plot but could not effectively use the entire extent of what she claimed. Others then squatted on the unused portions and gained title the same way she did.

The key to the controversy surrounding the Bennett claim is the amount of land the alcalde actually delivered to Mary in the judicial possession ceremony of early 1846. The actual grant, the deed from the Mexican governor, was lost by 1853 but must have been used in the alcalde's work showing Mary around the boundaries. Then too, the actual grant undoubtedly conformed to the *diseño* and the petition to the governor that called for a grant of 2,000 by 1,000 varas. That area of about 355 acres was far less than the approximately 1,600 acres Mary Bennett claimed she was given by the alcalde.

Surely an alert alcalde, whose duties regularly included giving judicial possession to land grantees, must have sensed this discrepancy between the

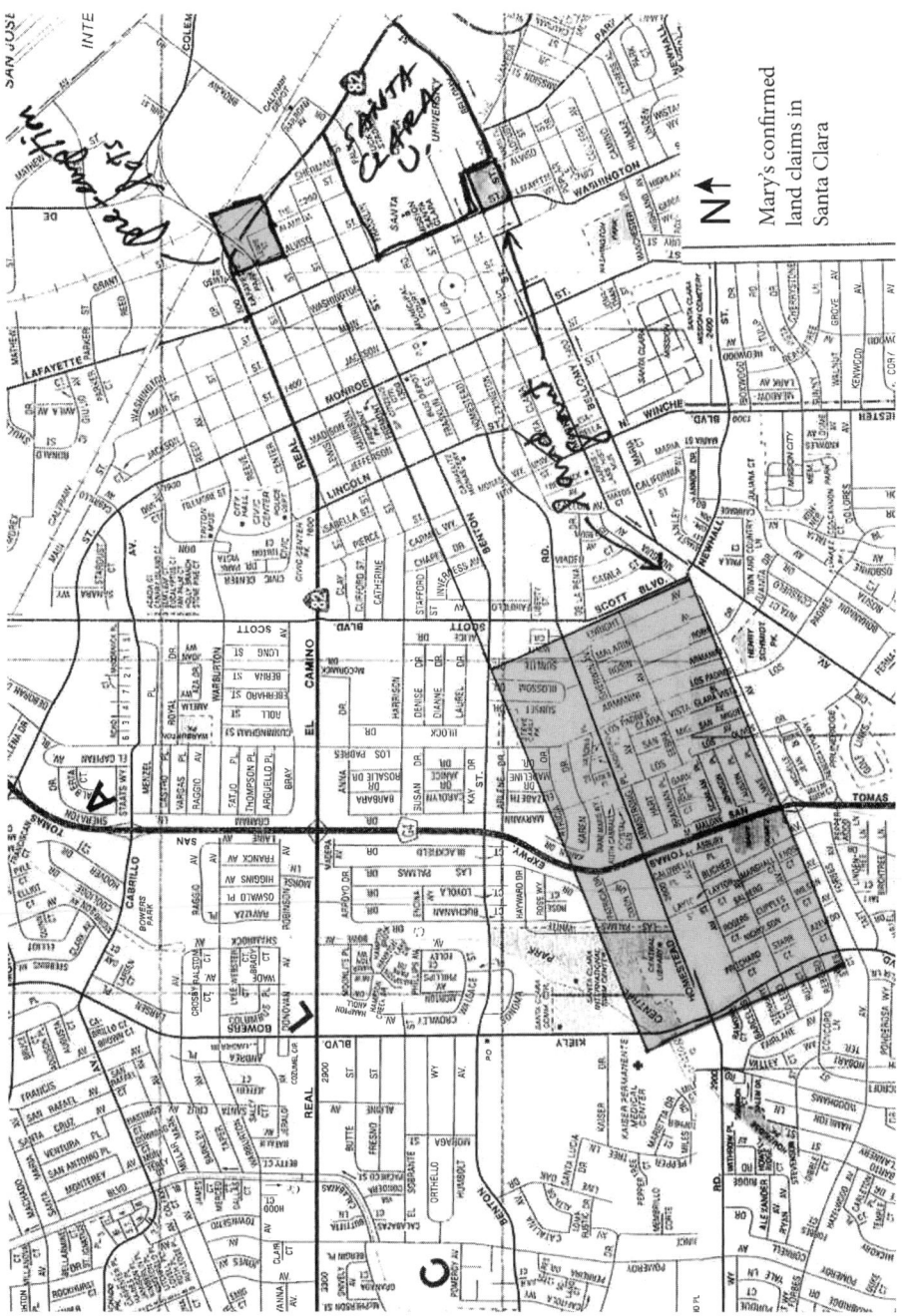

The approved Bennett land grant and preemption lots imposed on a map of modern Santa Clara. Courtesy of the Conrado Family Archives, with preemption lots added by author.

size specified in the grant and on the *diseño* and the much more extensive tract being pointed out to Mary that day they rode around the boundaries of her new grant. We either have a corrupt alcalde, colossal alcalde error, or corrupt witnesses. Every alternative, excepting significant error, points to an attempt at a colossal swindle, almost pulled off by Mary Bennett. The office of alcalde was appointed, paid no compensation, and the appointee had to accept his appointment. This would suggest that either corruption or the alcalde's casual indifference to the size of the tract was the culprit.

Yet this particular official, Dolores Pacheco, was an experienced alcalde and had served several terms previously. He did not testify himself. Could the testimony of others have been obtained improperly? Several Anglo witnesses testified that the Mexican witnesses were not of good character for truthfulness. However, Mexican witnesses were often maligned—not only in this case. Then too, we must remember Mary's acquisitive nature and her sometimes unscrupulous tactics. This would suggest that Mary Bennett attempted a nearly successful swindle by claiming more than the alcalde had given her or by inducing the alcalde to give her more than that to which she was entitled, or perhaps even more audaciously, by claiming a judicial possession that was never made at all. The fog that hovers over the Bennett claim may never be resolved.

Chapter 13

The Final Years

Mary Bennett Love was sixty-four years of age in December 1867 when her estranged husband, Harry Love, returned to Santa Clara. Mary had been obese for many years, but lately she had been eating even more, and she now weighed approximately 350 pounds.[1] Her daughter Catherine was worried that she might reach 400 pounds.[2] She had been ailing for the past few years from a heart condition[3] and was under the care of a physician.[4]

She still lived alone in the adobe house that she had built many years before on her preemptive claim to the north of the Santa Clara Mission, now fenced[5] and with a fine artesian well and an abundance of chickens, geese, and turkeys.[6] Then too, Mary had vegetables, including a corn field.[7] She now had a substantial income from the rentals of land on her grant, at least $1098 in 1868,[8] at a time when American average per capita income was approximately $200 per annum.

Santa Clara had become a bustling town, and the continuation of the old Alameda through Santa Clara, now renamed Grant Street, passed directly through her property. Stagecoaches and horseback riders going to and from San José and San Francisco would pass near her house, and there must have been considerable noise and even dust during the summer.

Her preemption claim was finally regularized. Pursuant to an act of Congress designed to quiet title to claimants of public lands within Santa Clara, the town deeded to Mary Love four city blocks,[9] about eleven acres, excepting the land required for streets. Her four blocks were bounded on the north by Clay Street, on the south by Harrison, and to the east and west, respectively, by Sherman and Alviso. The northern half of these blocks is in modern times consumed by the curve to the west by El Camino Real and the De La Cruz overpass. Dozens of other occupants of lands within the town were given deeds at the same time in a general cleansing of title to town lots.

Mary Bennett Love, 1865. Courtesy of the Conrado Family Archives.

This general store at the corner of Franklin and Main in Santa Clara was founded in 1849 and undoubtedly known to Mary. This image, in the public domain, has appeared in several sources, including Lorie García, George Giacomini, and Geoffrey Goodfellow, *A Place of Promise: The City of Santa Clara, 1852–2002* (Santa Clara, California: City of Santa Clara, 2002), p. 24 and Joan B. Barriga, "Mary Bennett: The Black Knight's Lady," *The Californians* 8 (Sept./Oct. 1990): 17, captioned as "Thompson & West's Historical Atlas Illustration of Santa Clara County, 1876."

The growth of Santa Clara and San José soon required that a railroad be built between San José and San Francisco. The route of the new San Francisco and San José Railroad cut off a very small amount of her town lands, the four blocks, at the very northeast corner. The railroad brought condemnation proceedings in 1864 for a width of twenty feet on either side of the center line of the track, containing an area of 18/100ths of an acre taken from Mary Love. In those years compensation for eminent domain was truly minimal. Of the dozens of landowners from whom property for this railroad's right-of-way was taken, a very few were awarded $75 or $125, but the majority received nothing.

With the consent of the parties, including Mary Love, the county court appointed commissioners to assess compensation, and after viewing the tracts and hearing the parties, they issued a report on July 26, 1864. Mary

Love was unfortunately within the majority of landowners for whom no compensation was allowed, the commissioners finding

> as a fact that there is no damage or compensation due to them or any of them and that said defendants [including Mary Love] have not suffered any damages and that they are entitled to no compensation for said premises or any part thereof.

The court approved the report on September 16, 1864, and it is notable that Mary Love filed no objection.[10] Perhaps she thought the amount of compensation that was even remotely possible was not worth the trouble. Perhaps, like many in the nineteenth century, she thought that the railroad was a blessing and might even increase the value of her land to the point where she had actually been benefited.

In April 1868 Mary began the construction of a new house. She hired a carpenter, Calvin Russell, to build a good-sized frame house, undoubtedly better and larger than the old adobe she had been living in. Russell ordered lumber in April and hired his crew, and construction was underway.[11] The new house was located right on Grant Street, while the adobe probably was somewhat off this main thoroughfare. Perhaps the plan was that she would live in the new house and eventually let Harry live in the old adobe.

As she grew older, Mary began making gifts to her children. In June 1866 she made a bargain sale of fifty acres in her land grant to Winston Bennett, her oldest child. The stated consideration was $500,[12] but raw land was then valued at about $100 per acre, so the price represented far less than the $5,000 approximate value of the land transferred. Then in 1867 she gave a plot of thirty acres adjacent to that she had given to Winston to her daughter Samantha, her youngest child. The deed specified that this was a pure gift.[13] The following year in August 1868 Mary had to regrant this parcel to put it into Samantha's married name of Hughes.[14] Mary may well have intended to make further gifts to her children, yet this is as far as she got.

Harry Love, now back in Santa Clara, must have been depressed by the sight of his estranged spouse's evident prosperity, especially as it contrasted with his own penury. According to his biographer, Harry was now morose and disheveled, borrowing money when he could and drinking, "a shabby old man in a battered hat driving his express wagon around town."[15] Mary meanwhile had hired a young German man, Christian "Fred" Eiversen, to help her. By this time she had grown so large and so heavy that she required help to get in and out of her buggy to take her frequent business trips into San José.[16] Stories circulated around town that Mary had hired Eiversen in large part to protect herself from Harry.[17]

A contemporary newspaper account describes the growing tension:

> Harry Love felt that he was only tolerated there, and he imagined that the great obstacle to the re-establishment of true marital relations in the family, was in the person of Christian Eiversen, a German laborer, employed by the wife to work upon the place. He told Eiversen to leave—he ordered him off the premises—he threatened his life if he did not go. Eiversen refused to go or to regard these threats. He said he was employed by the wife, who paid him, and he had nothing to do with Harry Love. While she desired his services on the place, he would remain. He tried to get Harry put under bonds to keep the peace, but we are told, failed in this for the magistrate held that the husband, although living on the wife's property, had a right to prevent persons obnoxious to him from coming there.[18]

By early June 1868, when the threat mentioned in the article was made, the new house was finished enough for Mary to live in it. Samantha was the only child still living with or close by Mary, and, although about to be married, apparently she was then living in the old adobe house. Presumably Harry was still in the barn. Her mother, Mary, told Samantha several times in the spring and early summer of 1868 that she was having trouble with Harry.[19] Events were building to a head. Calvin Russell remembered that on Saturday, June 27, he was working to finish up the new house when Harry Love came over "and kicked up a fuss and tackled Fred and then came upstairs and tackled me and I don't know what for."[20]

On the morning of June 29, 1868, Mary went on a morning business trip to San José. Fred Eiversen drove her in her buggy. Before leaving, Mary asked Samantha to go to the new house and watch it while she was gone. Apparently Harry Love saw them leave together. Something snapped and reason vanished. About eleven o'clock he came in his wagon to Mary's new house, armed with a double-barreled shotgun, a pistol, and a sheath knife. He locked the gate to the fence surrounding the house, then took up a position on the inside of the gate, and told Calvin Russell that "if that man Fred [Eiversen] came in there, he would have to walk over his dead body." Russell tried to defuse the obvious tension by inviting Harry to come into the house to help him, but Harry just "ripped out a great oath" and said he was going to stay at the gate. A man by the name of Owens came by and talked with Harry first and then Samantha. He told Samantha that Harry was an "old fool" who said he had come to take possession of the place. Calvin Russell urged Samantha to give her mother warning that Love was lying in wait for them.

About forty-five minutes later Mary Love and Fred Eiversen came along in her buggy. When they were about fifty yards from the gate, Samantha ran up to the buggy and caught the horse by the bit. At that point, Samantha testified, she

> told Iverson [i.e., Eiversen] to take mother straight to my house and told
> her Love was at the gate and I was afraid there would be trouble. I com-
> menced to tell him how to open the door of my house and was getting
> the key for him when mother said "there he comes, there he comes," and
> commenced screaming.

Mary showed a bit of her old form. Samantha heard Love say something but could not understand it because Mary's screaming was so loud that it frightened the horse. Then "Love dropped down on his knee and leveled his gun at them," Russell testified, "and Fred whirled on his heel and there was two shots fired so near each other that I can not tell which fired first." I. L. Duff, a painter working on the house, also saw the beginnings to the altercation. He also could not tell who fired first and added that while Love was somewhat excited, he did not appear to be intoxicated. Samantha was positive that Love fired first.

Love and Eiversen then exchanged three or four shots apiece, with both pistol and shotgun. Love retreated to the front door of the house; Fred climbed over the fence and followed. But then Love attacked. Fred knocked him down and repeatedly hit Love's head with the butt of his pistol and said he would kill him. At that point Russell and Duff stopped the fight.

Eiversen was bleeding, apparently from superficial shotgun wounds, while Love had suffered a serious gunshot wound on his arm below the shoulder. Russell and Duff carried Love to the back of the house and sum- moned doctors. While they were carrying him, Love said "he was a mur- dered man: that the wimen [women] were murderers and had hired this German to murder him."

Mary Bennett Love's new house in Santa Clara where Harry Love was killed. Courtesy of Lorie García and the San José *Mercury-News*.

Three doctors arrived to assist Harry. They found contusions on his head, although the skull was not fractured. The most serious wound was a hole to his right arm about two or three inches below the shoulder joint, with a compound fracture of the associated bones. The doctors agreed on the need to amputate Harry's arm at the shoulder joint. One doctor gave chloroform that apparently did not produce the appropriate effect. While the doctors were finishing the sutures on the arm, Love became very excited, rose up, fell back and expired, dead at age fifty-eight. The doctors found the cause of death to have been the gunshot wound, in part the loss of blood, and shock to the nervous system by the wound and the beating on the head. They disagreed on the effect of the chloroform.

The coroner's jury came to the conclusion that Harry Love "came to his Death by a Pistol Shot in the hand of Christian Iverson a german the same being in self Defense" [sic]. Eiversen was exonerated and released from jail, where he had been confined for a few hours pending the investigation. Harry was buried in the Santa Clara City Cemetery. The original headstone was unmarked, and as a matter of considerable irony, many thought the cemetery's register read "Mary Love" instead of "Harry Love." Eventually the error was rectified, and a proper headstone erected in 2003 to honor the final resting place of Harry Love.[21]

Long and thoughtful obituaries appeared in the Santa Cruz *Sentinel* on July 4, 1868, and the San José *Patriot* on July 2, 1868, which were then picked up by other papers throughout California. The *Sentinel*, especially, described Harry Love's character. It noted Love's long, matted hair, his generosity, intelligence, and considerable bravado, and that while he might have been negligent in person and dress, Harry Love was nevertheless the "ideal of a frontiersman. . . . In common with the many friends of the deceased, in the county and throughout California, we sincerely regret his untimely taking off."[22]

Harry left no will, and therefore his sole heir was Mary. A probate was opened in September 1868.[23] The inventory shows how impecunious Love truly was. His sole possessions consisted of two horses, one wagon, a shotgun and pistol, an express wagon, clothing, and $1.50. After sale and deducting the expenses of administration, only $44.50 remained to be divided among the doctors' claims.

The claims in his estate reveal that he had been caging money from at least two people, and one of them, a William Trenouth, had a judgment against Love for $1,025 and had loaned him an additional $500 or so. He filed claims on the theory that Harry had an additional asset—his community property share of the land deeded to Mary from the town of Santa Clara when her preemption claim was regularized. The administrator successfully argued that the four blocks in the town of Santa Clara were Mary's separate property because they had been acquired before marriage. Additionally she and Harry had been separated for five years before his death and were separated at the time the town lots were finally deeded to her.

Mary meanwhile continued to live in her new house on Grant Street, Santa Clara. She continued to feel poorly and saw her doctor, H. H. Warburton, M.D., on July 27, 1868, and December 3, 1868, for consultation and prescriptions.[24] Shortly after she saw Dr. Warburton for the second time, she went to her daughter Catherine's home for an extended visit. Catherine Bennett McCusker lived with her family on Elkhorn Slough near Moss Landing. Located just south of Watsonville in Monterey County, Elkhorn Slough would be very much quieter than the hustle and bustle of Santa Clara. Perhaps Mary's doctor suggested the change of pace.

According to her granddaughter, Josephine McCusker, Mary "seemed to be in no pain and was happier with my mother [i.e., Catherine] than she had been for many years."[25] Mary sat with her crocheting for hours, perhaps enjoying the peacefulness. Catherine continued to worry about Mary's over-eating, chiding Mary that she would soon weigh 400 pounds.

Then one day, December 19, 1868, Mary asked Catherine:

> "Get me that crocheting I was working on; I want to finish it." When it was finished she handed it to my mother, saying, "There, now, you see, I never did get to weigh four hundred pounds," lay back and died.[26]

Mary Bennett Love died at age sixty-five of her poor heart condition, after ailing from that disease for several years. She was buried at the Pioneer Cemetery in the village of Freedom, near Watsonville.[27] As with Harry, she received obituaries from newspapers throughout Northern California. They did not analyze her character or her difficulties with Harry Love. The obituary in the Santa Cruz *Sentinel*, the most complete, did mention that "she was sitting down when the fatal attack came . . . and died instantly, without a struggle." For a nineteenth-century reader, that meant that Mary had died a "good death," quietly and with family. Readers would be highly sensitive to the difference in style between her death and that of her estranged husband, Harry Love. The *Sentinel* also commented that "she leaves considerable property. No will is known to exist."[28]

Mary's probate opened on January 9, 1869,[29] with her son Winston Bennett as administrator. The petition listed as heirs the two sons, Winston and Mansel, and four daughters, Samantha A. Hughes (during the probate her husband died; she remarried and became Samantha A. Hicks), Mary A. Shelby, Julia A. Adams, and T. C. (Catherine) McCusker. Winston prepared a very detailed inventory of his mother's assets, as was typical of the nineteenth century. Personal property consisted primarily of household items and furniture, clothing, and assorted animals and implements. Only a few things are of interest in the personalty. She kept a bottle of brandy, a small fact in support of the previous supposition that her departure from Vardamon back in 1845 was not based upon an objection to all liquor. She owned a revolver and a double-gauge shotgun, which may have been Harry's, and for a town dweller kept the astonishing number of 120 chickens. Her real estate was intact. It consisted of the four blocks along Grant Street in town, the result of her preemption, and 263 acres of her original land grant. The *solar,* or house lot of three acres, had been previously sold in 1856. From the 355 acres given her by the approved and final survey, if we deduct the fifty acres sold to Winston, the thirty acres given to Samantha, and the twelve acres claimed by B. F. Watkins as a co-tenant in previous litigation, that equals the 263 inventoried in her estate. The probate account shows very clearly that, while Mary lost much of what she claimed to be hers by reason of the final survey, she lost nothing at all of her land grant to squatters. The total value of her estate was inventoried at $30,700, of which real estate was $30,000.

There were substantial taxes with respect to the estate, rents to be collected, and claims to be paid. Disputes remained to be settled. B. F. Watkins, as discussed previously, squatted on the land grant but then acquired a half interest in the first contingency contract with the attorneys who handled the land confirmation for Mary. She had sued to eject him in 1865, but Watkins claimed he was in effect a co-tenant by virtue of his purchase, since the land had been confirmed and he had purchased a half interest in the first attorney fee agreement, the one that was conditional on confirmation. Watkins cross-complained to make Mary honor her agreement by deeding his twelve and a half acres to him. The trial court ruled for Mary, but Watkins appealed. It is not clear why, but the appellate phase of this case extended for a long time and into the period of the Estate of Mary Love. The judgment for Mary Love was reversed in January 1871, and Watkins was held entitled to a deed for his twelve and a half acres.[30] Winston apparently refused to make the conveyance, so a commissioner appointed by the court deeded the twelve and a half acres to B. F. Watkins on June 3, 1871,[31] resolving that dispute.

On July 9, 1871, the federal government finally issued its patent to Mary Bennett Love's land claims.[32] Two claims against Mary Love's estate were affected by this. The second attorney fee agreement was based on the contingency that the patent be issued. Edward L. Goold, the third attorney who had joined Howard and Perley for the survey portion of the confirmation process, apparently had left the firm and now demanded his share of the fee. Winston Bennett raised the defense that this second-phase contingency contemplated fifty blocks of land within the developed areas of the town of Santa Clara, the survey did not confirm these to Mary Love, and therefore no fee was due. It was probably for this reason that Howard and Perley individually refused to join Goold in this lawsuit against the estate. This claim was still alive when the estate was settled but was dismissed by the plaintiff in 1877.[33]

Another claim affected by the patent was that of Hiram Shartzer. The reader will recall that he had purchased a promissory note that was due after the patent was issued. He sought to reopen Harry Love's estate to cover that base and established that his claim had mounted to $6,065. Then in March 1872 he filed a claim directly with the Estate of Mary Love. Winston rejected the claim on several technical grounds, including the standard marital disabilities always claimed by Mary. However, the principal reason was that the claim had not been filed against the estate within the statutory time after notice was made to creditors.

Mary's children proved to be almost as cantankerous as their mother. When Winston originally filed his petition in January 1869 to be appointed as administrator, all his siblings agreed to that in writing—except his sister Catherine. In December 1871 his sisters Samantha and Catherine and their husbands obtained a court order requiring Winston to show cause why he should not be discharged as the administrator. The estate had gone on too long, they felt. Winston staved them off, pointing out that there were still claims to be collected.[34]

Winston filed his final account on October 11, 1872, and a hearing was held a month later. Samantha and Catherine objected on the basis that Winston had used their mother's house as his own residence for thirteen months and should be charged in his accounts for rental at eight dollars per month. The court upheld their point. A more significant objection was that of the ever-diligent Hiram Shartzer, urging that he was still owed on the note Harry and Mary had executed (originally to William Lent) back in 1859.

Shartzer apparently obtained a judgment from the county trial court (not the probate court) on November 16, 1872, that the amount of $6,319 was then due on his note but that the Watkins claim was prior to his. That meant the twelve-and-a-half-acre portion could not be foreclosed upon. In 1874 a satisfaction of judgment was entered,[35] and on May 2, 1874, a final decree of distribution was entered. Shartzer either received full payment or compromised his claim.

Meanwhile Julia sold her one-sixth interest in the estate to Winston, and

Mansel and Mary sold their interests to a man named Isaac Smith. The final distribution was one-third to Winston, one-third to Isaac Smith, one-sixth to Samantha, and one-sixth to Catherine. Then in September 1874 Winston conveyed to Isaac Smith his one-third inherited interest together with the fifty acres he had previously received in the bargain sale from his mother. Winston received the sum of $10,000 for these lands, and Isaac Smith took them subject to the claims of Hiram Shartzer, Perley, Goold, and others.[36] In all likelihood Isaac Smith settled with Hiram Shartzer. In any event, by the end of 1874 almost all of the original Mary Bennett Love land grant had passed out of Bennett family hands.

Chapter 14

Epilogue and Conclusion

In 1888 Jesse Graham was tried for the murder of Dennis Bennett, thirty-eight years after the fact. The trial produced more sensational revelations and accusations directed at Mary and Catherine.

Following the 1850 shooting Jesse fled the Santa Cruz area, then went to Mariposa, California, where he joined a company engaged in fighting Indians. He apparently returned to Santa Cruz later that year and made some desultory efforts to seek out the lower-court judge to commence legal proceedings and clear his name. According to Jesse's account, the Santa Cruz officials he contacted were uninterested. He returned to Mariposa until 1859 and then left for Texas. At the outbreak of war, he enlisted in the Confederate forces and ultimately rose to the rank of general. He returned to California, lived for three months in Santa Cruz County, then moved to Southern California. It was clearly established at trial that from about 1872 he was a rancher in Fresno County.[1] He lived there under his own name and acquired an excellent reputation. Numerous character witnesses testified to his good character while he lived in Fresno County, including a constable and the sheriff of Fresno County.

A coroner's inquest was held in 1850, and a grand jury had indicted Jesse for murder in 1851. However, no real effort was made to track Jesse down until 1888. It is unclear why things were stirred up at long last, but of course, there is no statute of limitations on murder.

The essence of the prosecution evidence came through two witnesses, Samantha Bennett Hicks, sister to Dennis, and Lansing Haight, who in 1850 was a contractor building a dam at the Bennett sawmill. Jesse Graham came to the house where the girls lived, asked for Dennis, and was directed to the second house. Jesse called out for Dennis to come outside. Dennis did come outside, said "Jesse, you've got a new horse," and the two spoke a short while in a friendly manner. Dennis went up to the horse, as far as the witnesses could tell, to examine him. Graham raised the shotgun that he usually carried across his waist and shot Dennis with a single fatal shot.

The prosecution also offered evidence of threats made by Jesse in Santa Cruz after the April 1850 hearing on the peace bond that he would kill all the Bennetts and that only through their elimination would peace actually come, as well as evidence of his shooting of Mary Bennett and at David Jackson Bennett earlier in the day along the trail. The defense objected to evidence of the earlier shooting, but it was admitted on the theory that it showed Jesse's intent when he approached Dennis.

The defense was self-defense. As to the first shooting, Jesse related how, following the hearing before the town judge on the peace bond, he caught up with Mary and Jackson along the trail that led to their homes. The three of them traveled together for a while, but at one point, according to Jesse, Mary stopped, then "Jack [David Jackson] wheeled his mule, and she spoke to Jack in a language I didn't understand." Jackson then fired his gun at Jesse, the ball hitting his elbow. Jesse returned the fire, and looked over toward Mary. She had a "six-shooter in her hand pointed at me; I leveled my gun at her, and it went off, but I never did think I fired it on purpose."

Jesse testified that he then went to his father's house, had something to eat, and after some thought he decided to visit the Bennett house to explain to Dennis what had happened on the trail and try to quiet things down. Nevertheless, he admitted that once there he yet again asked Dennis where his father's gold was, a question not well-calculated to defuse tensions. When Dennis approached his horse outside his cabin,

> He [Dennis] grabbed the gun with the left hand with a steady grip and a savage look: I pulled the gun away, and he grabbed hold with the other hand; I was pushing the gun with one hand to get it away from his breast, and while I was trying to get it away I cocked it, fired, and he fell. . . . [when I fired] I knew that my life was in danger as much as ever a man's was.[2]

These specifics were shown to the jury against the backdrop of a major overriding theme offered by the defense. The defense alleged the existence of a Bennett family conspiracy to murder the Grahams so that Isaac's property would pass to Catherine and her children, that is, to the Bennett clan. According to Jesse's lawyer, it was none other than Mary Bennett who was "the prime mover in the conspiracy." Mary herself and not Catherine was the one who broke open Isaac's trunk, "took out $30,000 and divided it among her family, and forced her daughter to go to the Sandwich Islands [Hawaii] with the two children."[3] This was an entirely different version of the events of April 1850, but what was the evidence for it?

Jesse testified that many people had warned him that Dennis planned to murder him. After they returned from San José to discover Catherine and the gold missing and the children gone, Jesse took his double-barreled shotgun outside to shoot it off and then reload.

> I snapped it twice without result, but the third time it twisted at the breech: there was rock and sand in the gun, tamped down to the powder, about eight or ten inches from the muzzle, and I was badly burned, and it came near killing me.[4]

A young Indian girl who worked in Isaac's house spoke with Jesse when he and his father returned from San José. She told him that one morning while they were away Jackson and Dennis had come over to Isaac's house, and Mary Bennett arrived in the afternoon. The Indian girl told Jesse that she had noticed Dennis Bennett with that gun and saw him putting bullets in it, although the inference was that it was really the sand and rocks.

The star witness to establish the conspiracy was Jane Matilda Graham Rice, daughter of Isaac Graham and Catherine Bennett and granddaughter of Mary Bennett. She recalled a conversation in 1862 between her father Isaac and Mary Ann Bennett Shelby. Mary Ann had been there in Isaac's cabin visiting with Catherine while he was in San José with Jesse. Jane Matilda heard Mary Ann tell Isaac that she, Mary Ann, saw Dennis Bennett, her brother, "have hold of Jesse's gun [i.e., to tamper with it], and would have so stated, but her mother prevented her from saying so."

Jane Matilda had more. While Isaac and Jesse were gone to San José, but before Catherine had left with the two girls, including Matilda Jane as her name was then, she remembered "my grandmother, Mrs. Bennett, coming to the house and having a quarrel with my mother, whose heart seemed to fail her, and Mrs. Bennett slapped my mother in the face, and said 'God Damn you, go!' "[5] Jane Matilda Bennett Rice would have been four years old at the time of this conversation, which was remembered thirty-eight years later.

Mrs. Rice had almost unlimited capacity to remember conversations from when she was four years old, because there was still more. She recalled that Mary Bennett had advised her mother, Catherine, to do something that would damage Isaac and Jesse. Mary told Catherine, "If I was you, I would put a spider in their dumpling." Mary spoke to Catherine in a threatening manner. Shortly thereafter Catherine prepared dumplings, of which Isaac apparently was quite fond. Little Jane warned her father that he was about to be poisoned. She even remembered her exact words from thirty-eight years before, spoken as a four-year-old: "Papa, don't eat that dinner, because grandma told mamma to put a spider in the dumpling." There was an uproar at the table, and Catherine with tears admitted at least to her mother's request, saying "Mother did want me to do it."[6]

Jesse's cousin, J. H. Graham, a judge of some unspecified kind, testified that in 1854 he had a conversation with Jackson Bennett and that Jackson had told him that he "and Dennis had loaded a gun for the purpose of killing Jesse Graham. They knew that after Jesse had found out about the robbery he would take the gun. Jackson got the sand and Dennis loaded the gun."[7]

It was in the context of this conspiracy and Mary's role in spearheading it that the defense brought in the six male character witnesses, mentioned in the introduction, who testified that her reputation for peace and quietness was bad. In addition a woman, Mrs. Otis Ashley, testified that she too thought Mary Bennett's reputation for peace and quietness was bad. She first met Mary Bennett in 1846, and Mary was the first white woman that she met in California. She had some interesting comments about Mary's personality:

> When you contradicted her she was apt to fly off; she was always loaded. When she was Mrs. Bennett she was one of the most plausible, loving beings you ever saw in your life, but if you'd cross her she was an entirely different person.[8]

The linchpin evidence to establish the Bennett family conspiracy was a letter purportedly written by Catherine to Isaac Graham, dated November 6, 1854, that Jane Matilda claimed she found among Isaac's belongings after his death by natural causes in 1863. She kept it because she feared future legal problems for her brother Jesse. She was familiar with her mother's handwriting and the handwriting of the letter was that of her mother. The letter read:

Mr. Graham:—I am not going to justify you in the least, for you know when you consult your own conscience that I had good cause to leave you, but I should not have left you if it had not been for my mother. She laid the plan and got the man to go with me, and when the day came for me to go my heart rather failed me. She came and tried to unlock the trunk with other keys, and when she could not she . . . took the ax and broke it and took the money off [sic] and assisted me off that night, which was the last day of March, 1850. I have seen the day I would have died before I would have told upon her, but she treated me so mean, and is making her brags that she will get my children yet, and they will make both servants, and is reporting it around that I had laid a plan to have you shot, which I never thought of. I want you and the world to know what she done, but still, when I think of having her put into State Prison, feelings of pride and tenderness toward my mother rises in my heart, and it appears to be a worse punishment than I wish to put upon her. . . . There was $3,500 missing [of the purloined gold] when I got to the Islands and counted it. I knew that mother had got it . . . and when I came back she acknowledged that she took it and that she would pay me, and now she refuses to give me a dollar. . . . I can tell you if she had her way, you would not be here to-day, for she tried to get me to poison you, and when I would not she call me a fool and say if she was in my place she would put spider in your dumpling.[9]

Catherine denied under oath that her mother had ever mentioned poisoning Isaac. Significantly, she did acknowledge that Isaac had told her of Matilda's warning of poison.[10] She insisted her mother had never mentioned poisoning Isaac, and "such a thing never entered my head." Catherine testified that the decision to leave Isaac was hers alone but admitted that her mother had aided her departure. Catherine denied that her brothers touched Jesse's gun or that there was any sort of conspiracy to kill either Jesse or Isaac. After reading what purported to be her letter to Isaac, she pronounced it "false; false as the hair on Jacob's head. . . . I did not do that writing; I never saw that writing." She testified that she was positive she did not write the letter. "I could not sit down and write such a lie as is in that paper."[11]

Two of Catherine's sisters, Samantha Bennett Hicks and Julia Bennett Adams, then testified that to the best of their knowledge and belief the letter was not in Catherine's handwriting, although they also stated, at least as reported in the newspaper, that they were not very familiar with her handwriting.

Someone is lying here, either Jane Matilda Graham Rice or Catherine Bennett McCusker. Mrs. Rice's story seems a bit pat, her recollections too neatly dovetailing with the letter. It is difficult to believe there was ever any correspondence between Catherine and Jane, and therefore Jane's testimony that she was familiar with Catherine's handwriting is suspicious. It is also difficult to believe that she carried for thirty-eight years such a good recollection of events and conversations that she had and heard while she was four years old. However, as to some of those events, Catherine herself corroborated her recollection of a warning by testifying that Isaac told her directly that Jane had warned him of a poisoning.

After closing arguments and the court's instructions the jury began deliberations in the early evening of June 26. They came back and requested the letter and a copy of the judge's instructions, then went back to work. The Santa Cruz *Daily Sentinel* reported the next morning that "it was rumored that the jury stood nine for acquittal and three for conviction."[12] Indeed, it soon appeared that the jury could not reach a verdict. The judge declared a mistrial and began the procedures for a retrial. The *Daily Sentinel* editorialized on June 29 that too much time had passed and urged "that justice might be tempered with mercy."

> The skeleton of the dead past has been resurrected to serve no good purpose. The story of the vendetta has probably been kept alive by those only who delight to revel in the crimes and misfortunes of others. . . . The law need not stretch out its iron hand for a victim in this case. It can afford to be merciful towards the defendant and allow him to live the few short years allotted to him in peace.[13]

The editorial also referred to a petition in circulation, calling for Jesse's discharge from further prosecution. In the same issue a letter to the editor appeared, signed "Taxpayer." The point presented was that the trial just concluded was very full and fair to both sides, with all evidence presented and capably argued. Any "further prosecution of this case would be a reckless and useless expenditure of the people's money. . . . No fair-minded man, who heard the evidence, can believe for a moment that it is possible to ever secure a conviction, and it does seem to me that to further pursue the case would partake strongly of persecution."[14]

Within a short time the case was dismissed. The historian Doyce B. Nunis, Jr. has suggested that one of the thoughts behind, or at least a fig-leaf rationale behind, the dismissal was that the killing was committed during a twenty-day jurisdictional void between the time that California had become a state and the meeting of the first legislature. When California became a state, all prior Mexican law lapsed, it was argued, but because California had never been a territory, it had no law until the first legislature met.[15] That may well have provided some cover for the decision, but the evident reason was a community feeling that even though murder may have no statute of limitations, in this case and under these facts, too much time had run.

Conclusion

Mable Dorn Early became the Bennett family's keeper of family lore. She herself was the granddaughter of Catherine Bennett McCusker and therefore the great-granddaughter of Mary Bennett Love. She gave an interview to a writer named Frank F. Latta who was writing a book about Joaquín Murrieta and Harry Love and therefore needed to inquire a bit about Harry's wife Mary. Early told Latta: "Do not get the idea that Mary was an overbearing, quarrelsome woman. Grandmother (i.e., Catherine) always said that she (Mary) was fond of joking, very friendly and that everyone liked her."[16]

Mary surely was fond of jokes, especially practical jokes, and may have been quite friendly in a boisterous sort of way. She certainly was generous, depending on who you were. But it really is not true that everyone liked her. A total of six male witnesses and one female witness regarded her negatively in terms of peace and quietness. Simply put, although not expressly stated, they thought that Mary went too far, and especially too far for a woman. Beyond general boisterousness, the character witnesses felt she was often feisty with people. As we have seen, Mrs. Ashley thought Mary prone to fly off the handle. Another character witness added to his reputation testimony the observation that Mary "was generally in trouble with somebody."[17]

However, for all her feistiness, one has to admire Mary Bennett Love for living her life on her own stubborn terms. She wanted to acquire land from which she could derive a good income, and she was very successful in that. In the last few years of her life, she had a truly abundant income. She may have cut some corners with her attempts to aggrandize the contours of her land grant, but from Mary's viewpoint she was there first, and she was entitled.

We should use Mary's life to ask ourselves some broader questions. What does her life tell us about the American working class more generally in early California, in the years of transition from Mexico to the United States? About the working class's legal sophistication? And finally, what do Mary's experiences tell us about the position of American women in early California?

By looking at the men associated with Mary Bennett Love, either as family, tenants, workers, or poachers on her land and timber, it seems fair to say that most made their livelihood either by activities close to the soil or through small-scale retail operations, such as Vardamon Bennett's combination stable, bar, and bowling alley. At least in these early years, about 1843–1850, they tended not to be employees of other men.

Mary probably did not have any more knowledge of the law than the average nineteenth-century pioneer. She was illiterate, and there is no evidence that any of her ancestors or siblings had any legal training. In Mary's case the legal knowledge seems to come out of nowhere, but actually it came out of a common culture of nineteenth-century Americans that included a fair amount of legal knowledge, more than is true today. John Phillip Reid pointed out this extensive legal knowledge held as a common American cultural norm in his 1980 study of the use of the law on a very quotidian basis by the overland pioneers.[18] Mary was a part of that culture, quite literally, since she was an overlander herself.

What really made Mary different was not the knowledge of law but her ability to very actively and creatively use the law to advance her interests far beyond daily events. In her hands the law was not an idle interest but an active tool. Without any lawyer to guide her, she was aware enough of American preemption law to jump on an opportunity to acquire land for the taking by moving onto it quickly. She frequently used litigation to advance her interests. In the pre-American days that would have required her personal presence before the Mexican judges. Mary employed the legal disabilities of women as an active sword to defeat creditors' claims. She was able to shift legal positions flexibly when that served her ultimate purposes, as she did in the dismissal of her own divorce action. In short, Mary Bennett Love was a sophisticated consumer of the law.

The most admirable of Mary's traits was her uncanny ability to operate in what was still very much a male-dominated world, although she sometimes employed questionable tactics. From forging her son's name to a naturalization petition and the solicitation for the land grant, negotiating leases for her sawmill with sawyers and for various portions of her land grant with farmers, battling hard to expand her land grant beyond its original boundaries, to skillfully manipulating women's marital disabilities to make them an affirmative advantage for herself in litigation, she successfully made her way—sometimes bullied her way—through a male preserve of real estate and business.

What do Mary's experiences tell us more generally about the position of women in early California? Obviously, most American women in late Mexican and early American California did not have their own land grants, did not own their own sawmills. Nor did they speculate widely in real estate, rent out land, or engage in litigation to protect their interests. But if Mary Bennett Love did, other women could have. What stood between Mary and most other American women of her day was Mary's contrary nature. That does not mean merely that she was abrasive and contrary in that sense. She was contrary in another sense. Mary was willing to live contrary to the generally accepted norms of much greater domesticity for women and their lesser engagement, if any at all, within the world of business and enterprise. And because of this specific contrariness, Mary Bennett Love did what other women could have done but did not.

In sum, Mary Bennett Love was a multifaceted, complex person. She had some real faults, yet overbalancing these were the tremendous accomplishments that she achieved while operating in a world where male players and cultural norms were stacked against her.

Notes

Foreword

1. Reid, *Law for the Elephant*, 11.
2. Carolyn Stull, "Rindge, Rhoda May Knight (1864–1941)," in Gordon Morris Bakken and Brenda Farrington, eds., *Encyclopedia of Women in the American West* (Thousand Oaks: Sage Reference, 2003), 254.
3. Neal Lynch, "Ehmann, Freda (1839–1932)," in ibid., 120–21.
4. Craig Hendricks, "Callender, Marie (1907–1995)," in ibid., 43.
5. Michelle L. Oropeza, "Pleasant, Mary Ellen (1814–1904)," in ibid., 232–34. Also see Lynn M. Hudson, *The Making of "Mammy Pleasant": A Black Entrepreneur in Nineteen-Century San Francisco* (Urbana: University of Illinois University Press, 2003).
6. See Donna M. Lucy, *Photographing Montana 1884–1928: The Life and Work of Evelyn Cameron* (Missoula, MT: Mountain Press Publishing Company, 2000). Kristi Hager, *Evelyn Cameron: Montana's Frontier Photographer* (Helena, MT: Farcountry Press, 2007). Compare on woman photographers in the American West, Lori Ann Lahlum, "Mina Westbye: Norwegian Immigrant, North Dakota Homesteader, Studio Photographer, and 'New Woman,'" *Montana: The Magazine of Western History*, 60, no. 4 (Winter 2010): 3–15.
7. Jeannette M. Oppedisano, *Historical Encyclopedia of American Women Entrepreneurs, 1776 to the Present* (Westport, CT: Greenwood Press, 2000), 5–8.
8. Ibid., 22–24.
9. Ibid., 36–38.
10. Ibid., 68–70.
11. Ibid., 107–110.
12. Ibid., 128–30.
13. Ibid., 260–63.
14. Edith Sparks, *Capital Intentions: Female Proprietors in San Francisco, 1850–1920* (Chapel Hill: University of North Carolina Press, 2006), 112.
15. Ibid., 133.
16. Ibid., 166.

17. Ibid., 175.

18. Ibid., 206. Other biographies of women entrepreneurs continue to enrich the
    literature. Bob Luke's biography of Effa Manley is noteworthy because she too
    focused on a quality product, personnel improvement, and public relations.
    See Bob Luke, *The Most Famous Woman in Baseball: Effa Manley and the Negro
    Leagues* (Washington, D.C.: Potomac Books, 2011), 32, 42, 47, 62, 74, 95–114.

Chapter 1

1. Hague and Langum, *Thomas O. Larkin.*
2. Nunis, *Trials of Isaac Graham.*
3. Welter, "Cult of True Womanhood."
4. Scott, "Woman Worker."
5. Jeffrey, *Frontier Women*, 11.
6. Riley, *Place to Grow*, 231–43.
7. Jameson, "Women as Workers."
8. Interview with Winston Bennett, *Santa Cruz Daily Sentinel*, May 1, 1888, p. 3.
9. Testimony of T. W. Wright and H. B. Doane, *People v. Graham*, in *Santa Cruz
   Daily Sentinel*, June 19, 1888, p 3; testimony of Andrew Trust and John Daubenbiss, *Santa Cruz Daily Sentinel*, June 21, 1888, p. 3; testimony of Otis Ashley and
   Elihu Anthony, in Santa Cruz *Weekly Sentinel*, June 23, 1888, p. 3.
10. Barriga, "Mary Bennett"; Secrest, *Man from Rio Grande.*
11. García, Giacomini, and Goodfellow, "Mary Bennett."
12. Nunis, *Trials of Isaac Graham.*
13. Early, "Biographical Narrative of Bennett Family."
14. Reid, *Law for the Elephant.*
15. Langum, *Law and Community.*
16. McDermott, *Jury in Lincoln's America*, 6.

Chapter 2

1. In this chapter, unless indicated otherwise, "Bennett family lore," and similar
   expressions, refer to the first of two articles written by Mabel Dorn Early, the
   granddaughter of Catherine Bennett and the great-granddaughter of Mary
   Bennett, "Biographical Narrative of Bennett Family," *Pony Express* 17 (September 1950): 8.
2. United States Census for 1850, California, Santa Cruz County, page 263, sheet A,
   line 7, hereinafter cited as United States Census, 1850.
3. Letter, Mary Bennett to Thomas Oliver Larkin, June 6, 1845, in Larkin, *Larkin
   Papers*, 3: 223. 1852 California State Census, Santa Clara County, August 10,
   1852, in Daughters of the American Revolution transcription, microfilm ed.,
   reel 5, page 65.

4. 1852 California State Census, Santa Clara County, August 10, 1852, in Daughters of the American Revolution transcription, microfilm ed., reel 5, page 65.
5. A two-part series of memoirs, obviously prepared with the assistance of Winston Bennett, appeared as "Biographical Sketches." The reference to date and place of birth is in the piece of May 26, 1877, at p. 1.
6. For Dennis, 1825 is shown on the San Francisco *padrón*, Mexican census, of 1844. That same *padrón* indicated 1827 for David Jackson, but Winston Bennett testified in a later lawsuit that David Jackson was born on April 5, 1828, *Buzzell v. Bennett*, 2 California Reports 101, 102 (1852).
7. United States Census, 1850.
8. Winston Bennett, "Biographical Sketches," 1.
9. United States Census, 1850.
10. Early, "Biographical Narrative of Bennett Family," 8 (this is the second installment of the two-part narrative); "BENNETT, The Widow," *Riptide*, October 26, 1950.
11. Lindsay, "Lansford Hastings."
12. Hastings, *Emigrants' Guide*, 5.
13. Bennett, "Biographical Sketches," 1.
14. Unruh, *Plains Across*, 108, 118–20.

Chapter 3

1. The discussion in this chapter is drawn from these six diaries and recollections and two monographs. They will not be cited separately unless the Bennett family is directly mentioned or a quotation is made. The two monographs are: Unruh, *Plains Across* and Mattes, *Great Platte River Road*. The primary sources, diaries, and recollections are Winston Bennett, "Biographical Sketches"; Crawford, *Journal*; Hastings, *Emigrants' Guide*, 5–22; Lovejoy, "Lovejoy's Pioneer Narrative"; Matthieu, "Reminiscences; and White, *Ten Years in Oregon*.
2. Crawford, *Journal*, 10 (for June 25, 1842).
3. White, *Ten Years in Oregon*, 152.
4. Readers interested in the culinary aspects of overland travel might consult Williams, *Wagon Wheel Kitchens*.
5. White, *Ten Years in Oregon*, 148–49.
6. Crawford, *Journal*, 15 (for August 11, 1842).
7. Ibid., 12 (for July 17, 1842).
8. Hastings, *Emigrants' Guide*, 17.
9. When he prepared his recollections, Elijah White must have misremembered the boy's name, for in all probability it could be none other than Winston Bennett.
10. White, *Ten Years in Oregon*, 159.
11. Penter, "Recollections," 57, 60.

12. White, *Ten Years in Oregon*, 165.

13. Crawford, *Journal*, 20 (for September 14, 1842).

14. Bennett, "Biographical Sketches," May 26, 1877.

15. Ibid., 22 (for September 28 and 29, 1842).

16. Bennett, "Biographical Sketches," May 26, 1877.

17. Hastings, *Emigrants' Guide*, 64.

18. "Oregon Archives," 233.

Chapter 4

1. There appear to be only two primary sources to the 1843 journey from Oregon to California: Winston Bennett, "Biographical Sketches" and Hastings, *Emigrants' Guide*, 64–69. Discussion in the text concerning the journey to California is based on these sources.

2. Early, "Biographical Narrative of Bennett Family." Early was the great-granddaughter of Mary Bennett.

3. The most preeminent historian of California, Hubert Howe Bancroft, estimated 6,900 *gente de razón* and 3,180 ex-Mission Indians as of 1845. Bancroft, *History of California*, 4: 649. My detailed examination of local court records for my book *Law and Community* revealed many, many persons, primarily Mexicans and Californios but foreigners as well, who were obviously present in California but not identified in Bancroft's lists. I am therefore convinced that his estimates are too low.

4. Nye, *Sea Captain's Wife*, 156–57,

5. Doyce B. Nunis, Jr., makes this suggestion in ibid., 157n48.

6. Ibid., 157–58.

7. Bancroft, *History of California*, 4: 387.

Chapter 5

1. General historical discussion follows Bancroft, *History of California*.

2. Dwinelle, *Colonial History*, 113–14.

3. Bancroft Reference Notes.

4. Mawn, "Framework for Destiny," 168, 175n8, 176n13.

5. Davis, *Seventy-five Years*, 149. These reminiscences first appeared in 1889 as *Sixty Years in California*. Davis later expanded them to include seventy-five years, with the later book published in several editions over the years.

6. Bancroft, *History of California*, 2: 716.

7. Ibid., 4: 669n.

8. Osborn, "Narrative of a Visit."

9. Downey, *Filings From an Old Saw*, 8, 41, 78.

10. Ibid., p. 5.

11. Brown, *Early Days*, 92. This work has appeared in earlier obscure publications.
12. Davis, *Seventy-five Years*, 149.
13. Downey, *Filings From an Old Saw*, 5.
14. Winston Bennett, "Biographical Sketches," June 2, 1877. This is the second of a two-part series, the first appearing May 26, 1877.
15. Davis, *Seventy-five Years*, 149–50.
16. Ibid., p. 151.
17. Ibid.
18. Petition, Mary Bennett to Thomas O. Larkin, June 6, 1845, in Larkin, *Larkin Papers*, 3: 223–24.
19. Quoted in Latta, *Joaquín Murrieta*, 306.
20. Early, "Biographical Narrative of Bennett Family."
21. Interview with Winston Bennett, *Santa Cruz Daily Sentinel*, May 1, 1888, p. 3.
22. Deposition of Stephen A. Wright, Land Case #361, Mary S. Bennett, Claimant, Federal District Court (Northern District, California), on deposit with Bancroft Library, Berkeley, California.

Chapter 6

1. Much of the discussion about the California procedures for separation is drawn from Langum, *Law and Community*.
2. Letter, Susan Biggerton to William Leidesdorff, December 31, 1845, in Larkin, *Larkin Papers*, 4: 136.
3. Markoff, *Russians on the Pacific Ocean*, 45.
4. Ibid., 52–53.
5. Geiger, *Franciscan Missionaries*, 249–51.
6. Quoted in García, *Santa Clara*, 17, 18.
7. Paraphrase of letter of the Rev. Doroteo Ambris, July 16, 1859, in Geiger, *Franciscan Missionaries*, 250–51.
8. Letter, James Alonzo Forbes to Zephyrin Engelhardt, December 30, 1905, quoted in Geiger, *Franciscan Missionaries*, 251.
9. Deposition of Silvería Pacheco de Cole, January 31, 1863, Land Case #361, pp. 321–28, Mary S. Bennett, Claimant, Federal District Court (Northern District, California), on deposit with the Bancroft Library, University of California, Berkeley, California, hereinafter Land Case #361 N.D., then pagination.
10. Letter, Thomas O. Larkin to Antonio María Pico, June 6, 1845, Larkin, *Larkin Papers*, 3: 225–26.
11. Letter, Larkin to Alcalde of Yerba Buena, June 6, 1845, Larkin, *Larkin Papers*, 3: 226.
12. Letter, José de la Cruz Sánchez to Larkin, May 12, 1845 (error in MS, probably June 12, 1845), Larkin, *Larkin Papers*, 3: 182–83 (trans. by author).

13. Letter, Larkin to Alcalde of Yerba Buena, June 25, 1845, Larkin, *Larkin Papers*, 3: 248.

14. *Griswold v. Penniman*, 2 Conn. 564, 565–66 (1818).

15. Larkin to José María del Real, June 6, 1845, Larkin, *Larkin Papers*, 3: 224–25.

16. Deposition of George W. Bolling (Bellomy), February 2, 1854, Land Case #361 N.D., pp. 7–8.

17. See, e.g., deposition of Charles Brown, February 15, 1855, Land Case #361 N.D., pp. 35–37.

18. Secrest, *Man from Rio Grande*, 178.

19. Book G, pages 310, et seq., Official Records of Santa Clara County, California; also part of District Court Record, Land Case #361 N.D., p. 100.

20. Depositions, George W. Bolling (Bellomy), February 2, 1854, and Charles Parr, April 4, 1862, Land Case #361 N.D. pp. 7–8 and 166–75.

21. Deposition, George W. Bolling (Bellomy), February 2, 1854, Land Case #361 N.D., pp. 7–8.

22. Affidavit of Mary Bennett, Land Case #361 N.D., p. 101; deposition of George B. Tingley, Land Case #361 N.D., pp. 64–65.

23. Petitions A & B, with notations that petitions found in archives, Land Case #361 N.D., pp. 87–88, 92.

24. Opinion of the Board of Land Commissioners, Land Case #361 N.D., pp. 103–109.

25. Petition A of Narciso Bennett for land grant, September 4, 1845, Land Case #361 N.D., pp. 87–88.

26. Deposition of Andres Pico, June 9, 1854, and marginal notes on Petition B, Land Case #361 N.D., pp. 77–89 and 92.

27. Depositions of Pedro Hernández, February 2, 1854; Antonio Bernal, January 20, 1855; and Secundino Robles, January 19, 1855, Land Case #361, N.D., pp. 9–11, 11–21, and 22–28.

28. Affidavit of José Antonio Bernal, March 11, 1862, Land Case #361 N.D., pp. 282–87.

Chapter 7

1. Letter, Julius Martin to Thomas O. Larkin, July 11, 1845, Larkin, *Larkin Papers*, 3: 268.

2. Consular Records of Thomas Oliver Larkin, p. 12. These records were formerly on deposit with the Monterey County Recorder's Office, Salinas, California, and are believed to be among those transferred to the Monterey County Historical Society, Salinas, California.

3. Winston Bennett, "Biographical Sketches," June 2, 1877 (2nd installment).

4. This biographical discussion of Isaac Graham is largely taken from Nunis, *Trials of Isaac Graham*.

5. Ibid., 18n55.

6. New York: Saxton and Niles, 1844.

7. A. Robinson, *Life in California*, 187.

8. Bancroft, *California Pioneer Register*.

9. Watson, *Journals*, 124. I am indebted to Paul Conrado and Paul Puppo for this reference.

10. Clyman, "James Clyman," 134. This diary has also appeared in book form, including *Journal of a Mountain Man* (1984). Clyman's comment may have been consciously imitative of Cooper. Clyman was a remarkable man and was everything most mountain men were not—educated, reasonably literate, and with a refined mind.

11. Quoted in *Graham v. Bennet*[t], 2 California Reports 503 (1852).

12. Nunis, *Trials of Isaac Graham*, 62.

13. Donald Munro Craig in editor's introduction to Garner, *Letters from California*, 34–35.

14. Petition Against Isaac Graham, presented to the Prefect of the 2nd District, no date, in Savage, *Documentos*, 192–95, and also in Archives of Santa Cruz, p. 51, both in Bancroft Library, University of California, Berkeley, California.

15. Letter, Thomas O. Larkin to José Antonio Bolcoff, November 19, 1845, Larkin, *Larkin Papers*, 4: 101–2.

16. Letter, José Antonio Bolcoff to Thomas O. Larkin, December 4, 1845, Larkin, *Larkin Papers*, 4: 115–16.

17. Nunis, *Trials of Isaac Graham*, 84.

Chapter 8

1. Depositions of George James Alexander Forbes, May 22, 1862; Pedro Hernández, February 2, 1854, Transcript of Land Claim Proceedings before United States District Court of the Northern District of California, Case #361 (hereinafter Land Case #361 N.D.), pp. 7–8 and 9–11.

2. Deposition of Ignacio Sibrician (probably Cibrian), August 30, 1863, Land Case #361 N.D., pp. 340–43.

3. Deposition of Pedro Hernández, February 2, 1854, Land Case #361 N.D., pp. 9–11.

4. Depositions of James Alexander Forbes, May 22, 1862; Stephen A. Wright, March 30, 1855, Land Case #361 N.D., pp. 221–40 and 67–75.

5. Depositions of James Alexander Forbes, May 22, 1862; Charles Parr, April 4, 1862, Land Case #361, pp. 221–40 and 166–77.

6. Depositions of George W. Bolling (Bellomy), February 2, 1854; James Alexander Forbes, May 22, 1862; Pedro Hernández, February 2, 1854; Ignacio Sibrician (probably Cibrian), August 30, 1863; and Stephen A. Wright, March 30, 1855, Land Case #361 N.D. , pp. 7–8, 221–40, 9–11, 340–43, and 67–75.

7. Depositions of José Fernández, February 8, 1855; Sebastian Peralta, February 8, 1855, Land Case #361 N.D., pp. 28–31 and 31–34.

8. Opinion of the Board of Land Commissioners, Land Case #361, N.D., pp. 108–9.

9. Affidavit of José Antonio Bernal, March 11, 1862, Land Case #361 N.D., pp. 282–87. Depositions of George W. Bolling (Bellomy), February 2, 1854; Benjamin Campbell, February 27, 1855; Silvería Pacheco de Cole, January 31, 1863; James Alexander Forbes, May 22, 1862; Pedro Hernández, February 2, 1854; and Antonio Bernal, January 20, 1855, Land Case #361 N.D., pp. 7–8, 37–40, 321–28, 221–40, 9–11, and 11–21.

10. Deposition of James B. Taber, January 30, 1863, Land Case #361 N.D., pp. 350–57.

11. Depositions of Antonio Bernal, January 20, 1855; Pedro Hernández, February 2, 1854, Land Case #361 N.D., pp. 11–21 and 9–11.

12. Deposition of Charles Brown, February 15, 1855, Land Case #361 N.D., pp. 35–37.

13. Watson, *Journals*, 115–16. I am indebted to Paul Conrado and Paul Puppo for this reference.

14. Depositions of Pedro Hernández, February 2, 1854; Secundino Robles, January 19, 1855, Land Case #361 N.D., pp. 9–11 and 22–28.

15. Deposition of José Antonio Bernal, March 11, 1862, Land Case #361 N.D., pp. 282–87.

16. "Petition C, Petition of Mrs. Mary McSwain," found in Land Case #361 N.D., pp. 95–100.

17. Deposition of Joseph Aram, February 28, 1855, Land Case #361 N.D., pp. 44–48.

18. Bancroft, *History of California*, 4: 683n.

19. Deposition of Antonio Bernal, January 20, 1855, Land Case #361 N.D., pp. 11–21.

20. Bryant, *What I Saw*, 298.

21. See note 17 and accompanying text.

22. Lancey, "Biographical Sketch," 154.

23. Unruh, *Plains Across*, 119 (table 1).

24. Aram, "Reminiscences," 623, 629–30.

25. Deposition of Stephen A. Wright, March 30, 1855, Land Case #361 N.D., pp. 67–75.

26. Aram, "Reminiscences," 629.

27. Adna A. Hecox, "Crossing the Plains," 2.

28. Margaret M. Hecox, *California Caravan*, 45–46.

29. A composite view derived from the Joseph Aram, Adna Hecox, and Margaret Hecox accounts.

30. Margaret Hecox, *California Caravan*, 48, 50.

31. Deposition of James B. Taber, January 30, 1863, Land Case #361 N.D., pp. 350–57.

32. Ibid.

33. Discussion about the events surrounding the battle of Santa Clara drawn from Bancroft, *History of California*, 5: 377–83, and Regnery, *Battle of Santa Clara*.

34. Brown, *Early Days*, 51.

35. Report of the commanding officer, Ward Marston, reprinted in Regnery, *Battle of Santa Clara*, 91–92.

36. Margaret Hecox, *California Caravan*, 54.

37. Brown, *Early Days*, 51.

38. Deposition of Joseph Aram, February 28, 1855, Land Case #361 N.D., pp. 44–48.

39. Deposition of James Alexander Forbes, March 30, 1855, Land Case #361 N.D., pp. 60–61.

40. Affidavits of E. F. Fitts, May 20, 1862, and of Stephan A. Wright, March 30, 1855, Land Case #361 N.D., pp. 205–12 and 67–75.

41. Deposition of Stephen A. Wright, March 30, 1855, Land Case #361 N.D., pp. 67–75.

42. Affidavit of William Campbell, April 4, 1862, Land Case #361 N.D., pp. 190–95.

43. Deposition of James Alexander Forbes, March 20, 1855, Land Case #361 N.D., pp. 60–61.

44. Letter, José María del Real to John Burton, February 1, 1847, among uncataloged manuscript letters in the California Room, Martin Luther King Library, San José State University, San José, California. I am grateful to Professor Damian Bacich for alerting me to this letter.

45. Letter, John Burton to José María del Refugio Sagrado Suárez del Real, February 15, 1847, in Larkin, *Larkin Papers*, 6: 23.

46. Deposition of Stephen A. Wright, March 30, 1855, Land Case #361 N.D., pp. 67–75.

47. Letter, José María del Real, March 3, 1847, quoted in *Riptide Centennial Edition* 22 (October 19, 1950) (unpaginated). Although this source does not indicate the location of the original letter, I am convinced that it is genuine, because it refers to the February 15, 1847, order that Real could take possession. That February 15 letter is authenticated beyond doubt and was included in the published *Larkin Papers*.

48. Skowronek, *Situating Mission Santa Clara de Asís*, 328.

49. Munro-Fraser, *Santa Clara County*, pp. 775–76. When Peckham went into law practice in fall 1851 in Santa Cruz, one of his first clients was Mary Bennett.

50. Ibid., 546.

51. Baldwin, *Peace Keepers*.

52. See generally, Bancroft, *History of California*, 5: 462–68.

53. 30th Cong., 1st sess., *Report of Senate Committee on Military Affairs*, February 23, 1848.

54. 34th Cong., 1st sess., *Senate Executive Document # 63*, May 5, 1856, Report of Secretary of War, including report of "Board for Examination of Claims Contracted in California Under Lt. Col. Frémont," 13 (Claim #300).

55. Bennett Papers, miscellaneous documents, Bancroft Library, University of California, Berkeley, California.

56. Matilda (Graham) Rice, the daughter of Isaac Graham and Catherine Bennett, told a reporter in 1888 that "the old woman's [Mary Bennett] first husband lived in San Francisco, but they couldn't get along, and she couldn't get a divorce. Finally they came together again. It was only a little while after this that Bennett, the elder, died under suspicious circumstances," *Santa Cruz Daily Sentinel*, April 29, 1888, p. 3. On the other hand, Winston maintained that his father died in San Francisco of alcoholism. For reasons explained in the epilogue, I question Mrs. Rice's credibility. There is another slight strain of evidence suggesting a possible reconciliation in a few Santa Clara residents' passing recollections of Vardamon and Mary Bennett moving over to Santa Cruz in 1847. I think these recollections may be a misreading of Vardamon's efforts to help his sons rebuild the sawmill at that approximate time. Mary may well have once or twice traveled over the mountains with Vardamon in connection with that rebuilding, but a true reconciliation, even for a short period of time, seems unlikely.

57. Winston Bennett, "Biographical Sketches," p. 1.

58. Interview with Winston Bennett, *Santa Cruz Daily Sentinel*, May 1, 1888, p. 3.

59. Hittel, *History of California*, 2: 596–97.

60. Wheeler, *Land Titles*, 40.

61. Letter, Josiah Belden to Thomas Oliver Larkin, September 2, 1847, Larkin, *Larkin Papers*, 6: 306–7.

62. Fritzsche, "San Francisco," 17, 29.

63. *Lestrade v. Barth*, 19 California Reports 660 (1862). See also, for this litigation, *Lestrade v. Barth*, 17 California Reports 286 (1861).

64. *Sacramento Daily Union*, February 19, 1856, p. 1; *Love v. Watts*, 1 California Unreported Cases 24 (1856).

65. *Love v. Waltz*, 7 California Reports 250 (1857).

66. *Daily Alta California* (San Francisco), May 13, 1855, p. 4.

67. *Lestrade v. Barth*, 19 California Reports, 660, 668 (1862).

68. Ibid., at 663, 675.

69. Interview with Winston Bennett, *Santa Cruz Daily Sentinel*, May 1, 1888, p. 3.

70. Thomas O. Larkin, former American consul to Mexican California and a leading businessman in northern California, sold fifty-vara-size lots in San Francisco, in September, 1848 for $10,000. Hague and Langum, *Thomas O. Larkin*, 195–96. Within two months their sale value had jumped to $15,000. Larkin, *Larkin Papers*, 8: xii (preface by editor). Admittedly, the value of lots may have increased even more as the Gold Rush progressed, but we also must remember that Vardamon had sold one-third of his fifty-vara lot before his death and also that his property was not in the immediate downtown but on Pacific between Kearny and Grant. It seems that $15,000 must be the figure intended in the newspaper's account.

Chapter 9

1. See, "Forest Use in Spanish-Mexican California," in Clar, *California Government and Forestry*, 3–52, and Wilson, "Early Lumber Operations," 12–15.

2. Harrison, *Santa Cruz County*, 63.

3. Letter, Mansel V. Bennett to John Wilson, September 22, 1857, John Wilson Papers, Bancroft Library, University of California, Berkeley, California.

4. Winston Bennett, "Biographical Sketches," 1.

5. Interview with Winston Bennett, *Santa Cruz Daily Sentinel*, May 1, 1888, p. 3.

6. Testimony of Samantha A. (Bennett) Hicks and Lansing Haight, *People v. Graham, Santa Cruz Daily Sentinel*, June 14, 1888, p. 3.

7. *Santa Cruz Weekly Sentinel*, June 16, 1888, p. 2.

8. Hoover, *Historic Spots*, 436.

9. Defendant's Index, Santa Cruz District Court, suit # 3, *Willard Buzzell v. Jackson Bennett*.

10. Recitals in deed, David J. Bennett to William Fogg, March 16, 1852, Book 1 of Deeds, p. 291, Santa Cruz County Records, Santa Cruz County Recorder's Office, Santa Cruz, California.

11. Deed, David Jackson Bennett to Thomas Byrd, March 15, 1852, p. 270, Santa Cruz County Records.

12. Deed, David J. Bennett to William Fogg, March 16, 1852, Book 1 of Deeds, p. 291, Santa Cruz County Records.

13. Plaintiff's Index, Santa Cruz District Court, suit #58, *Mary Bennett v. Thomas Byrd*.

14. Mary Bennett to John Wilson, June 7, 1852, John Wilson Papers.

15. *Daily Alta California* (San Francisco), October 7, 9, 10, 11, 13, and 15, 1852.

16. Winston Bennett to John Wilson, October 8, 1852, and Mary Bennett, October 9, 1852, John Wilson Papers.

17. *Santa Cruz Riptide* 22 (October 19, 1950): 21.

18. Mary Bennett to John Wilson, November 12, 1852, John Wilson Papers.

19. Harry Love & wife to Maury W. Smith, December 8, 1856, lease for three years, Book 1 of Deeds, p. 356. The "wife," was of course Mary, and legal conventions of the time required that a lease or any other conveyance be in the name of the husband together with the wife.

20. Testimony of Samantha A. (Bennett) Hicks, *People v. Graham, Santa Cruz Daily Sentinel*, June 14, 1888, p. 3.

21. Mary Love to John Wilson, November 30, 1858, John Wilson Papers.

22. "Santa Cruz Yesterdays," Santa Cruz *Sentinel-News*, August 22, 1954, p. 20.

23. Early, "Biographical Narrative of the Bennett Family," 8.

24. Santa Cruz County Probate Court, file #23, Santa Cruz County Records.

25. Testimony of Lansing Haight, *People v. Graham, Santa Cruz Daily Sentinel*, June 14, 1888, p. 3.

26. Interview of Winston Bennett, *Santa Cruz Daily Sentinel*, May 1, 1888, p. 3.

27. Deeds, Winston Bennett to Mary Love, September 20, 1860, Book 5 of Deeds, p. 41 (lots 11 & 15 of Block 15), and Winston Bennett to Mary Love, December 18, 1860, Book 5, p. 142 (lots 1 and 5 of Block 14), Official Records of Santa Cruz County.

28. Deed, David Jackson Bennett to Mary Love, July 20, 1854, Book 4 of Deeds, p. 127, Santa Cruz County Records.

29. Deed, Lambert B. Clements to David Jackson Bennett, April 1, 1850, Book 1 of Deeds, p. 126, Santa Cruz County Records.

30. Deed, David Jackson Bennett to Mary Ann Amanda Shelby, October 20, 1851, Book 1 of Deeds, p. 221, Santa Cruz County Records.

31. Deed, Harry Love, et al., to B. C. Whiting, October 7, 1854, Book 2 of Deeds, p. 491, Santa Cruz Country Records.

32. Deed, B. C. Whiting to Harry Love, September 29, 1855, Book 3 of Deeds, p. 126, Santa Cruz County Records.

33. Deed, Harry Love & Mary Love to Jonathan Guild, January 2, 1856, Book 3 of Deeds, p. 188, Santa Cruz County Records.

34. Santa Cruz County Probate Court, file 27, Santa Cruz County Records.

35. Deed, James and Pauline Williams to David Jackson Bennett, August 23, 1855, Book 3 of Deeds, p. 132, Santa Cruz County Records.

36. Deed, David Jackson Bennett and James and Pauline Williams to Adeline Matilda McHenry, October 13, 1855, Book 3 of Deeds, p. 148, Santa Cruz County Records.

37. Deed intended as a mortgage, October 13, 1855, Book 3 of Deeds, p. 169, Santa Cruz County Records.

38. Deeds, David Jackson Bennett to David and Mary Jones, October 13, 1855, and

David Jackson Bennett to Joseph Dinet, October 13, 1855, Book 3 of Deeds, pp. 242 and 220, respectively, Santa Cruz County Records.

39. Notice of Action Records, *James P. Treadwell v. Joseph Denet* [sic], *et al.*, dated January 30, 1857, Book 1, p. 11.
40. Letter, Harry Love to John Wilson, May 24, 1848, John Wilson Papers.
41. Santa Cruz Probate Court, file 27, Santa Cruz County Records.
42. Lease, Harry Love and Mary Love to George Liddell, November 17, 1858, Book 4 of Deeds, p. 137, Santa Cruz County Records.
43. Letter, Mary Love to John Wilson, November 30, 1858, John Wilson Papers.
44. Letter, Mansel V. Bennett to John Wilson, September 22, 1857, John Wilson Papers.

Chapter 10

1. In this chapter I am generally following the interpretation of Nunis in his *Trials of Isaac Graham*, 61–62, 64–71, of Santa Cruz County Cases 35 (the damages case) and Cases 36 and 46 (the custody case) and the affidavits therein, Santa Cruz County Clerk's Office, Santa Cruz, California. Exceptions are where I have found additional evidence and also the suit for damages, as distinct from custody, where I have a different reading of the evidence than Nunis.
2. San Francisco *Pacific Daily News,* May 16, 1850, p. 2, col. 3 (hereinafter *PDN).*
3. Letter, Mary Bennett to Editor, May 7, 1850, published in *PDN*, May 16, 1850, p. 2., col. 3.
4. Letters, Isaac Graham to Editor, from Santa Cruz, April 3, 1850, published in San Francisco *Alta California*, April 20, 1850, p. 3, col. 4.
5. *PDN*, April 27, 1850, p. 2., col. 2.
6. Mary Bennett to Editor, May 7, 1850, published in *PDN*, May 16, 1850, p. 2., col. 3.
7. *PDN,* May 16, 1850, p. 2., col. 3.
8. *PDN*, November 20, 1850, p. 4., col. 1.
9. Testimony of Catherine (Bennett) McCusker, *People v. Graham, Santa Cruz Weekly Sentinel*, June 23, 1888, p. 3.
10. *PDN*, November 20, 1850, p. 4, col. 1.
11. *PDN,* April 27, 1850, and May 16, 1850.
12. *PDN,* November 20, 1850.
13. Eliza W. Farnham, *California, In-Doors and Out*, 89.
14. Testimony of Mary Bennett, Santa Cruz County Coroner's Inquest into Death of Dennis Bennett (1850), printed in *Santa Cruz Daily Sentinel*, April 27, 1888, p. 3.
15. Again, I am following Nunis, *Trials of Isaac Graham*, for his reading of the local

Santa Cruz County 1850–1852 cases, excepting his interpretation of the damages case brought by Catherine against Isaac Graham.

16. Testimony of O. K. Stampley, *People v. Graham, Santa Cruz Daily Sentinel,* June 15, 1888, p. 3.

17. Testimony of Mrs. John Woods, *People v. Graham, Santa Cruz Daily Sentinel,* June 16, 1888, p. 3.

18. *PDN,* April 27, 1850.

19. *PDN,* May 16, 1850.

20. *Graham v. Bennet[t],* 2 California Reports 503, 504 (1852). Therein the California Supreme Court describes the lawsuit.

21. Hartog, "Marital Exits," 125 (1991). Doyce Nunis characterized the damages lawsuit as one for "ruining her good name and for assault and battery," *Trials of Isaac Graham,* 67. It did have express allegations of assault and resultant damages, but the balance of the lawsuit was for damages due to expenses that followed Isaac's alleged wrongful abduction, not for loss of reputation.

22. *Graham v. Bennet[t],* 2 California Reports 503, 506–7 (1852).

23. Affidavit of Isaac Graham, June 30, 1852, published in *Santa Cruz Daily Sentinel,* April 28, 1888, p. 3.

24. 1860 U.S. Census, population schedule. Santa Cruz, Santa Cruz, California; Roll: M653–66; p. 601, image 77; Family History Library Film: 803066.

25. *Santa Cruz Riptide,* 22 (October 19, 1950): 21.

26. "Jane Matilda Rice," Pioneer Card File, California State Library, Sacramento, California.

Chapter 11

1. Secrest, *Man from Rio Grande,* 187.

2. Complaint, *Love v. Love,* Santa Clara District Court # 2357, venue changed to Santa Cruz District Court # 627.

3. San José *Patriot,* July 2, 1868.

4. This biographical sketch follows Secrest, *Man from Rio Grande.*

5. Letter, Harry Love to John Bigler, John Bigler Correspondence & Papers.

6. Secrest, *Man from Rio Grande,* 187, 192.

7. *Maclay v. Love,* 25 California Reports 367, 373–74 (1864).

8. Ibid., at 375.

9. Complaint, *Love v. Love,* # 2357, Santa Clara County, August 9, 1866; deposition of Julia A. Adams, # 627, Santa Cruz County, November 12, 1857.

10. Ibid. and Answer, *Love v. Love,* # 627, Santa Cruz County, October 3, 1866.

11. Secrest, *Man from Rio Grande,* 215.

12. Paul Anthony Conrado, August 2005 newsletter, published online at nifty-gadgets.com/Puppo_Family/Records,II579.html, accessed June 13, 2010. Mary

Bennett is the g-g-g-grandmother of Mr. Conrado; he is the keeper of the few surviving photographs of Mary and Catherine Bennett and other early relatives. This seems to be based on a statement made to the writer Frank F. Latta by Mable Dorn Early, great-granddaughter of Mary Love and quoted in Latta, *Joaquín Murrieta*, 306.

13. This description of Harry Love's life at the sawmill site, 1858–1868, follows Secrest, *Man from Rio Grande*.

14. Santa Cruz *Pacific Sentinel*, January 30, 1862, as quoted in Secrest, *Man from Rio Grande*, 233.

15. Santa Cruz *Sentinel*, January 14, 1864, as quoted in Secrest, *Man from Rio Grande*, 234.

16. Santa Cruz *Sentinel*, "Santa Cruz Yesterdays," August 8, 1954, and August 22, 1954, as cited in Milburn, *Selected Papers*, 42–55.

17. Santa Cruz *Sentinel*, June 2, 1866, as quoted in Secrest, *Man from Rio Grande*, 239.

18. Secrest, *Man from Rio Grande*, 240. Secrest claims that this was a sale, yet acknowledges that it was recorded in the mortgage books of the Santa Cruz County Records.

19. Santa Cruz *Sentinel*, June 15, 1867, as quoted in Secrest, *Man from Rio Grande*, 240.

20. *Love v. Love*, # 2357, Santa Clara County; # 627, Santa Cruz County.

21. Santa Cruz *Sentinel*, October 12, 1867, as quoted in Secrest, *Man from Rio Grande*, 245.

22. Complaint, *Love v. Love*, # 2357, Santa Clara County, # 627, Santa Cruz County.

23. Answer, *Love v. Love*, October 3, 1866, # 2357, Santa Clara County, # 627, Santa Cruz County.

24. Transcript of testimony taken before commissioners in action no. 627, *Mary Love vs. Harry Love*, Third District Court for the County of Santa Cruz.

25. Judgment, December 14, 1867, *Love v. Love*, # 627, Santa Cruz County.

26. Probate of Mary Love, Deceased, Probate 499, Register B (commenced January 9, 1869), Santa Clara County (as to 1868 and 1869), and Miscellaneous Records of Probate Court of Santa Clara County, 2: 646–49 (as to 1870). These records are now with the San José Historical Museum, San José, California.

27. The accounts in her estate show, for the period March 1870 through January 1871, that the estate had five different tenants for portions of her land grant and also five separate tenants for her preemptive claim. During this time Winston Bennett was living in Mary's house, so this probably represents close to the tenant structure during Mary's later years, 1865–1868. Second Annual Account of the Administrator in the Estate of Mary Love, Deceased, Miscellaneous Records of the Probate Court of Santa Clara County, 2: 646–49, Santa Clara County Records, now on deposit with the San José Historical Museum.

28. Code provisions taken from a reprinted version in the *Standard Civil Code of the State of California* (Albany, CA: Hanna Legal Publications, 1961). Of course, there are several other editions of the Civil Code.

29. From Inventory, Estate of Harry Love, Probate # 449, Santa Clara County (1868).

30. Secrest, *Man from Rio Grande*, 250.

31. San José *Patriot*, July 2, 1868.

Chapter 12

1. Article 8, Treaty of Guadalupe Hidalgo, signed February 2, 1848, ratifications exchanged May 30, 1848, and proclaimed July 4, 1848.

2. Langum, *Law and Community*, 22–23.

3. 1850 and 1860 population figures from geography.about.com, accessed January 16, 2012.

4. Discussion of land claim procedures and quotations of the statute are taken from W. W. Robinson, *Land in California*.

5. Ibid., 67, 69.

6. Petition of Mary Bennett, Land Case # 361 N.D. Federal District Court (Northern District, California).

7. Miscellaneous Records, County of Santa Clara, Book A, Page 360.

8. Book G of Deeds, p. 310, Santa Clara County Records.

9. Opinion of the Board, July 10, 1855, Land Case # 361 N.D., pp. 103–109.

10. District Court Proceeding on Confirmation, Land Case # 361, N.D., pp. 112–19; Hoffman, *Reports of Land Cases*, 281–84.

11. *Maclay v. Love*, 25 *California Reports* 367, 368 (1864).

12. Affidavit of Chief Clerk, Office of Surveyor General, Land Case # 361, N.D., p. 484.

13. "Historical Census Population of Counties and Incorporated Cities in California, 1850–2010," California State Data Center, dof.gov/research/demographic/ State_census_data_center/historical_census_1850-2010, accessed online January 16, 2012.

14. Depositions of J. H. Morgan and Peleg Rush, Land Claim # 361 N.D., pp. 159–164 and 177–188.

15. Reprinted in García, *Santa Clara*, 43.

16. Agreement, January 5, 1861, Miscellaneous Records, Book A, Pages 378–81, Santa Clara County Records.

17. Deed Harry & Mary Love to John Darmeyer, October 6, 1857, copy in Land Claim # 361 N.D., pp. 374–78.

18. Deed Book K, Pages 164–65, Santa Clara County Records.

19. *Love v. Shartzer*, 31 California Reports 487, 489–90 (1867).

20. Affidavit of E. F. Fitts, Land Case # 361 N.D., pp. 205–12.

21. *Love v. Shartzer*, 31 California Reports 487 (1867).

22. *Love v. Watkins*, 40 California Reports 547 (1871).

23. *Bostic v. Love*, 16 California Reports 70 (1860).

24. Secrest, *Man from Rio Grande*, 228–29.

25. Mortgage Book C, Pages 628–29 and Miscellaneous Records Book A, Pages 206–8, Santa Clara County Records.

26. Mortgage Book H, Pages 32–33, Santa Clara County Records.

27. *Shartzer v. Love*, 40 California Reports 93 (1870).

28. Reprinted in *Daily Evening Bulletin*, April 19, 1861.

29. Land Case # 361 N.D., pp. 128–33.

30. Land Case # 361 N.D., pp. 141–42.

31. Land Case # 361 N.D., p. 157.

32. Lounsbury, "Mexican Land Claims," 11.

33. Bancroft, *California Pioneer Register*, 271.

34. Bennett Survey Opinion, Land Case # 361 N.D., pp. 383–97, August 22, 1863.

35. Land Case # 361 N.D., pp. 404–6.

36. W. W. Robinson, *Land in California*, 106 (relying on J. N. Bowman).

Chapter 13

1. *Eating even more*, interview with her granddaugher, Josephine McCusker, in Latta, *Joaquín Murrieta*, quoted in Barriga, "Mary Bennett," 16, 25. *Weighed 350 pounds*, Early, "Biographical Narrative of Bennett Family," 9, 10.

2. Josephine McCusker interview quoted in Barriga, "Mary Bennett," 25.

3. Santa Cruz *Daily Sentinel*, January 2, 1869, p. 1.

4. Claim of Dr. H. H. Warburton in her estate shows visits of July 27, 1868, and December 3, 1868. Doubtless she had already paid for earlier visits. Estate of Mary Love, Deceased, Probate Court of Santa Clara County, Probate No. 499, Register B, now housed at the San José Historical Museum, San José, California.

5. List of town lots accompanying J. J. Bowen's "Map of the Town and Sub-Lots of Santa Clara," July 1866, reprinted in García, *Santa Clara*, 96–101.

6. Early, "Biographical Narrative of Bennett Family," 10.

7. Testimony of Calvin Russell and I. L. Duff, Coroner's Inquest into Death of Harry Love, June 29, 1868, pp. 2, 5, Santa Clara, California, located at San José Historical Museum.

8. Receipt from U.S. Internal Revenue for tax, based on income for year 1868 of $1,095. Estate of Mary Love, Deceased.

9. Deed, Town of Santa Clara to Mary Love, August 30, 1867, Book Y of Deeds, p. 414, Santa Clara County Records.

10. Miscellaneous Records of Santa Clara County, Book B, Pages 219–28.

11. Claims of Calvin Russell, contractor, and James G. Barney, lumberman, in Estate of Mary Love, Deceased.

12. Deed, Harry Love and Mary Love to Winston Bennett, June 27, 1866, Book V of Deeds, Pages 354–55, Santa Clara County Records.

13. Deed, Harry Love and Mary Love to Samantha A. Bennett, April 15, 1867, Book Z of Deeds, Pages 401–3, Santa Clara County Records.

14. Deed, Mary Love to Samantha A. Hughes, August 31, 1868, Book 9 of Deeds, Pages 571–72, Santa Clara County Records.

15. Secrest, *Man from Rio Grande*, 250, 252, 256.

16. Early, "Biographical Narrative of Bennett Family," 10.

17. Secrest, *Man from Rio Grande*, 251.

18. San José *Weekly Patriot*, July 3, 1868, p. 3.

19. This incident and later events immediately leading to Harry Love's death and results of official investigation are based on testimony of witnesses identified in text (Samantha Bennett misidentified as "Cementhia"), before *Coroner's Inquest into Death of Harry Love*, June 29, 1868.

20. The doctors were A. B. Caldwell, Whipple (who administered the chloroform), and L. Robinson.

21. Secrest, *Man from Rio Grande*, 258–59n24, 260; Barriga, "Mary Bennett," 25.

22. Santa Cruz *Sentinel*, July 4, 1868, p. 2. Obituaries appeared in the San José *Patriot*, July 3, 1868, p. 3; Napa *Register*, July 11, 1868; San Francisco *Alta California*, July 2, 1868, p. 1; San Francisco *Times*, June 30, 1868; and Sonora *Democrat*, July 4, 1868.

23. Probate of Harry Love, Deceased, Probate # 449, Register C, p. 76, et seq., Santa Clara County Records, now housed at San José Historical Museum, San José, California.

24. Claim in Probate of Mary Love, Deceased.

25. This is from an interview of the writer Frank F. Latta with Mable Dorn Early, keeper of the Bennett family lore; Ms. Early was apparently quoting her mother, Josephine, granddaughter of Mary Bennett, quoted in Latta, *Joaquín Murrieta*, 308.

26. Ibid.

27. This is not entirely free from doubt. Her probate records show she was buried in Pajaro Cemetery, nearby to Watsonville. The family lore historian, Mable Dorn Early, identifies Pioneer Cemetery in "Biographical Narrative of Bennett Family, 10, and also in her statement to Latta, *Joaquín Murrieta*, 308. The author has verified that her monument is in the Pioneer Cemetery.

28. Santa Cruz *Sentinel*, January 2, 1869, p. 2. Other obituaries include: Santa Clara *News*, December 26, 1868; San Francisco *Alta California*, January 1, 1869; San Francisco *Times*, December 28, 1868; and Sacramento *Union*, December 30, 1868.

29. References to the events of her probate are all to Probate of Mary Bennett, De-

ceased, No. 499, Register B, now housed at the San José Historical Museum, San José, California, except where otherwise specifically noted.

30. *Love v. Watkins*, 40 California Reports 547 (1871).

31. Commissioner's Deed to B. F. Watkins, Book of Deeds, 22: 222–25, Santa Clara County Records.

32. Land Case # 361, Northern District of California, pp. 148–52, on deposit with Bancroft Library, Berkeley, California.

33. Summaries from abstract of title to "Watkins and Mary Bennett Tract Near the Town of Santa Clara," Sam P. Howes, Searcher of Records, November 26, 1877, pp. 89, 94, 104, on file with Bancroft Library, University of California, Berkeley, California.

34. Materials in this citation are in Miscellaneous Records of Probate Court, 4: 128–33, 277, Santa Clara County Records.

35. Howes, "Abstract of Title," pp. 69–78.

36. Ibid., 178–80 (distribution), 215 (sale, Winston Bennett to Isaac Smith).

Chapter 14

1. Santa Cruz *Daily Sentinel*, April 27, 1888, p. 3. The developments of his trial are all based on detailed articles in the Santa Cruz *Daily Sentinel* for the dates June 14, 15, 19, 21, 22, 23, 24, 26, 27, and 29, 1888, and will not be separately noted except for quotations. The weekend editions of the Santa Cruz *Weekly Sentinel* repeated the coverage. An excellent secondary analysis of the trial is in Nunis, *Trials of Isaac Graham*, 73–97.

2. Santa Cruz *Daily Sentinel*, June 19, 1888, p. 3.

3. Ibid., June 14, 1888, p. 3.

4. Ibid., June 19, 1888, p. 3.

5. Ibid.

6. Ibid., June 21, 1888, p. 3.

7. Santa Cruz *Weekly Sentinel*, June 23, 1888, p. 3.

8. Ibid.

9. Santa Cruz *Daily Sentinel*, June 24, 1888.

10. Santa Cruz *Weekly Sentinel*, June 23, 1888, p. 3.

11. Santa Cruz *Daily Sentinel*, June 22, 1888, p. 3.

12. Ibid., June 27, 1888, p. 3.

13. Ibid., June 29, 1888, p. 2.

14. Ibid., p. 3.

15. Nunis, *Trials of Isaac Graham*, 95–96.

16. Quoted in Latta, *Joaquín Murrieta*, 308.

17. Testimony of Thomas W. Wright, Santa Cruz *Weekly Sentinel*, June 23, 1888, p. 3.

18. Reid, *Law for the Elephant*.

Bibliography

Manuscript Sources

Bancroft Reference Notes, vol. 20, "Bennett." Bancroft Library, University of California, Berkeley, California.

Bennett Papers. Miscellaneous documents. Bancroft Library, University of California, Berkeley, California.

Bigler, John. Various correspondence and papers. Bancroft Library, University of California, Berkeley, California.

California State Census for 1852, Santa Clara County. In Daughters of the American Revolution transcription, microfilm edition.

Coroner's Inquest into Death of Harry Love, June 29, 1868. Manuscript on deposit with San Jose Historical Museum, San Jose, California.

Deed Books, Official Records of Santa Clara County, California.

Deed Books, Official Records of Santa Cruz County, California.

District Court Records of Santa Clara County, California.

District Court Records of Santa Cruz County, California.

Howes, Sam P. "Abstract of Title to Watkins and Mary Bennett Tract near the Town of Santa Clara," November 26, 1877. On file with Bancroft Library, University of California, Berkeley, California.

Larkin, Thomas O. "Consular Records of Thomas Oliver Larkin." Monterey County Historical Society, Salinas, California.

Lounsbury, Ralph. "Mexican Land Claims in California." Paper on file with National Archives, Washington, D.C.

Milburn, Rosemary H. *Selected Papers on the History of Santa Cruz County* (1967) (student work), on file with the Santa Cruz Public Library.

Miscellaneous manuscript letters. California Room, Martin Luther King Library, San Jose State University, San Jose, California.

Miscellaneous Records of Santa Clara County, California.

Mortgage Books, Official Records of Santa Clara County, California.

Notice of Action Books of Santa Cruz County, California.

Osborn, W. B. "Narrative of a Visit to San Francisco, 1844." Manuscript in Bancroft Library, University of California, Berkeley, California.

Probate Records of Santa Clara County, California. On deposit with the San Jose Historical Museum, San Jose, California.

Probate Records of Santa Cruz County, California.

Rice, Jane Matilda. Pioneer Card File. California State Library, Sacramento, California.

Santa Cruz [California] Archives. Bancroft Library, University of California, Berkeley, California.

Savage, Thomas. *Documentos para la Historia de California II*. 4 vols. Bancroft Library, University of California, Berkeley, California.

United States Census for 1850. California, Santa Clara County, and Santa Cruz County.

United States Census for 1860. California.

Wilson, John. Various correspondence. Bancroft Library, University of California, Berkeley, California.

Printed Primary Sources

Aram, Joseph. "The Reminiscences of Captain Aram." *Journal of American History* 1 (Fall 1907): 623–32.

Bennett, Winston. "Biographical Sketches: Winston Bennett—A Pioneer of '43," [memoirs]. *San Jose Pioneer*, May 26, 1877, and June 2, 1877.

Brown, John Henry. *Early Days of San Francisco*. Oakland, CA: Biobooks, 1949.

Bryant, Edwin. *What I Saw in California*. Santa Ann, CA: Fine Arts Press, 1936 (reprint ed.).

California Reports. Decisions of the California Supreme Court, various cases and dates.

California State Data Center. "Historical Census Population of Counties and Incorporated Cities in California." dof.gov/research/demographic/State_census_data_center/historical_census_1850–2012.

California Unreported Cases.

Clyman, James. "James Clyman: His Diaries and Reminiscences." *California Historical Society Quarterly* 5 (June 1926): 109–38.

Crawford, Medorem. *Journal of Medorem Crawford*. Fairfield, WA: Ye Galleon Press, 1967.

Davis, William Heath. *Seventy-five Years in California*. San Francisco: John Howell, 1967.

Downey, Joseph T. *Filings from an Old Saw: Reminiscences of San Francisco and California's Conquest*. San Francisco: John Howell, 1966.

Early, Mabel Dorn. "Biographical Narrative of Bennett Family," *Pony Express* 17 (September 1950): 8–15, and 17 (November 1950): 9–10.

Farnham, Eliza W. *California, In-Doors and Out; How We Farm, Mine, and Live Generally in the Golden State.* New York: Dix, Edwards, 1856.

Farnham, Thomas Jefferson. *Travels in the Californias, and Scenes in the Pacific Ocean.* New York: Saxton and Niles, 1844. Reprint, Oakland: Biobooks, 1947.

Garner, William Robert. *Letters from California, 1846–1847.* Edited by Donald Munro Craig. Berkeley: University of California Press, 1979.

Griswold v. Penniman, 2 Connecticut Reports 564 (1818).

Hastings, Lansford W. *The Emigrants' Guide to Oregon and California.* Cincinnati, OH: George Conclin, 1845. Reprint, New York: Da Capo Press, 1969.

Hecox, Adna A. "Crossing the Plains," *Santa Cruz County Times,* August 20, 1870.

Hecox, Margaret M. *California Caravan: The 1846 Trail Memoir of Margaret Hecox.* San Jose, CA: Harlan-Young Press, 1966.

Hoffman, Ogden. *Reports of Land Cases.* San Francisco: Numa Hubert, 1862.

Lancey, Thomas C. "Biographical Sketch of Thomas C. Lancey." *San Jose Pioneer,* February 7, 1880.

Larkin, Thomas O., et al. *The Larkin Papers: Personal, Business, and Official Correspondence of Thomas Oliver Larkin, Merchant and United States Consul in California.* Edited by George P. Hammond. 10 vols. and index. Berkeley: University of California Press, 1951–1968.

Lovejoy, Asa L. "Lovejoy's Pioneer Narrative, 1842–48." Edited by Henry E. Reed. *Oregon Historical Quarterly* 31 (1930): 237–60.

Markoff, Alexander. *The Russians on the Pacific Ocean.* Translated by Ivan Petroff. Los Angeles: Glen Dawson, 1955.

Matthieu, F. X. "Reminiscences of F. X. Matthieu." Edited by H. S. Lyman. *Oregon Historical Quarterly* 1 (1900): 73–104.

Munro-Fraser, J. P. *History of Santa Clara County.* San Francisco: Alley, Bowen, 1881.

Napa Register, July 11, 1868, Napa, CA.

Nye, Lydia Rider. *The Journal of a Sea Captain's Wife, 1841–1845.* Edited by Doyce B. Nunis, Jr. Spokane, WA: Arthur H. Clark, 2004.

"Oregon Archives, 1841–1843." Edited by David C. Duniway and Neil R. Riggs. *Oregon Historical Quarterly* 60 (June 1959): 233.

Penter, Samuel. "Recollections of an Oregon Pioneer of 1843." *Oregon Historical Quarterly* 7 (March 1906): 57ff.

Riptide Centennial Edition 22 (October 19, 1950). Santa Cruz, CA.

Robinson, Alfred. *Life in California.* New York: Wiley and Putnam, 1846. Reprint, New York: Da Capo Press, 1947.

Sacramento Daily Union. Various dates.

San Francisco Alta California. Various dates.

San Francisco Pacific Daily News. Various dates.

San Francisco Times, June 30 and December 28, 1868.

San Jose Mercury. Various dates.

San Jose Patriot. Various dates.

Santa Cruz Daily Sentinel. Various dates.

Santa Cruz Weekly Sentinel. Various dates.

Sonora Democrat, July 4, 1868, Sonora, California.

Standard Civil Code of the State of California. (1872; printed in many editions).

Treaty of Guadalupe Hidalgo, 1848. Various editions.

United States Congress, 30th Cong., 1st session. *Report of Senate Committee on Military Affairs,* February 23, 1848.

United States Congress, 34th Cong., 1st session. Report of "Board for Examination of Claims Contracted in California Under Lt. Col. Fremont." *Report of Secretary of War, Senate Executive Document # 63,* May 5, 1856.

Watson, Henry Bulls. *The Journals of Marine Second Lieutenant Henry Bulls Watson: 1845–1848.* Edited by Charles R. Smith. Washington, D.C.: History and Museums Division, U.S. Marine Corps, 1990.

Wheeler, Alfred. *Land Titles in San Francisco.* San Francisco: Alta California Steam Co., 1852.

White, Elijah. *Ten Years in Oregon: Travels and Adventures of Doctor E. White and Lady.* Compiled by A. J. Allen. Ithaca, NY: Mack, Andrus, 1848.

Secondary Sources

Baldwin, C. L. *The Peace Keepers: A History of Santa Clara Law Enforcement.* Santa Clara, CA: Santa Clara Police Department, 1973.

Bancroft, Hubert Howe. *California Pioneer Register and Index, 1542–1848.* (Baltimore, MD: Regional Publishing, 1964) (extracted from Bancroft, *History of California*).

———. *History of California.* 7 vols. In *The Works of Hubert Howe Bancroft.* 39 vols. San Francisco: History Co., 1874–1890. Reprint, *History of California.* Santa Barbara, CA: Wallace Hebberd, 1963–1970.

Barriga, Joan B. "Mary Bennett: The Black Knight's Lady." *The Californians* 8 (September/October 1990): 16–25.

Clar, F. H. Raymond. *California Government and Forestry from Spanish Days until the Creation of the Department of Natural Resources in 1927.* Sacramento: State of California, Department of Natural Resources, Division of Forestry, 1959.

Dwinelle, John W. *The Colonial History: City of San Francisco.* San Francisco: Towne and Bacon, 1867. Reprint, n.p.: Ross Valley Book Co., 1978.

Fritzsche, Bruno. "San Francisco, 1846–1848: The Coming of the Land Speculator." *California Historical Quarterly* 51 (Spring 1972): 17–34.

García, Lorie. *Santa Clara: From Mission to Municipality.* 2nd ed. Santa Clara, CA: Beyond Buildings, 2001.

García, Lorie, George Giacomini, and Geoffrey Goodfellow. "Mary Bennett: A Mind of Her Own," in *A Place of Promise: The City of Santa Clara, 1852–2002.* Santa Clara, CA: City of Santa Clara, 2002.

Geiger, Maynard. *Franciscan Missionaries in Hispanic California, 1769–1848.* San Marino, CA: Huntington Library, 1969.

Hague, Harlan, and David J. Langum. *Thomas O. Larkin: A Life of Patriotism and Profit in Old California.* Norman: University of Oklahoma Press, 1990.

Harrison, E. S. *History of Santa Cruz County.* San Francisco: Pacific Press, 1892.

Hartog, Hendrik. "Marital Exits and Marital Expectations in Nineteenth Century America." *Georgetown Law Journal* 80 (1991) 95–129.

Hittel, Theodore H. *History of California.* San Francisco: N. J. Stone, 1897.

Hoover, Mildred Brooke. *Historic Spots in California.* Rev. ed. by Douglas E. Kyle. Palo Alto, CA: Stanford University Press, 1990.

Jameson, Elizabeth. "Women as Workers, Women as Civilizers: True Womanhood in the American West," in *The Women's West,* edited by Susan Armitage and Elizabeth Jameson, 146–64. Norman: University of Oklahoma Press, 1987.

Jeffrey, Julie Roy. *Frontier Women: The Trans-Mississippi West, 1840–1880.* New York: Hill and Wang, 1979.

Langum, David J. *Law and Community on the Mexican California Frontier: Anglo-American Expatriates and the Clash of Legal Traditions, 1821–1846.* Norman: University of Oklahoma Press, 1987. Reprint, San Diego: Los Californianos, 2006.

Latta, Frank F. *Joaquin Murrieta and His Horse Gangs.* Santa Cruz, CA: Bear State Books, 1980.

Lindsay, Robert. "Lansford Hastings and His California Dream." http://robertlindsay.wordpress.com, accessed June 4, 2010.

Mattes, Merrill J. *The Great Platte River Road.* Lincoln: Nebraska State Historical Society, 1969.

Mawn, Geoffrey P. "Framework for Destiny: San Francisco, 1847." *California Historical Quarterly* 51 (Summer 1972): 165–78.

McDermott, Stacy Pratt. *The Jury in Lincoln's America.* Athens: Ohio University Press, 2012.

Nunis, Doyce B., Jr. *The Trials of Isaac Graham.* Los Angeles: Dawson's Book Shop, 1967.

Regnery, Dorothy F. *The Battle of Santa Clara.* San Jose, CA: Smith and McKay, 1978.

Reid, John Phillip. *Law for the Elephant: Property and Social Behavior on the Overland Trail.* San Marino, CA: Huntington Library, 1980.

Riley, Glenda. *A Place to Grow: Women in the American West.* Arlington Heights, IL: Harlan Davidson, 1992.

Robinson, W. W. *Land in California.* Berkeley: University of California Press, 1948.

"Santa Cruz Yesterdays." *Santa Cruz Sentinel-News,* August 8 and 22, 1954.

Scott, Joan W. "The Woman Worker." In *A History of Women in the West.* Vol. IV: *Emerging Feminism from Revolution to World War,* edited by Genevieve Fraisse and Michelle Perrot, 399–426. Cambridge, MA: Harvard University Press, 1993.

Secrest, William B. *The Man from the Rio Grande: A Biography of Harry Love, Leader of the California Rangers Who Tracked down Joaquin Murrieta.* Spokane, WA: Arthur H. Clark, 2005.

Skowronek, Russell K., with Elizabeth Thompson. *Situating Mission Santa Clara de Asís: 1776–1851, Documentary and Material Evidence of Life on the Alta California Frontier: A Timeline.* Berkeley, CA: Academy of American Franciscan History, 2006.

Unruh, John D., Jr. *The Plains Across: The Overland Emigrants and the Trans-Mississippi West, 1840–1860.* Urbana: University of Illinois Press, 1979.

Welter, Barbara. "The Cult of True Womanhood, 1820–1860," *American Quarterly* 18 (Summer, 1966): 151–74.

Williams, Jacqueline. *Wagon Wheel Kitchens: Food on the Overland Trail.* Lawrence: University Press of Kansas, 1993.

Wilson, R. C. "Early Lumber Operations in the Santa Cruz Region." *Timberman* 38 (May 1937): 12–15.

Index

Page numbers in *italic* refer to illustrations.

About the Author

David J. Langum, Sr. is Research Professor of Law at Samford University's Cumberland School of Law in Birmingham, Alabama. He has written eight books in the field of legal history and biography, with a concentration in western America. Among his titles are *Law and Community on the Mexican California Frontier: Anglo-American Expatriates and the Clash of Legal Traditions, 1821-1846* (1987), *Thomas O. Larkin: A Life of Patriotism and Profit in Old California* (1990), and *William M. Kunstler: The Most Hated Lawyer in America* (1999).